D1006454

Praise for

THE MYTH OF MORAL JUSTICE: WHY OUR LEGAL SYSTEM FAILS TO DO WHAT'S RIGHT

"As a diagnostician, Thane Rosenbaum is on target. He paints a picture of a frosty system that blasts the emotion, subjectivity, and complexity out of every dispute brought to its doorstep. Citing the 'bureaucratic efficiencies' governing decisions, 'winner-take-all' mentality drummed into lawyers and the profession's ethics, which bear only a glancing familiarity with human morality, he exposes a system that encourages lying, permits truth to be stifled, and allows evil men to roam free. . . . Rosenbaum should be read by every law student in America."—*New York Times Book Review*

"Thane Rosenbaum's moral critique is considerably enriched and enlivened by the connections he makes between our contemporary legal system and our ideas of justice as they have been influenced by the whole of Western arts and letters. . . . His book ought to be required reading in law schools and continuing legal educations classes, if only because at least a few of his readers will be humanized by the experience."—*Washington Post Book World*

"Thane Rosenbaum bravely attempts to bring philosophy into the courtroom. . . . If Rosenbaum is serious about reforming the hearts of all people, his best hope is to continue to use his gifts as a novelist to do it. As he surely knows, the world does not need more lawyers. But it can always use a good storyteller."—*Los Angeles Times Book Review*

"An engaging critique of the legal system. . . . Making broad cultural and political references—to Kafka, Camus, Dickens, Shakespeare, Seinfeld, the *Sopranos,* the O. J. trial, *Bush v. Gore*, and the 9/11 Victim's Compensation Fund—Mr. Rosenbaum argues for a legal system that embodies a kind of humanist morality, a system in which the participant's emotional need to be heard is given as much credence as grievances, crimes and bank accounts."—*New York Observer*

"Thane Rosenbaum has done a great service for those of us who love the law but don't like it. He has grabbed the legal system and, like an old purse, shaken out all the detritus from its depths, then carefully put back in a few essential things. A truly compelling book."—Stephen J. Dubner, author of *Freakonomics* and *Turbulent Souls*

PAYBACK

PAYBACK

the case for revenge

THANE ROSENBAUM

The University of Chicago Press
Chicago and London

THANE ROSENBAUM is a novelist, essayist, and law professor. He is the author of *The Myth of Moral Justice: Why
Our Legal System Fails to Do What's Right*, as well as four
novels, *The Golems of Gotham*, *Second Hand Smoke*, the
novel-in-stories, *Elijah Visible*, and the novel for young
adults, *The Stranger Within Sarah Stein*. His articles,
reviews, and essays appear frequently in the *New York
Times*, *Los Angeles Times*, *Wall Street Journal*, *Washington Post*, and *Huffington Post*, among others. He lives in
New York, where he is the John Whelan Distinguished
Lecturer in Law at Fordham Law School and directs the
Forum on Law, Culture, and Society.

The University of Chicago Press, Chicago 60637
The University of Chicago Press, Ltd., London
© 2013 by Thane Rosenbaum
All rights reserved. Published 2013.
Printed in the United States of America

22 21 20 19 18 17 16 15 14 13   1 2 3 4 5

ISBN-13: 978-0-226-72661-8 (cloth)
ISBN-13: 978-0-226-04369-2 (e-book)

Library of Congress Cataloging-in-Publication Data

Rosenbaum, Thane.
   Payback : the case for revenge / Thane Rosenbaum.
     pages cm.
   Includes bibliographical references and index.
   ISBN 978-0-226-72661-8 (cloth : alkaline paper)
ISBN 978-0-226-04369-2 (e-book)   1. Punishment—
Philosophy.   I. Title.
   K5103.R674 2013
   364.601—dc23

                                       2012043341

♾ This paper meets the requirements of
ANSI/NISO Z39.48-1992 (Permanence of Paper).

For Danny and Alex,
who, in friendship,
always go beyond even

CONTENTS

INTRODUCTION

Human beings all long for justice. We are drawn to fairness. All is not right in the moral universe when those who have caused harm go unpunished, when the killers and the cheaters, the rule breakers and advantage takers, are not required to pay for the damage they leave behind.

Nicole Brown Simpson, the wife of O. J. Simpson, and Caylee Anthony, the daughter of Casey Anthony, are tragic symbols of justice denied, of legal failure, of the false promise that it is possible to right a wrong. Bankers and traders, who risked the money, homes, and livelihoods of others without ever having to spend a night in jail for their own excesses, provided the inspiration and resentments of the Occupy Wall Street movement. The assassination of Osama bin Laden and the imprisoning of Bernard Madoff to an unprecedented 150 years were appreciated by most people as just deserts.

These were not mere news items, tidbits of tabloid fodder for the culturally informed. These stories were obsessively followed because we are all sensitive to unfairness that has gone too far. During such times we zero in on moral outrage knowing that the difference between justice and injustice is very much a zero-sum game. We all gain when wrongdoers are punished, and we all lose when they are not.

Justice is not an abstract concept; it also evokes palpable feelings. Believing that wrongs should be righted is not a matter merely of personal opinion. The idea that people can get away with murder or highway robbery epitomizes moral revulsion at its most revolting. Injustice summons forth feelings that are deeply visceral—causing minds to race and emotions to stir. No one is casual about it, and no one is indifferent to it. Injustice strikes at the core of what it means to live in a just society, to live in a world that makes moral sense.

And the same is true with revenge. Victims who have been unavenged elicit strong emotional sympathies, sensations that suggest that something has gone seriously and terribly awry. It pulls at the same heartstrings, strikes similar nerve endings, as feelings of injustice. The gut-wrenching sensation of justice denied is precisely what sickens the soul of victims whose payback went unredeemed. Emotionally we all appreciate that victims cannot be expected to forget what happened to them. No one should be forced to accept that wrongdoers will not receive their due. Whatever debt was created surely cannot remain forever unsettled, written off like a bad loan that the victim can ill afford to let go.

Justice is not as dispassionate as the legal system has instructed us to accept. And vengeance is not as irrational as we have been taught to believe. They are not polar opposites but, rather, codependencies. Their moral appeal is lodged in the same sectors of the human brain. Actually, justice and vengeance are mirror images of one another. There is no justice unless victims feel avenged; and vengeance that is disproportionately taken is not just.

We accept legal rulings when justice is served—not simply when the law has spoken. If we don't feel the just in justice, we will walk away from the law like any unavenged victim who knows that the score remains unsettled and that payback is still owed. This is why running away from revenge, pretending that reclaiming honor is not an honorable pursuit, presents similar moral consequences as living in a society where the guilty go unpunished while citizens are asked to accept that justice was done.

Justice and vengeance arouse the same emotional feelings and spring from the same moral imperatives. Revenge justly owed and justly taken feels morally right not because humankind has a voyeuristic fetish for violence but because vengeance is one of the ways in which human beings demonstrate their commitment to moral order and just treatment. Yet in civil society revenge is taboo while justice operates beyond the sway of human feeling, only vaguely connected to the emotional life of victims who come before the law precisely to *be* avenged.

It's time to finally humanize justice by restoring the face of vengeance. Doing so is not an invitation to lawlessness but a mandate that the law must act with the same moral entitlement, and the same spirit of human fulfillment, as the righteous avenger.

ONE RUNNING AWAY FROM REVENGE

Let's take a tour through the head-spinning, backpedaling, morally ambiguous alleyways of revenge. Don't be afraid. I know vengeance conjures many mixed feelings and raw emotions. It's more acceptable to confess to having a kinky taste for porn than to acknowledge harboring feelings of revenge. Vengeance occupies a dark and deeply buried shelf inside the closet of cultural taboos. Rarely is it discussed openly where reputations can be ruined and bad opinions formed. We tend to speak about revenge hypothetically, jokingly, as if we're not to be taken seriously:

"What I am about to say is just between you and me."
"Surely you know I would never do such a thing."
"I'm ashamed to even think it. But I wouldn't mind seeing —— receive what is coming to her."

For Jews around the world who are members of the Conservative denomination, the High Holy Days of 2010 represented yet another death blow for revenge. After nearly forty years (when it comes to the Old Testament, forty years does seem to possess certain magical, symbolic significance), the prayer book, known as the *mahzor*, which is used during the Days of Awe—the period in the Jewish calendar extending from Rosh Hashanah to Yom Kippur—was updated with a new edition. Aside from its more user-friendly appearance there were some significant changes in substance, too. For instance, no longer would God be described as "awesome," since, in modern times, awesome is the word of choice—for Chosen teenagers as well as Gentiles—to describe just about anything. God shouldn't have to compete with pizza or a pair of jeans, and that's why the *mahzor* now refers to God simply as "awe-inspiring."

As for other modernizing changes, the prayer book is now more gender neutral and even acknowledges the death of a gay partner. What's more, God himself was not spared a makeover. Apparently, a vengeful God no longer favorably represents the Jewish faith well enough. In the solemn prayer, *Avinu Malkeinu*, a line that asked God to avenge the killing of Jews, was deleted.

Louis D. Levine, a congregant of Temple Israel in White Plains, New York, wondered about the wisdom, not to mention historical accuracy, of this drastic change in the liturgy. "I am not a warmongering, right-wing nut," he said, "but that line represented a real historical response to the horrors visited upon Israel."[1]

But it also made God look unhinged, so it was removed. The God of the Jews was almighty and, apparently, unavenging, as well. For several thousand years, religions, and then governments, issued commandments, edicts, dire warnings, and, ultimately, mixed signals about vengeance. Now Conservative Jews were being asked to edit their own central texts lest they be reminded that the language of revenge had once been very much part of the prayers of the Jewish people.

Vengeance: expunged from ancient texts, ridiculed as a holdover from a primitive past, and yet longingly stored in the memory bank of humankind. The advance of civilization marches on while the revenge impulse stubbornly refuses to civilize and subside, to simply give up its enduring influence on the human psyche. Vengeance can be curtailed and suppressed, but it can never be truly undone, nor should it. Whether we admit it or not, whether we are permitted to act on it or not, revenge brings order to the moral universe, establishes the proper measurement of our loss, gives voice to indignity, and serves as a necessary equalizer when victims have been rendered low.

Despite all the warnings about revenge and the prohibitions against it, everyone practices it on some level, applauds it when properly exercised, and even dreams about it in their sleep. We see it daily in schoolyards, sports arenas, and halls of Congress; we know that it lurks within the messy details of international affairs, domestic relations, business dealings, and, of course, legal battles. Revenge is life's ultimate dirty little secret and guilty pleasure. In so many dramatic and unavoidable ways it has defined our civilization, influenced our politics and culture, informed our literature, and dominated our private fantasies.

And, yet, there is also a curious schizophrenia about revenge, loopholes where vengeance slips through even amid all the proclamations that revenge is wrong and that justice is a far more important human value than getting even.

A few recent stories of revenge will reveal a culture in conflict with itself when it comes to the proper role that revenge plays in society and in the lives of individuals. They also demonstrate a fundamental confusion about the relationship between vengeance and justice. Everyone makes distinctions between them, with the search for justice widely accepted while the pursuit of vengeance roundly condemned. But are these two concepts so very different? When individuals are in desperate need for justice they qualify their obsession by categorically denying that they are out for revenge. Yet in a very real and unacknowledged sense they believe that they are entitled to both; they simply can't say so in polite company. And that's where the distinction between justice and revenge becomes more of a linguistic exercise than a hard truth. Every effort to mask the human impulse to feel avenged by hiding behind the robes of justice is like a bait and switch among the morally wounded. We know what we mean; we just can't express it openly and honestly.

Several weeks after 9/11, with plans already underway to bomb Afghanistan in retaliation for the most devastating act of terrorism committed against the United States on its own soil, President George W. Bush addressed a large gathering of employees of the Federal Bureau of Investigation (FBI)—the very same body, along with the Central Intelligence Agency (CIA), that had failed to gather the necessary information and take the appropriate measures to foil al-Qaeda on 9/11.

In explaining the reasons behind the "shock and awe" that America would soon visit on the Taliban in Afghanistan, the president said, "Ours is a nation that does not seek revenge, but we do seek justice."[2]

The audience erupted with applause, and millions of Americans watched highlights of the speech on their nightly news broadcasts or read about it in the morning newspapers. An auditorium packed with FBI agents who despised Osama bin Laden for murdering nearly three thousand American citizens in less than two hours cheered the president for the actions our nation was about to assume and the purported reasons for doing so. Surely the FBI had taken the murderous events of 9/11 personally—almost as personally as the families of the firemen, office workers, and airline passengers and personnel who lost loved ones on 9/11. After all, the FBI had been made to look like bumbling bureaucrats who allowed terrorists to learn how to fly commercial jets under their watch. Naturally they would have profound feelings of anger and hatred. The auditorium may have been filled with men and women of the law, but those badges and shields weren't going to temper their more immediate and impassioned cries for revenge.

Nevertheless, the president was careful to couch our retaliatory response as an act of justice and not as a demonstration of American vengeance.[3] Applause would naturally follow the words of someone who sought justice rather than revenge, even though the feelings that justice and vengeance provoke, in many cases, feel similar. The Taliban were not going to be taken to trial. Conventional justice, as reflected in the powers of subpoena and the procedures of due process, was being subordinated to the more immediate powers of war. Indiscriminate bombing sure looks a lot more like vengeance than like the more measured application of the rule of law.

Why all the misdirection and doublespeak? Why not simply say what was on everyone's mind anyway? The president pulled his punches and chose to recast the reasons why America now found itself duty-bound to unleash such a lethal spectacle. George W. Bush made a distinction between justice and revenge as if everyone was in agreement that the former was socially acceptable while the latter was morally despicable.

The FBI may have grossly mismanaged its intelligence gathering prior to 9/11, but the agents who cheered the president were not stupid. Surely they knew that what was about to happen in Afghanistan wasn't being done in the name of justice alone. Constitutional protections weren't on anyone's mind at that time—including the leadership of Human Rights Watch and the ACLU. Neither the Taliban nor al-Qaeda were going to be given an opportunity to testify in a court of law, to explain why America was Satan and Americans were infidels who all deserved to die.

Moreover, the massive monetary reward that would soon be placed on the head of Osama bin Laden through the Rewards for Justice Program would be claimable by any bounty hunter who could successfully infiltrate the caves of Tora Bora and make certain that bin Laden never made another trash-talking video again.[4] This government-sponsored, nonjudicial program of targeted assassinations resembled vengeance more than justice. It might as well have been titled Rewards for Revenge.

Justice in Afghanistan would come in the form of lethal bombs, not legal tribunals. And ten years later, the war in Afghanistan, and America's progressive withdrawal, still didn't approximate anything that looked like Nuremberg, The Hague, or the International Criminal Court—the familiar faces of "justice" in the global community. The war in Afghanistan, not unlike all retaliatory wars, was to be fought as a legitimate expression of just deserts, a term of art that is often synonymous with revenge—but revenge that is fully legalized and morally accepted.

And yet the president addressed an audience that had been conditioned to view revenge—no matter what form it took—as unbecoming of a great nation. "Shock and awe," for better or worse, sounds like the language of revenge, with those declarative vowels that easily collapse into a closed fist. These words don't evoke the tranquil inner sanctum of courtrooms were judgment is based on reason and deliberation and where punishment is neither random nor immediate. The president was forcing a distinction between justice and revenge that sounded presidential and diplomatic but in the moral universe didn't actually exist. He was speaking in code, feeding his constituents a familiar line, winking at the nation all the while. The assembled FBI agents, and the rest of America, for that matter, acted as if they were in denial—mindlessly clapping in favor of justice, signaling to the world that we were most assuredly *not* a vengeful nation. But in the chaos of post-9/11 hysteria, who could really tell the difference anyway?

When Osama bin Laden was finally assassinated by a team of Navy Seals that had infiltrated his Pakistani compound on May 1, 2011, many people in the United States pumped their fists in the air and even celebrated in the streets. Were they cheering the delivery of justice, or merely releasing the emotions associated with vengeance? Some criticized the celebrations as undignified, as if America were a nation of brutes with a bin Laden blood-lust. But just because they felt jubilation didn't make them very different from decent, fair-minded citizens who knew that justice was finally being done and bin Laden was receiving the payback he richly deserved.

Many, however, were left confused, not exactly sure how to feel. President Bush had promised that we would one day have our justice, and when it finally arrived it would most definitely not be in the form of revenge. We would take pride that we had forsaken our vengeful impulses in favor of the justice worthy of a great nation. Years later, however, a new president, Barack Obama, a former professor of constitutional law, was able to announce triumphantly that justice was, indeed, finally done—bin Laden had been judged and punished by a sharpshooting Navy Seal.[5] Apparently a bullet to bin Laden's head was the justice we had all been waiting for. Nonetheless, most people experienced the assassination with all the emotion and exhila-ration that generally accompanies revenge.

Others wondered how President Obama could possibly frame the killing of bin Laden in the language of justice when the terrorist wasn't captured and brought back to stand trial in the United States. Fifty American commandos overtook the compound, which was fortified only by bin Laden's wives and a teenage son, with little resistance. Surely he could have been abducted and tried in a civil courtroom as a criminal defendant (or as an enemy combat-ant before a military commission). Such a trial, any trial, would have dis-played more of the attributes of justice than did the summary judgment that took place in Pakistan. And there still would have been cheers after a guilty verdict was announced, and that, too, would have seemed a lot like revenge.

Now a detour from the roving battlefields of counterterrorism to the gridiron of America's favorite sport.

National Football League (NFL) quarterback Brett Favre already had a Hall of Fame career with the Green Bay Packers when he retired from foot-ball in 2007, only to change his mind several months later. The problem was, the Packers didn't want him back. They had committed themselves to Aaron Rogers, Favre's backup, who several years later would lead them to another Super Bowl victory. It was Rogers's team now. Favre went on to sign with the

New York Jets for one year, and then, after that season was over, retired once more only to change his mind, yet again. This time, however, rather than signing with a team from a different conference, Favre returned to the National Football Conference—to the very same division in which the Packers played—and joined their most dreaded rival, the Minnesota Vikings. As the newly installed Viking quarterback, Favre would have to play his old team at least twice during the 2009 NFL season.

Wearing the purple uniform of the Vikings before his first game against Green Bay's green and gold, Favre said the following in response to whether he was motivated by revenge: "No. That has nothing to do with it," but he soon added, "it's human nature to feel, I didn't use the word revenge, but to prove that you still could play. To prove someone wrong, . . . So you can call it what you want."[6]

Terry Bradshaw, himself a Hall of Fame quarterback, said on Fox's *NFL Sunday*, "Oh, really Brett? It's not about revenge? I'm sorry but no one believes that this time around."[7] Another former NFL quarterback, Ron Jaworski, said on ESPN's coverage of the NFL, "Brett Favre is going to approach this game and he's going to be angry, he's going to be vindictive and he will come out smoking."[8] And his partner on ESPN, former NFL coach Jon Gruden, said, "I can only imagine how Brett Favre is (feeling). He's going to be so excited to compete against the team that let him go. There's going to be a lot of emotions that go into this. Is it revenge? Whatever you want to call it, this is really going to be appealing."[9]

At the end of the game, with the Vikings having won and with Favre having delivered one of the finest performances of his career, Jaworski was asked how he thought Favre was feeling at that moment: "I don't think he would admit it," he replied, "but I'm sure Brett is feeling that he finally got his revenge."

All this hemming and hawing and backpedaling from quarterbacks who are usually more nimble in dropping back to pass, and yet here, with so little on the line—unlike America's response to 9/11—they were so visibly clumsy, fearful to admit that there are scores to be settled that never show up on a scoreboard. There is pay dirt, which is part of the game, and there is payback, which can be just as important. What did these football TV analysts expect:

When it was time to finally face the team that cast him aside, Favre would have no special feelings about it, no incentive to prove the Packers wrong, that he would treat the game as any other on the Vikings' schedule?

Obviously, it's not just NFL quarterbacks. We are all, seemingly, invested—if not culturally programmed—in the self-denial of revenge. It's difficult if not impossible to have honest conversations about revenge. Retaliation must be reserved for more noble and lawful reasons than mere vengeance. And so we memorize the disclaimers and rehearse the verbal gymnastics. We want revenge but know not to ask for it. Instead, we demand justice, which we can safely say without appearing demented. The distinction between justice and revenge may actually be artificial, but it is undeniably everywhere.

Clara Schnorr's daughter was murdered outside of Chicago in 1985. After the man who killed her was sent to prison, Ms. Schnorr said, "There is no way that he can be punished enough for taking our Donna away from us. Yet we want justice, not revenge."[10] Another grieving mother shared a similar view. In 2008, Hudson Post, from Nevada, was killed by a drunk driver who was sentenced to five years in prison but ended up released on house arrest after serving only three months. Post's mother, outraged by the lack of accountability for those who commit vehicular manslaughter, said, "It's the system that's the problem. It's not about revenge. It's about justice."[11] In 2009, Ellen Harrington's son was murdered in Oakland when he refused to hand over his wallet during an armed robbery. Her son's murderer was sentenced to life imprisonment without parole. Ms. Harrington said, "I don't believe in vengeance. . . . But I'm glad that no other mother will have to go through this."[12]

In these measured words spoken by anguished relatives lies a concession that justice is not to be taken privately through self-help[13]—no matter how wounded or aggrieved the victims might be. The rule of law must prevail, and citizens will accept the verdicts that emanate from courts of law. But the very foundation of justice that is being invoked in these statements shares the same qualities of vindication that is found with revenge. In proclaiming that they seek justice and not revenge, these victims are speaking not to the formalism of legal trials but to the human longing for justified payback, in whichever way it is delivered, so long that it *is* delivered. For them, justice must produce the same levels of emotional satisfaction as revenge. It is for this reason that, for most people, justice is just revenge by another name.

The state of Connecticut tested its moral tolerance for the death penalty in 2010 when jurors convicted Steven Hayes of numerous capitol felonies in connection with the brutal murder of a mother and her two daughters. Working with a partner, Hayes broke into the Cheshire home of the Petit family, beat the father senseless, raped the mother and eldest daughter, and sexually abused the youngest daughter, age eleven. He then strangled the mother and tied the girls to their beds, dousing them with gasoline before setting the home on fire. The father, Dr. William Petit, survived the attack only to discover that his entire family had been tortured and sadistically murdered.[14]

The jurors ultimately sentenced Hayes to die by execution while his accomplice, Joshua Komisarjevsky, received a subsequent, separate trial that resulted in the same outcome. Komisarjevsky instigated the home invasion and was, admittedly, the more irredeemable of the two—if such a distinction can even be made when dealing with men who were truly first among equals in their evil. For this reason, the jurors showed little hesitancy in scheduling them to die. Dr. Petit said that he favored the death penalty over life imprisonment without parole, but not because it would avenge the loss of his family. "That's between Mr. Hayes and the Lord. Vengeance belongs to the Lord. This is about justice." But he also said on hearing the verdict, "I'm glad for the girls that there was justice."[15] These statements appear contradictory, or at least suggest a man in conflict over how he was expected to respond to the legal system's decision to execute the men who he had every moral right to execute on his own. His daughters surely received "justice," but it was not so very different from the vengeance that their murders warranted.

In the same year, a Kansas City family faced a similar vindication and an equal aversion to loose talk about vengeance. Bob and Janel Harrison finally received the sentencing decision they believed their daughter's killer deserved. Robert Nunley was scheduled to be executed for kidnapping fifteen-year-old Ann Harrison while she waited for her school bus. Along with an accomplice who today remains on death row, the two men brought Ann to a house, raped her, then coaxed her into getting inside the trunk of the car where they each used kitchen knives in stabbing her to death. The

Harrisons were pleased that at least one of Ann's killers would finally pay the ultimate penalty for the ultimate crime. But like so many, they weren't quite sure how to characterize their true feelings, as if they, too, were being judged—not for wanting to see justice done, but for celebrating the delivery of that justice. "Some people call this seeking revenge," Janel Harrison said about her daughter's murderer now facing his own death. "I call it seeking justice for the victim."[16]

Why isn't that the same thing? From the point of view of a grieving mother, a murderer is going to die for having raped and then taken the life of her teenage girl. All the same, Harrison believed that the justice owed to her daughter was somehow incompatible with the sense of vengeance that she and her husband understandably felt but could not freely admit.

When bestselling writer of thrillers Tom Clancy was asked whether his fictional character Jack Clarke was motivated by revenge for the death of his wife in an earlier novel, Clancy, not wishing to offend anyone who might think him an intemperate man, joked, "Have you been reading books in psychology or something? It's justice, not revenge."[17]

Jenny Sanford was publicly humiliated when her husband, South Carolina governor Mark Sanford, carried on an affair with an Argentine woman and, along the way, misappropriated state funds. The governor did not seek reelection but chose to serve out the remainder of his term as both a lame duck and an even lamer husband. His wife, however, the first lady of South Carolina if not the first lady in her husband's heart, ended up writing a book about her experience as the victim of marital betrayal. She insisted, however, that the book was not written out of any personal need for vengeance. "It was really written to help other women," she said without any bitterness or irony.[18]

Sometimes there is a slip of the tongue and citizens forget themselves. Their true feelings surface as they cry out for justice with the more genuine tears of revenge.

In 2009, New Yorkers faced the possibility of a civilian trial against Khalid Shaikh Mohammed, the mastermind of 9/11. The trial was to be held in Foley Square, just a few short blocks from where the World Trade Center once stood. There was widespread disagreement, however, in New York City and all throughout America, whether terrorists should even receive civilian trials. Many believed that military commissions were more appropriate, largely because suspected terrorists were enemy combatants in the war against terror. They did not deserve the full sweep of constitutional protections offered to ordinary defendants in federal courthouses.

Michael Curatola was one New Yorker who wanted to see justice for the atrocity that was 9/11. In fact, he very much wanted to participate in the delivery of that justice—as a juror in a civilian trial should one have been convened in Foley Square. For him the trial was a symbolic way to honor and remember his former neighbor, Pablo Ortiz, who was forced to leap from the eighty-eighth floor to his death. Here is what he said about wanting to stand in judgment of those who killed his neighbor: "Just to get vengeance for my dead friend who's not here anymore." But then he quickly caught himself and restated his intentions. "But the word 'vengeance' sounds too much like a personal vendetta. I mean justice."[19]

One of the DC snipers who, during a three-week period in 2002, terrorized the area around the nation's capital by killing ten people, died from lethal injection in November 2009. Robert Meyers wanted to watch the execution of the man who murdered his brother, Dean, who had been shot in the head while filling up his car at a gas station. But he was careful not to come across as bloodthirsty when he said, "We're expecting justice being done, but not from a vengeful standpoint. It is more about the payment of his debt to society, because that was decided by others."[20] For Meyers, by allowing others to decide the fate of the man who murdered his brother, he could not experience the sensations of just deserts from a "vengeful standpoint." He simply had to embrace the concept of justice alone, without the emotional satisfaction that comes with revenge. But no one can reasonably believe that the execution wasn't satisfying on an emotional level, as well, since it vindicated his brother's memory. He surely was allowed, if not altogether expected, to savor the justice his brother's murderer received—regardless of the form in which that justice was delivered. And the savoring would share all manner of common features with the sweetness of revenge.

Sometimes score settling can't be so easily framed in the language of justice. Sometimes it's just garden-variety revenge. This can happen when the insult or injury isn't technically a crime. There are many injuries that result in wounded pride and diminished self-worth, but despite all the damage, no laws are broken. The wrongdoer is deserving of some comeuppance, but legal justice isn't the appropriate avenue for achieving it. The avenger will have to devise another way of getting even. Words matter, but the one word never uttered is revenge.

Kenneth G. Langone, the billionaire cofounder of Home Depot, Inc., had been the head of the compensation committee for the board of directors for the New York Stock Exchange. In 2004, New York Attorney General, Eliot Spitzer, had named Langone in a lawsuit in connection with the $187.5 million pay package that the committee had approved for the former chairman of the Exchange, Richard Grasso. In 2006, when Spitzer was seeking the Democratic nomination in his election campaign for governor of New York, Langone and his family gave $64,000 to Spitzer's opponent, Tom Suozzi, and urged friends and associates to donate to him as well. The problem was that Suozzi didn't have a chance of winning. Langone and his friends and family were throwing away their money. For someone so good at making money, Langone's behavior was irrational. But he didn't seem to care. In fact, he admitted that the impossible odds of a Suozzi upset were irrelevant to him. "I thought it was time to stand up to [Spitzer] and demand accountability," he said. "It wasn't revenge, it was principle."[21]

But what's more principled than vengeance? The endgame for the avenger is always a matter of principle—and that principle is, in fact, vindicated by revenge. As many people now know, Eliot Spitzer ultimately won that election but resigned in scandal not long thereafter when it was revealed that he was Client 9 in a high-priced prostitution ring. Many on Wall Street who Spitzer had prosecuted when he was known as the Sheriff of Wall Street gloated, shamelessly, at the governor's downfall. (Eliot is a friend, and, to my mind, New York lost a most talented public servant.) But none would have dared to admit that his misfortunes resulted in their vicarious revenge. Yet some actual principle was being vindicated (honor over hypocrisy?), but no one knew what to call it.

It's not just Wall Street titans who become tongue-tied when forced to recast the feelings of revenge into the loftier ideals of justice. In 2010, Thomas Blatt, an elderly Holocaust survivor from a Nazi death camp, flew from his home in California to Berlin to witness the trial of John Demjanjuk, who was a guard at the Nazi concentration camp, Sobibor, in 1943. Demjanjuk was accused of participating in the mass murder of 27,900 people. In an interview, Blatt wanted to make clear that he was seeking "justice, not revenge."[22] He provided the expected disclaimer, but he shouldn't have had to, and surely no one bought it. He survived a death camp, after all. It was an added miracle that he lived until 2010 to witness Demjanjuk finally about to be punished for his crimes. Just because he sat in a courtroom didn't mean that he had to have been stripped of all vengeful feeling. Such a compartmentalized division between justice and vengeance is not only unlikely but inhuman as well.

When the Nazi death camps were first liberated soon after the end of World War II, Jewish prisoners—essentially human corpses with a pulse—were sometimes given an opportunity to take vengeance against the guards who had tortured and tormented them. An escaping guard would be brought back to the camp by either the Russian or American liberators, thrown inside one of the barracks, and greeted by a number of Jewish skeletons who proceeded to tear the guard to pieces. Vichy collaborators experienced a similar fate when they were strangled on the streets of Paris shortly after the city was liberated—not by Jews, but by French citizens. Whether these lawless acts of retribution are examples of justice or revenge didn't seem to matter much to anyone since no one—except Nazi guards and Vichy collaborators—complained about it. Most people believed that these sporadic, improvised acts of vengeance were completely just and justified given the enormity of evil, and the scale of mass death, that the Nazis and their abettors had visited on Europe.

In spite of that, sixty-five years later, Blatt, a Holocaust survivor, sat in a German courtroom and with an accusing finger pointed at a mass murderer, wanting everyone to know that his reasons for attending the trial were all the more credible because he was motivated by justice solely. Doesn't that make his explanation sound incredible? Surely he must have been guided by the emotions of vengeance, too. Either his desire for revenge had dissipated after six decades of waiting for Demjanjuk to finally receive his due, or he simply did not allow himself to have such feelings—even for Nazi guards. It's more likely he was certain that civilized society would not grant even a Holocaust survivor the satisfaction of having his revenge and stating it so unabashedly. Ironically, one of the Israeli judges who sat in judgment of

Demjanjuk when he was tried and convicted before an Israeli court in 1988 (only later to have won his release on appeal) recalled that when the verdict was announced, cheers erupted in the courtroom. "They were survivors, what could you do?" she said knowingly. "They wanted vengeance."[23]

When it came to the postwar fate of Nazis who managed to escape justice and live quietly in nations that didn't seem to mind giving sanctuary to mass murderers, no one spent more time documenting their crimes, pinpointing their locations, and compiling evidence against them, than the famed Nazi hunter Simon Wiesenthal. Wiesenthal devoted his entire life after being liberated from the concentration camp Mauthausen to tracking down Nazis, the most infamous of whom was Adolf Eichmann, the architect of the Final Solution. Yet, Wiesenthal titled one of his books *Justice Not Vengeance*, in case anyone should doubt that the dossiers he kept on ninety thousand Nazi fugitives was inspired by the former and not the latter. And all that time, haunted by the moral outrage of unpunished murderers, somehow all he managed to think about was the unbearable injustice rather than the unrealized revenge.

Susan Jacoby, in her groundbreaking book *Wild Justice: The Evolution of Revenge*, recalled that in 1972 a number of Holocaust survivors testified in a deportation proceeding against Hermine Braunsteiner Ryan, an officer of the Maidanek death camp. (She, too, was identified by Wiesenthal.) Braunsteiner Ryan's lawyer accused the victims who had been called to testify about his client's brutality as being "out for revenge."[24] His argument, apparently, was based on the premise that vengeful people are not reliable truth-tellers. Their jittery, wrathful emotions will cancel out whatever oath they are required to take before settling into the witness stand. Objectivity is impossible for them. They can't, or simply won't, think clearly and rationally. They may be eyewitnesses to a crime, but what they purport to have seen will quite possibly be contrived, their eyes clouded with rage, their memories contaminated by loss.

Faced with this accusation and sensing that the legal burden had somehow shifted to them—as if they had to reestablish their credibility as impartial witnesses to a genocide—the survivors of Maidanek were compelled to say that all they wished to see was justice done. This would satisfy the judge and the jury that they could be trusted to speak the truth, their testimony protectively sealed away from the emotional influences of revenge. Victims are always placed on the defensive whenever they testify against wrong-doers who are being judged under the law rather than through the quick fix of self-help. Once legal proceedings commence, vengeance can no longer be what victims hope to achieve. Placing their faith in the law means playing by a different set of rules. They must, humbly, stand in the line that waits for justice and hope that justice comes.

In the case of these Maidanek survivors, they were being asked to recall the horrors they had once experienced without betraying any personal desire for vengeance. A long-overdue reckoning with a mass murderer was imminent. But it was not to be enjoyed. Such is the emotional paradox that exists in revenge-averse societies.

More recently, during the criminal sentencing of Bernard Madoff in 2009, the attorney who represented the world's greatest Ponzi schemer argued that his client should be spared having to serve 150 years in prison. Nearly all of Madoff's victims, however, made plain their wish, either through their written letters or in their remarks before the court during the sentencing hearing, to see him receive the maximum penalty allowable under the law. Madoff's attorney, Ira Sorkin, said that these requests amounted to a "type of mob vengeance," given the fact that his client, already seventy-one years old, surely would not be able to serve out the entirety of a sentence that would end in 2159.[25]

Judge Denny Chin, then a federal district judge who presided over the Madoff case, disagreed, reminding Sorkin that rather than resort to mob vengeance, the victims "are doing what they are supposed to be doing—placing their trust in our system of justice." For Judge Chin, the mere presence of a courtroom signifies the very opposite of revenge. Vengeance, after all, takes place outside of courtrooms. But just because the law is being given an opportunity to run its course doesn't mean that victims are not relying on the law to achieve the private vengeance they were forced to surrender when they placed their faith in the legal system to avenge their losses. And that's precisely what made Judge Chin's ruling just: it properly and symbolically addressed the moral outrage of the community and private pain of victims, which satisfied both justice and vengeance.

Two years later Judge Chin reflected on the Madoff sentence and the reasons why he rejected any consideration that Madoff should receive a lighter punishment. The reasons for mercy may have been trite, but they were not without some appeal. Madoff was an old man, after all. There was a numerical limit to how much he could be punished. An even more fundamental question was whether the maximum penalty would do society any good. Why not give him the hope of one day emerging from his confinement? It was here that Judge Chin invoked the word "retribution," the principle that "a defendant should get his just deserts" and "be punished in proportion to his blameworthiness." This was especially true here, he added, given the "extraordinary evil" of Madoff's crimes.[26]

Judge Chin distinguished retribution from revenge, the latter he rejected in favor of the legality of the former. This is the way the legal system ordinarily makes these distinctions. Retributive justice and vengeful impulses cannot coexist in the same system. In choosing the law, one necessarily selects legal retribution over moral revenge. Retribution becomes the weapon of choice. But make no mistake: it, too, is a weapon. It is not to be lightly regarded as a weaker cousin in the family of punishments. To exact retribution is to avenge, although apparently with more elegance. Retribution is vengeance made respectable, vengeance stripped of emotional commitments and removed from the responsibility of avengers, taken up, instead, by austere and impassioned jurists. Retributive justice is not something the public can experience personally. It just happens, like garbage collection and postal delivery. Justice is done for the benefit of all without anyone in particular savoring any personal victory.

But it is simply not true that human beings have no emotional involvement in how they experience justice. Crime victims, and even the general public, have their own personal investments in seeing punishment carried out. No one is indifferent to injustice. Retribution carried out by legal systems can't be neatly divorced from the feelings that justice, true justice, evokes in former victims and ordinary citizens. At the time of sentencing, Judge Chin dismissed the idea that his harsh symbolic punishment of Madoff was vengeance with a legal face. Two years later, however, he made it plain that Madoff received no mercy; legal retribution required a sentence consistent with just deserts. Madoff deserved a 150-year sentence regardless of whether his victims fortuitously derived some emotional benefit from this strictly legal outcome. Legally, Madoff got what he deserved. Morally, his victims were avenged. So wasn't Judge Chin's retributive objective somehow advancing their vengeful one? Victims invariably partake in the ancillary benefits of retribution, getting their revenge secondhand, but it is still potently felt. Legal retribution indirectly placated the vengeful wishes of Madoff's victims. Perhaps their letters to the judge, and the statements they made in open court, were indicative of mob vengeance after all.

The judge who sentenced Madoff proved himself as a dispassionate jurist handing down a sentence in keeping with the retributive mandate. Madoff's victims accepted the court's decree without resorting to self-help. Justice was thereby served. But so, too, was revenge.

The judge who sentenced Madoff is not alone in running away from revenge while anchoring himself securely within the big-top tent of legal justice. All judges routinely invoke the cool, rational disclaimer that revenge plays no role in their decision making.

Most recently, the judge who sentenced Jerry Sandusky to thirty to sixty years in prison for having molested ten boys over a fifteen-year period was, not unlike Judge Chin, faced with a high-profile trial and an equal moral outrage that cried out for revenge. Sandusky, a former assistant football coach at Penn State, all but single-handedly brought down its storied program, and ended Joe Paterno's once illustrious career, on account of acts of molestation that had taken place on university grounds and under its watch.[27] Many people, however, wondered whether Sandusky's punishment didn't send a strong enough message to him and to others contemplating such despicable crimes. Judge Chin had sentenced a seventy-one-year-old Madoff to 150 years in prison; Judge John M. Cleland, who presided over the Sandusky trial, stated that he was "not going to sentence you to centuries. It makes no sense for a 68-year-old man. This sentence will put you in prison for the rest of your life."[28]

But what about the feelings of the victims—their need to be vindicated—and the moral disgust of the community? Here Judge Cleland made it clear that "we do not consider vengeance, and we do not consider retaliation."[29]

Lester Munson, a writer for ESPN.com, wondered why the judge felt it so necessary to project such an aura of circumspection, if not emotional obtuseness. He wrote, "Cleland's sentencing calculus would work well in garden variety cases. But there is nothing garden variety about the crimes of Jerry Sandusky. How about a little vengeance? How about some retaliation? Is there anyone who would object? Would a higher court criticize 'centuries of incarceration' for Sandusky?"[30]

Judges all over the world are quick to assert their legal gravitas whenever there is a need to explain away a jail sentence that appears to be both morally vindictive and legally vindicating. In such cases they will utter all the right words to automatically confer the public legitimacy extended to law, all the noble reasons why governments punish its citizens. And they will distance themselves from any possibility that their judicial temperament has betrayed a vengeful streak.

In 2009, twenty-seven defendants, all French Muslims, were prosecuted in a French courtroom for having participated in kidnapping, torturing, and murdering a young Jewish man, Ilan Halimi, in 2006. The justice minister of France, Michele Alliot-Marie, persuaded the public prosecutor to appeal the sentences of fourteen of the defendants that were patently unjust (some only of six months long, which were then suspended), given the brutality, gruesomeness, and anti-Semitic nature of the crime. Halimi's family, along with French Jewish associations, praised the actions of the justice minister.

Hundreds of demonstrators marched the streets of Paris carrying white flowers, French flags, and portraits of Halimi, shouting "Justice for Ilan!" But the magistrate's union, comprised of the French judiciary, strongly disagreed with this Euro do-over, this attempt to punish the defendants even after they had already been sentenced in a court of law. The law, after all, exists not to placate victims but to render justice. "Justice is different from vengeance," said Emmanuelle Perreux, the union's president.[31]

Sometimes a victim will invoke an even more specific value than justice, something even more altruistic and impersonal to justify revenge. In 2010, in England, a twenty-nine-year-old DJ, Sami Sharif, was beaten so severely by two men outside of a London nightclub that he was left paralyzed and unable to speak—all because of an argument over a spilled drink. One of his attackers was sentenced to a mere three-and-a-half years in prison. Decrying the punishment as a "miscarriage of justice," Sharif's father, Joseph, said, "I have no feelings of revenge—all I want is to make sure that other people do not fall victim to the leniency of this sentence. It doesn't act as a deterrent."[32]

Anguished parents are often placed in the awkward position of having to downplay their vengeful feelings by adopting a more dignified, law-abiding stance. The call for justice is infused with altruism. Preventing others from experiencing the same fate becomes the overriding societal value. Private pain is subordinated to the greater good. Justice radiates for the benefit of all, and the deterrence of future crimes is how most people receive that benefit. Deterrence becomes the primary calling card of justice. Grieving parents can demonstrate their commitment to justice by reconfiguring their vengeance as deterrence. Who can really tell the difference anyway? Justice seems to be malleable enough so that avengers can easily avoid any unfortunate slip of the tongue.

A former Indonesian government official, Antasari Azhar, was convicted in 2010 of plotting the murder of a businessman. He was sentenced to eighteen years in prison. In handing down this punishment, Judge Herri Swantoro said, "The sentence is not intended as revenge, but to make the defendant aware of his mistakes."[33] Yes, legal systems do offer wrongdoers an opportunity for self-reflection. Long jail sentences give criminals a lot of time to contemplate where they went wrong. There is justice in setting an example, and there is justice in taking personal responsibility. But these lofty virtues of justice are never far removed from the more lowly vices of vengeful fury.

These statements of legal purpose betray the Janus face of the justice/ vengeance paradox, rationalizations that depend on mixing metaphors and taking cover inside the legitimacy of the law. Harsh punishments are not awarded merely to deter future crimes by drunken louts who loiter outside of British nightclubs. Sami Sharif's father wanted revenge for his son's senseless loss of a precious life; the shocking leniency that the wrongdoer received offended the moral universe. And the punishment of a murderous politician was justified for reasons apart from merely notifying him that he had made a mistake. Revenge colored these rulings just as much as any other retributive, legalistic value.

At least there's one candid government official who is without the forked tongue that slides all too easily into the doublespeak between justice and revenge. In urging the incoming administration of the Philippines to recover the ill-gotten wealth stolen by former president Ferdinand Marcos, Benigno

Aquino III said in 2010, "Justice has a nice ring to it but what critics really want is revenge."[34]

Why does talk of revenge bring out the hypocrite in so many of us? Why is the revenge impulse worn like a grotesque mask that isn't allowed to see the light of day? So many people, from American presidents to NFL quarterbacks, from grieving mothers to anguished Holocaust survivors, twist themselves in knots in order to avoid having to admit that only vengeance will satisfy their loss and relieve their suffering.

Biblical people didn't bother with these distinctions. For them, justice and vengeance were synonymous. Long before imaging technology allowed for pictures of and insights into the human brain, and even before governments decided that human beings could no longer be trusted to help themselves to vengeance, the people of the Bible and tribal societies developed their own systems for getting even with wrongdoers. They equally knew how to balance the consequences of going beyond even—when the scales of justice tipped unfairly in favor of the avenger.

The Bible was not averse to establishing ground rules for punishing those who have done wrong. God tells Noah after the flood: "Whoso sheddeth man's blood, by man shall his blood be shed" (Gen. 9:6). The Torah lists more than thirty offenses for which death is the prescribed penalty. Biblical tribes understood that the consequence of harming another meant that the victim, or his family, would be morally entitled, if not duty-bound, to retaliate.

In cases of homicide, two separate laws specifically impose the responsibility to punish a wrongdoer who has committed intentional murder on a single individual—the "avenger" (Deut. 19:1–13) or the "blood avenger" (Num. 35:9–28). Such a job is not for the community. The avenger is an individual charged with a duty to right a wrong. There is no reason to appoint a governing authority to commence a public trial, pronounce a judgment, and deliver a sentence. All you need is a blood relative. If the victim is unable or unwilling to avenge himself, the blood avenger will know what to do.

And he will also know what he is. Not all avengers are alike. Biblical laws distinguished between murder and manslaughter. When it came to the former there were no exceptions—the wrongdoer who intentionally took a life must himself die at the hands of the avenger. With regard to the latter, the unintentional, inadvertent killer is exiled to a city of refuge where he will be safe from either the avenger or the blood avenger.[35] A *beth din*, or rabbinic court, often pronounced judgment on who was entitled to remain in the city and who, given the intentionality of their crime, should receive no protection and must be tossed out. And as for the unintentional killer who misguidedly decided to leave the city, he would become a marked man, always vulnerable to vengeance, always in the sightline of the justified revenge taker.

Cities of refuge were established not only as safe havens but also as places for atonement. The Bible leaves room for repair and rehabilitation in the aftermath of manslaughter. Such is not the case for the cold-blooded murderer, however. Nothing more is expected or demanded of him other than to run and hide.

Most important, the very fact that biblical people created cities of refuge serves notice that the murder victim—and by mandated proxy, his avenger—has rights. He or she is entitled to redress. A victim is not to be forgotten or ignored. And the primary right he or she possesses is one of revenge. The intentional murderer will lose his own life; the unintentional murderer will lose his freedom. There are no exceptions, no biblical plea bargains, and no deal-cuttings that will leave the victim un-vindicated. And when carrying out this duty the avenger isn't crazy, or deluded, or irrational, or especially lusting for blood. He is merely doing his job, a job that must be done because it is owed to the victim, and it is the very thing that a balanced moral universe requires.

Whether one looks to the Old Testament, the Koran, or even Hammurabi's Code, ancient people treated revenge not as an expression of irrational madness but, rather, as a quite rational, self-regulating necessity that ensured fairness and justice. It also kept the peace by deterring future crimes, as wrongdoers realized that their misdeeds would not be forgotten, that someone would be deputized to avenge the wrong. Observing that justice and vengeance were not incompatible ideas in early civilization, philosopher Robert C. Solomon has pointed out that "vengeance is the original meaning of justice. The word 'justice' in the Old Testament and in Homer virtually always refers to revenge.... Not that the law and the respect for the law are unimportant, of course, but one should not glibly identify these with justice and dismiss the passion for vengeance as something quite different and wholly illegitimate."[36]

Yet, several thousand years later President George W. Bush and NFL quarterback Brett Favre repeated the "justice not revenge" mantra as if it had always existed as a biblical alternative to "an eye for an eye." But it hadn't. The people of the Bible didn't maintain such artificial lines, stripping justice of its vengeful dimensions. Justice, in order to be just, had to include the moral clarity, emotional closure, and symbolic vindication that comes with revenge. Vengeance was an article of faith among the newly faithful; the only consideration was who was to perform it, whether it was deserved, and how it was to be measured.

Ultimately as civilization advanced, from biblical tribes to the Dark Ages and then on through the Enlightenment, human beings were forced to surrender their right and obligation to seek revenge. The march of time resulted in the retreat of vengeance. The eighteenth-century philosopher of the Enlightenment Cesare Beccaria wrote in his 1764 treatise, *On Crimes and Punishment*, "The right of punishing belongs not to any individual in particular, but to society in general, or the sovereign."[37] This theory of the social contract, which has many fathers from John Locke to Jean-Jacques Rousseau to Thomas Jefferson, required citizens to give up certain individual rights in exchange for the government's promise to assume responsibility for the liberties that citizens would come to forfeit. Revenge is one of those rights of man that gave way to the rule of law. Governments assumed the role of surrogate avenger, minus the emotional involvement that a true avenger would naturally possess.

The drum roll for revenge turned into its own death march. Civilization gave up on vengeance and replaced it with something altogether different: judgment and punishment that is state sanctioned, emotionally dispassionate, victim insensitive, and procedurally obsessed. Governments maintained a monopoly on revenge by substituting something far more inaccessible, impersonal, and all too often innocuous—justice. And, in doing so, it turned justice into something that bore little resemblance to the vengeance that had sustained humankind from time immemorial.

Justice, and all that it implied, exerted a magical hold on modern man. The mere mention of justice triggers a Pavlovian response, an instant sense of public legitimacy and purpose. By contrast, talk of revenge nowadays leaves many repulsed. Given the distinction that everyone seems to make between justice and revenge, it would appear that their differences are vast, that they lie on opposite ends of a continuum of human behavior that defines how we respond to loss and right another's wrong. On the one end is justice, with its cool judgment, level-headedness, emotional detachment, and strict focus on the general welfare of all citizens; and on the other lies revenge, stewing in the hot juices of personal resentment and private pain, unwilling to reason, implacably committed to a course of action that leads to spilled blood, broken bones, and the recycling of still further revenge.

Ultimately, though, this is a false distinction. The call for justice is always a call for revenge. Despite all the wordplay and mind games, there is no difference between justice and vengeance. They are one and the same no matter how much we run away from revenge while falling into the arms of justice. There is no justice if wrongdoers go unpunished and victims do not feel avenged; and revenge—restoring honor, evening the score, ensuring that wrongdoers receive their just deserts—is inseparably linked to living in a just society, one that is honest about what must be done to those who do harm, and the opportunity that must be given to individuals to redress the indignity caused by another.

Speaking to the fundamental role of revenge in our conception of justice, Robert C. Solomon writes, "to seek vengeance for a grievous wrong, to revenge oneself against evil—that seems to lie at the very foundation of our sense of justice, indeed, for our very sense of ourselves, our dignity, and our sense of right and wrong."[38]

Yes, wrongdoers must serve their debt to society. But there is yet another debt—one that exists on the balance sheet of the moral universe—the one that is personally owed to the victims of that wrong. In the moral universe such debts are not dischargeable simply by making the wrongdoer repay the public at large. A wrongdoer cannot get away with paying less than what is owed, and he cannot ignore his personal obligation to the one who he has wronged.

All ledgers remain open, but the primary debt is always owed to the victim, and victims are usually in no mood to offer discounts. He or she is the proper lien holder; only the victim can decide whether the ledger gets wiped clean. Legal systems can serve as repositories of grief and resolvers of disputes, but the power to punish—the very reasons to punish—cannot be exercised without the victim foremost in mind. Societies that treat moral injury too blithely and focus only on legal retribution end up with victims who are forever resentful, untrusting of courtrooms, and unable to live with injustices that have only compounded the original injury.

Those who do harm must be held to account. Payback is not optional but obligatory. Victims must be vindicated—their dignity restored and honor reclaimed. These are not just idle wishes of the spiritually wounded. They are basic human needs and moral imperatives. And vindication cannot be performed by proxy alone. Courtrooms are fine for blind justice, but victims have to see what's going on, they must be reassured that the crimes committed against them are being taken seriously. Some emotional investment is necessary to make certain that justice has, indeed, been done. The assurance and delivery of justice is always the correct outcome because it is what both the victim and his wrongdoer rightly deserve.

But this is not what we are told. The law, we are told, runs its course on an assembly line of shared societal values, each one disconnected from private pain. We can look to the law for justice, but we can't expect it to satisfy our desire for private vengeance, nor should we. If revenge is so wrong, however, why do human beings find the settling of scores so emotionally and morally satisfying? We are not all savages at heart, consuming beverages but secretly thirsting for blood, our revenge impulse unquenchable. We simply expect to see wrongs righted and moral balance restored. Instead, the law denies victims the satisfaction that would otherwise accompany revenge. And, in doing so, legal systems ultimately fail in the delivery of justice. It is an incomplete justice; the satisfaction of the state is not shared by the true targets of the injury. What the public sees is a self-congratulatory justice that is without the moral closure of revenge. Perhaps this is why so many victims walk away from courtrooms disgusted, or refuse to enter them in the first place.

And so the public is forced to look elsewhere, somewhere other than a court of law. And that search for moral clarity is often conducted inside, of all places, movie theaters. The longing for justice has, over the centuries and across cultures, found expression in the world of art. This is where fairness is reinforced, wrongs get righted, and those who deserve be punished receive their due. The purpose of such art is not to achieve a happy ending but rather a righteous one. Avengers are paid back what they are owed because that's what the moral universe demands. Sadly, and all too often, no such similar mandate emanates from courts of law.

In art, revenge is played out in overdrive, and revenge is, undoubtedly, the artist's best friend. The legal system insists that we seek justice only through its corridors and always accept its decrees, which often means reconciling ourselves to unjust outcomes. Our culture, however, tells a different story. All forms of art—low and high, literary and pulp, theatrical and cinematic—have glorified the fate of the ordinary person who refuses to accept the law's failure, cannot ignore his loss, and is forced into a life of revenge.

It's probably safe to say that there has been an inverse relationship between injustice under the law and the abundance of revenge novels, plays, and films that spring from the imagination of artists. If the legal system didn't treat emotion as contraband, if it better appreciated the human need to feel avenged, vengeance wouldn't have become such a staple of our common culture. Our revenge cravings become ravenous whenever justice is left undone. These very same emotions are quarantined from courtrooms, a consequence of the state's monopoly over revenge and the mandate that crimes not be personalized. Tears of human emotion are not permitted to rust the grinding gears of justice. But these primal human instincts are permitted an outlet—one that is lawful—and open for business during weekend matinees.

Art comes to the rescue, not unlike the avenger himself. Artists have supplied humankind's revenge fix, feeding an addiction that has the virtue of being both emotionally necessary and entertaining. Perhaps it would be better for judges to simply convert their courtrooms into arenas where revenge can be played out emotionally and harmlessly. At the very least it would reduce our dependence on fictional stories of revenge, our only assurance that justice is, indeed, possible. Courtrooms, after all, rarely showcase such emotional power and moral purpose; damaged dignity is scarcely, if ever, given a day in court.

Cultural depictions of vengeance are the only reliable way for scores to be settled fairly and finally. But while tantalizing when projected onto screens, revenge can be deadly and destabilizing if practiced freestyle as unregulated self-help. We don't want citizens unleashing their revenge instincts onto the world like crazed vigilantes. Surely it is best for courts to handle the messy business of prosecution and punishment. After all, what is morally necessary for the individual may not be best for all of society. A victim might end up vindicated and avenged at the expense of the general welfare of everyone else. Vengeance can escalate into blood feuds and honor killings, a problem more commonly found in developing nations, but the presence of the Hatfields and the McCoys of an earlier era (adapted recently into a TV movie for the History Channel), and the Crips, Bloods, and Latin Kings of present times, demonstrates that America, too, has glimpsed the revolving consequences of unchecked revenge.

And, yet, the very idea of vengeance shouldn't remain such a cultural taboo and social stigma. That has not served us so well, either. There are moments when the taking of revenge is necessary, when there is no choice but to retaliate. For this reason, the judicial system must recognize that citizens can't be expected to so casually accept unjust outcomes. The law should always be given the first chance to balance the scales of justice, and victims should be allowed to participate in that justice. But if justice is not done, then justice must be made possible in some other way. Injustice invites a second chance, and vengeance is the realization of that chance.

Most important, we must take more seriously what it means to be victimized—first by a wrongdoer and then once more when snubbed by the law. Everything must be done to spare victims a lifetime of victimhood. But that can't happen when legal systems remove the matter from the hands of the victim and then pronounce justice to have been achieved—in name alone. Justice occurs only when, reasonably, the victim says so, when the victim declares himself to be satisfied. Robert C. Solomon has written that "the problem is not that in vengeance we take the law 'into our own hands' but rather that without vengeance justice seems not only to be taken out of our hands but eliminated as a consideration altogether."[39]

And we also have to be honest about the ways in which we permit the law to sneak revenge through the back door, creating revenge exceptions that confuse us even further. Capital punishment, victim impact statements, self-defense laws, and temporary insanity pleas are all ways in which revenge resides inside courtrooms without acknowledging that the moral need to feel avenged—and its attendant feelings of satisfaction—is, in fact, understandable and proper.

The hope with this book is to liberate vengeance from all the silence and hypocrisy that prevents it from openly informing public debate about the deficiencies of the legal system. Vengeance teaches a great deal about the moral development of mankind, and the interplay between humanity and inhumanity. And, beyond that, its denial is futile. Vengeance is everywhere, as a stealth human instinct, deeply internalized and powerfully felt. It was present in the war in Afghanistan and in the sentencing of Bernard Madoff.[40] We see it in the barely concealed satisfaction that many experience when watching those who break laws and breach the public trust receive their due. And vengeance provides the backdrop for so much of our popular culture and high art. Rooting for the avenger has become an American pastime—the fictional revenge taker is allowed a life that we all too willingly deny ourselves.

In the hit CBS TV series *The Mentalist*, Patrick Jane is a former con man psychic who now, as an independent consultant, assists California homicide detectives in solving crimes through his astute powers of observation and insight into human behavior. He's also determined to find the serial killer who murdered his wife and daughter. With his unorthodox methods and ulterior motive, he often finds himself at philosophical odds with the head of the police unit to whom he has been assigned, Teresa Lisbon. In one scene, Jane, the aggrieved husband and father, speaks honest words of moral injury that Lisbon is trained to cancel out in her line of work:

TERESA LISBON: Jane, we're officers of the law.

PATRICK JANE: You are. I don't care about the law. I care about justice. And justice says Machado deserves to suffer.

TERESA LISBON: That's not justice; it's vengeance.

PATRICK JANE: What's the difference?[41]

Revenge is the one human instinct that dares not speak its name. The mere mention of it is widely regarded as undignified—barbarism at its most naked, one of those nasty impediments to civilization itself. And yet, even as our better angels whisper that we should look away from revenge, our human nature reminds us that we cannot.

Throughout history rubbernecking at revenge has remained a beguiling spectator sport. Vengeance brings out the voyeur in each of us—even in the best among us. That's largely because revenge, like love, is a human instinct that doubles as an addiction. From neuroscience and the anatomy of the human brain we have learned that the very same sectors that respond to addictions are similarly primed to react to altruistic punishment—the impulse to see a score settled even if it produces no direct personal benefit and even if there are costs to the punisher. The knowledge that a wrongdoer has been punished is its own reward—punishment for altruistic, rather than selfish reasons. We are all better off when the bad guy is punished. Revenge is, indeed, sweet. It's not just a metaphorical saying; it's a scientific fact. The consumption of chocolate and the witnessing of justified payback register similar levels of neural satisfaction in the human brain.

Yet society has worked especially hard to eradicate revenge or, at least, to suppress the desire to retaliate. As proverbs go, "don't get mad, get even," doesn't stand a chance against the more measured voices intended to diffuse the taking of revenge, such as, "what goes around comes around"; "forgive and forget"; "let bygones be bygones"; "living well is the best revenge"; and "I wouldn't give him the satisfaction of knowing that he hurt me."

Revenge is a response to a moral injury, an attack on a human dignity. We all know the vital importance of maintaining one's dignity. The legal system, however, is far more concerned with the rights owed to the accused than with the honor that must be restored to the victim. The debt that is created from a criminal act requires a form of repayment not fully addressed by a jail sentence, and surely not from compensatory damages. The physical loss always has a spiritual dimension. And the damage done to the human spirit is what animates the impulse to avenge. The moral universe is in the business of measuring hurts and grievances, where feelings are registered and moral debts repaid. Vengeance has always been with us, a partner in our evolutionary history, a mainstay of our DNA. The tension between what is in our nature and what is purportedly in our best interest goes to the very heart of why civilization has worked so hard talking us out of our need for revenge. And it is also why, against all odds, we have been conditioned to run away from it—all the while doubling back, in demand of justice.

TWO   JUST DESERTS

Revenge is not unlike the eating habits of people at mealtime—the appetite should stop on satisfaction. It's far healthier to eat only to the point of reaching satiety. The appetite is satisfied and the body has had enough. Americans, however, are known for their big serving portions—Big Macs, Whoppers, foot longs, extra scoops, double-deckers. Buffet tables are for people who like to walk away feeling stuffed. Paradoxically, however, when it comes to vengeance, at least against common criminals, Americans are dainty eaters.

The taking of revenge has much in common with the consumption of food. There is an upper limit for eating after which one becomes a glutton; and there is a bottom limit where the intake is insufficient, where the body has, in fact, not had enough to sustain the same weight. So, too, is the case with revenge. There are indelicate and indecent avengers who shamelessly stuff themselves beyond the breaking point of justified vengeance; and there are those so decorous, forgiving, or cowardly that they refuse to partake in revenge—honor anorexics who push themselves away from the table of just deserts. Counting calories is to good health as just deserts is to justice: it's all about balance and proportion. Just deserts require that wrongdoers receive what they deserve—with precision. No arbitrary penalty, and surely not a devalued one. Only then can the punishment be deemed just.

Justified revenge—moral vengeance—is not possible unless the avenger is able to exercise restraint, has a specific measure of payback in mind, and knows not to take too much. To be an avenger rather than a hotheaded vigilante is to know when to stop, to set limits, to take what one is entitled to and no more.

As an artifact of American culture, the movie *The Godfather* is one of the most celebrated if not frequently quoted films. In fact, the film occupies a transcendent place within film history. In romanticizing the underworld activities of the Cosa Nostra, with its elegant gangsters, decapitated horses, dead bodies swimming with fish, and all of those offers that can't be refused, it's easy to overlook what the film has to say about family honor, business vendettas, and how we should all feel about the legal system. The opening scene, in fact, is a cautionary tale for lawyers and judges. And yet many miss the message.

The film begins with Bonasera, an undertaker, visiting the Godfather, the head of the Corleone crime syndicate, on the day when the Don's daughter is to be wed. Bonasera is there to ask a favor, knowing that among the various Sicilian rituals that traveled over from the old country, a man cannot refuse a favor on the day his daughter becomes a bride. Bonasera's request concerns his own daughter who was brutally beaten by two neighborhood boys who tried to rape her. Like any good, law-abiding American, the undertaker first looked to the legal system for justice.

That proved to be a mistake. The boys were given a light sentence, which was ultimately suspended, and they were returned to the street, but not before sneering at the father whose daughter they victimized. Surely this was not justice; those who had damaged his daughter were not made to pay for their crime. Bonasera felt the great insult and sense of outrage that arises when a crime goes unpunished, when loss of honor remains lost. As cognitive scientist and linguist Steven Pinker has observed, in many languages around the world, the word "honor" itself means to avenge insults, even if it requires bloodshed to do it.[1]

For most of his life the undertaker had made sure to stay clear of the Godfather. He didn't want to get mixed up with illegal business; he wanted to stay on the right side of line that divided the lawless from the lawful. Now, however, he found himself with little choice but to place himself in the Godfather's debt in return for the assurance that his daughter would be avenged. But, in doing so, Bonasera acknowledged a bitter truth about his adopted country: "For Justice, we must go to the Godfather."[2]

Many have seen the film but few recognized the moral implications of its opening scene. Chastened by the law's failure, the undertaker comes to realize that despite the trappings and promises of the law, the Mafia is, ultimately, a far more reliable dispenser of justice. And we all know the narrow and specific range of justice within which the Mafia operates. The Cosa Nostra does not preside over prisons or convene courtrooms; nor are they known for maintaining precise ledgers in keeping their books. Their world is largely confined to ending life swiftly and leaving no trace of evidence of the finality of their work.

When Don Corleone asks Bonasera what he proposes as the proper punishment for the boys who got away with the crime, the undertaker unblinkingly says vengeance: He wants the two boys killed. Don Corleone immediately replies that killing them is not fair vindication. His daughter, after all, is still alive. When Bonasera leaves, the Don instructs his lawyer Tom Hagen, "Give this to, uh, Clemenza. I want reliable people, people who aren't going to be carried away. After all, we're not murderers, in spite of what this undertaker thinks." The Godfather will only ensure that the boys will be beaten up, measure for measure, in the same way as they had beaten Bonasera's daughter—but no more.

There is a healthy dose of movie irony having a hardened killer, a Mafia chieftain, no less, someone gainfully involved in the death business—even more so than Bonasera, the undertaker—making distinctions among attempted rape, assault, and premeditated murder. Who knew the Cosa Nostra was so meticulous about punishment? The Godfather could have simply given Bonasera what he wished for: an old-fashioned Mafia death sentence for the boys who assaulted his daughter. Instead, he went to the trouble of fashioning an appropriate remedy. "We're not murderers," the Godfather proclaims. He didn't say: "Hey, I'm the Godfather. I kill for a living. I can't refuse a favor on the day of my daughter's wedding. Let's just kill the boys and be done with it."

The fact that a professional killer, even a fictional one, observes the rules of retaliation is more than just a neat movie anecdote. It's also an object lesson about justice. Retaliation is obligatory, but so, too, is a standard for measuring the amount of retaliation that is allowed. Precision is essential; proper measurement counts. Revenge is a balancing act that is steadied by a fine sense of proportion. An avenger is not required to possess the math skills of a CPA, but neither can he be a spatial moron, a spastic when it comes to arithmetic.

The opening scene from *The Godfather* speaks to the age-old difficulties of getting vengeance right, especially in cases where the crime doesn't suggest a perfect eye-for-an-eye symmetry. What is the proper punishment for rape? The fathers of modernity have had no less an easy time of getting it right than did the patriarchs of the Bible. Indeed, Bonasera is not the first father who was faced with this moral dilemma. Biblical forefathers had daughters, too, and the Old Testament has its version of loutish, roguish street thugs who tried to take advantage of young women. In fact, all modern narratives about rape, a father's anguish, and what should be done about it, have their origins in the rape of Dinah from the book of Genesis.[3] These questions arose from the very beginning; the proper punishment owed to the rapist has always been one of humanity's great imponderables. Everyone agrees that retaliation is required. But what form should the punishment take?

From Genesis and beyond, fathers understood the duty that Bonasera owed to his daughter. And the Godfather was correct in reminding this aggrieved father that the price of vengeance cannot exceed the cost of the original crime. Don Corleone intuitively understood how revenge can be made lawful, and how lawless revenge is bad business—even for the Mafia. The people of the Bible had already figured it all out. Bonasera had a predecessor in Jacob.

Jacob, one of the three patriarchs of Judaism, had many sons (remember Joseph and his brothers?) and a daughter named Dinah. One day while out on an apparent date with Shechem, the son of Hamor the Hivite, the ruler of a neighboring tribe, Dinah is raped and returns to her father's tent humiliated and damaged. Like all stories in the Bible, this one begins with a wrong turn that leads to a moral lesson.

Shechem is no ordinary sexual predator. He may, in fact, be the first date rapist of any historic note. It turns out that he loves Dinah and wants to marry her. The problem is that their first date got off to a very bad start. Although a prince, his courtship skills were prehistoric—even for biblical times. Shechem asks his father, Hamor, whether anything can be done to help win Dinah back. Hamor visits Jacob and offers him the right for Jews to own land where the Hivites have lived for generations, in return for Jacob granting Shechem's marriage proposal to Dinah. Shechem even goes so far as to double his father's offer.

Jacob's sons, known to be both wily and wild, make a counteroffer. They agree to allow their sister to marry into the Hivite tribe, but only after all of its males agree to be circumcised. Dinah's brothers want their new extended family to become Jews—to actually join their tribe. Circumcision, of course, is a painful ritual—especially for grown men and especially in the absence of anesthetics. The entire male Hivite population was being asked to make this enormous sacrifice simply to enable Shechem to marry Dinah. Hamor agrees to the proposal and returns to his tribe to give them the news. Shortly thereafter, while each Hivite male is recovering from the removal of his foreskin, two of Jacob's sons, Levi and Simeon, enter the city, kill all the men, and loot the tribe of its riches.

Jacob was not aware of what Levi and Simeon had in store for their future brother-in-law and tribal brothers. He may have realized that his sons never intended to dance at Dinah's wedding, but he is furious when he discovers what his sons have done to avenge the rape of their sister. He tells them that their family will now forever be targets of retaliatory vengeance. The brothers, however, are neither apologetic nor fearful. Dinah's rape had to be avenged. To do anything less would dishonor their family and send a disastrous message to all neighboring tribes that Jacob and his children—and all Jews, for that matter—could be violated with impunity.

The problem was not that Levi and Simeon had suckered the Hivites into a marriage that would lead to payback. Shechem had it coming. Yet Jacob knew that what Don Corleone would one day tell Bonasera was correct: when vengeance is taken to excess it ceases to be revenge and can turn into a blood feud that knows no end. It becomes unjustified revenge and loses its moral authority. And when that happens, the retaliation—wholly out of bounds and lawless—is neither vengeance nor justice. Worse still, it will invite a new series of disproportionate reprisals. Rather than settling the score, unmeasured revenge runs up the score and a new game of vengeance begins.

Dinah's brothers went well beyond even. In repayment for the rape, they not only killed the rapist, they also killed every male member of his tribe. And then, as an added bonus, they stole all of the tribe's possessions.

The imposition of collective responsibility for Shechem's crime by killing the entire Hivite male population and stealing all of their wealth surely was not a just outcome. Dinah was not killed, after all. She was raped, but she was alive. Don Corleone made the same distinction in scaling back Bonasera's desire for vengeance.

In the intervening millennia since the story of the rape of Dinah, killing the rapist has been understood as not being the proper payback for the crime of rape. Criminal statutes in the Western world continue to regard the murder of the rapist as a far more culpable crime than the underlying rape itself. The US Supreme Court, in *Coker v. Georgia*, barred the execution of rapists as "grossly disproportionate and excessive punishment" in violation of the Eighth Amendment.[4] The rule, not so very different from the Bible's treatment of Dinah, seems to be based on the principle that adult women are expected to recover from the trauma of rape. The very fact that the rape victim survived the attack means that the rapist cannot be put to death. Rules vary more widely with regard to the rape of children, however. But is the presumption that the killing of the rapist constitutes disproportionate punishment necessarily right? When it comes to the proper balancing of the scales of justice, the weights and measurements are sometimes in dispute.

Law professor Peter French, for instance, in his important book, *The Virtues of Vengeance*, wonders why the death of the rapist is not an appropriate punishment for the lifetime of psychological damage inflicted on the rape victim.[5] The crime of rape has always presented measurement problems in fashioning the correct penalty for the rapist. Susan Jacoby has observed that women, historically, did not receive the same right of revenge as was allowed their fathers and husbands to avenge the rape. Women avengers, apparently, were too threatening to patriarchal visions of female helplessness. And the manly duty to defend honor applied exclusively to men.[6]

What is not permitted under the law is often accepted in art, however. Feature films such as *Hannie Caulder* (1971), *A Time to Kill* (1996), *Kill Bill* (vols. 1 and 2, 2003 and 2004, respectively), and the fourth season of the TV series *Dexter* present the apparently more emotionally satisfying idea that the death of the rapist is the equivalent punishment for the crime of rape—whether performed by the rape victim herself or by her husband, boyfriend, or father.

The rape of Dinah in the book of Genesis assumes a right of revenge. But it is more a cautionary tale than a blanket license to avenge. Murdering an entire tribe of men and sacking their city as payback for the rape of a sister is vastly disproportionate and unmeasured. Levi and Simeon were gluttons at the revenge table. Shechem was guilty of neither murder nor theft. In a legal sense, Levi and Simeon are now guilty of both. Jacob was right in fearing that the liberties his sons had taken would likely unleash a new wave of retaliatory violence.

Yet, if the people of the Bible were on notice that a right of retaliation always lurked behind a contemplated crime, how would they know how much revenge to take without igniting a blood feud? It is an especially complicated arithmetic when dealing with revenge among nations.

This was exactly what Steven Spielberg had in mind in his film *Munich* (2005), which was inspired by the murder of the entire Israeli Olympic team by Palestinian terrorists during the 1972 Olympic Games. In an early scene in the film, Israeli prime minister Golda Meir is consulting with her advisers on what Israel's response should be to the killings. One of her generals reminds her that Israel had already succeeded in bombing a Palestine Liberation Organization (PLO) training base in retaliation. Many terrorists were killed, far more than the number of murdered Israeli athletes. Was that the appropriate and proportionate response? In the sober, unemotional language of real politik, the general explains that the attack against the PLO base is precisely what nations do in such circumstances.

Aaron Sorkin, the creator of the dramatic television series *The West Wing*, gave his fictional president an opportunity to weigh in on what constitutes a "proportional response" when it comes to vengeance among nations. With great agitation and impatience, the president asks his military advisers what are the virtues of a proportional response. Terrorists have attacked America; the president is taking the offense personally and shows little desire to tailor the retaliation so as not to exceed the original assault. What he wants is to dial up the kind of "shock and awe" (code words for unmeasured, disproportionate retaliation) that an actual American president, George W. Bush, ultimately unleashed on Afghanistan. The privilege of commanding a superpower makes it possible to send a message that the cost of attacking the United States will result in the kind of payback that can truly scorch the earth. The measure of America's resolve is always an infinite number. But presidents and prime ministers surround themselves with advisers in situation rooms, and the advice they give is to stay the hand of vengeance. Accept the customary reprisal and move on to the others matters of state. The American president in *The West Wing* remains unconvinced. A Navy admiral responds to the president by saying, "It isn't virtuous, Mr. President. It's all there is."[7]

But is that true? Nations, apparently, are bound by clearly defined protocols where retaliation is permitted but only to the extent that it is proportionate. There are rules, and one such rule is that a nation is not permitted to simply go berserk. How does a state know when its retaliation will be regarded as disproportionate and unjustified? There is no shortage of national security experts who advise world leaders as to what is appropriate and proportional and what violates international norms. Are America's drone strikes on the border between Pakistan and Afghanistan in proportion to the crimes of 9/11? Were Allied bombings of Hiroshima, Nagasaki, and Dresden a measured response for the Japanese bombing of Pearl Harbor and the German bombing of London?

In the film *Munich*, Prime Minister Golda Meir, surrounded by her military advisers, is equally unconvinced that proportion is measurable, that balance is at all possible, and that a ratio can be found. For the prime minister, a proportional response that is limited to an attack against a PLO base does not feel sufficiently retaliatory, much less emotionally satisfying. She wants to get the actual killers. Her people, the Israeli public, watched their Olympic team kidnapped and slaughtered on national TV. They will regard an isolated, nonspecific act of vengeance to be insufficient, even if that is how nations exercise revenge on the global stage.

The prime minister orders the targeted assassinations of a rogue's gallery of Palestinian terrorists all throughout Western Europe, consisting of the men who actually plotted the murder of the Israeli Olympic team. She says, "Every civilization finds it necessary to negotiate compromises with its own values."[8] Revenge, in this instance, cannot be achieved by killing PLO terrorists indiscriminately—regardless of where they live and who they are.

Even in international affairs, accuracy matters. Those responsible for the crime must be discovered and held fully accountable. At the same time, the point of view of the film as it reaches its conclusion is that indiscriminate killings have led to a blood feud between the Israelis and the Palestinians, achieving little except for an endless recycling of revenge.

In 2009, Israel's invasion of Gaza led to a United Nations investigation by its Human Rights Council. The resulting "fact-finding report" primarily blamed Israel for a three-week incursion that produced a disproportionate number of Palestinian casualties: As many as fourteen hundred Palestinians were killed during the campaign as compared with just thirteen Israelis. Israel was also condemned for apparently failing to distinguish between civilians and combatants in targeting its victims.

The Gaza campaign lasted for twenty days, and during that time period the Palestinians clearly suffered more than the Israelis did. But since 2001, Hamas, the terrorist group that governs Gaza, launched eight thousand rockets into Israel. The rain of rockets continued even after 2005 when Israel withdrew from Gaza as a first step toward achieving peace. Meanwhile, Hamas never wavered from its proclaimed intention to rid the region of all its Jews and claim Israel for itself. A Palestinian statehood that includes all of greater Israel minus all the Jews is precisely what Hamas sought. That's the scorecard that Hamas was using and the endgame of its intentions: not coexistence between Israelis and Palestinians, but no existence at all for Israelis.

From the Israeli perspective, that's how proportion needed to be measured when the Gaza campaign began. And it was not unlike the choice its prime minister (the real Gold Meir, not just the fictional one portrayed in *Munich*) made in 1972 following the murder of Israel's Olympic team. Any discussion about proportion had to take into account the larger Palestinian objectives. The Gaza War—short as it was, and apparently as uneven as it was—was a snapshot of a far more complicated and murderous landscape where proportion can easily grow all out of proportion. In such zero-sum circumstances, one-to-one ratios are no longer the standards by which reprisals are measured. The two sides can't agree about when the scales of justice are balanced, when will the scores finally be settled?[9]

In the world's estimation, the Gaza War, known in Israel as Operation

Cast Lead, was conducted as if Israel had a lead foot on the accelerator of immeasurable force. But when it comes to international affairs and the strife between nations, a proportional response must always take account of the past. Revenge is, by definition, a response to some *prior* action that resulted in great harm, loss, or dishonor. Vengeance is all about the past; it is fixated entirely on what happened and what must now be done about it. Without stubbornly long memories, the impulse to avenge would lose its moral urgency. Even preemptive strikes require a concrete provocation, and that provocation is sometimes embedded in past memories.

It is precisely a nation's collective memory—and the sanity of its individual members—that makes revenge indispensable to achieving justice. Revenge is as much about memory as it is an instrument of just deserts. There is no reason to balance the scales of justice if they were never believed to be unbalanced to begin with. Something had already tipped the scale. Only then does the state of affairs appear to be out of proportion, all on account of the unilateral act of another. But the vilest of all provocations occurs when one nation draws a line in the sand and says: "Everything behind this line no longer counts. Our sins and your grievances are forever erased. But everything going forward will result in our nation screaming bloody murder."

Such are the psychodynamics and mind games of the Middle East: New lines are drawn in the desert sand, and no nation wishes to take responsibility for the actions of the past—to faithfully remember what had happened. Every day is Groundhog Day in Gaza and the Galilee; the odometer of grievance always rolls back to zero.[10] Proportion has a way of looking all lopsided, the fuzzy math of the Middle East never adds up. The enduring conflict is as much a tragedy about keeping score as it is one of failed opportunities. Israel's recent eight-day excursion into Gaza in November 2012, to retaliate against the one thousand missiles Hamas had launched at the Jewish state, produced similar dynamics and disproportions.[11]

It becomes nearly impossible to remember who started what and when. One nation's retaliation is another's provocation. Revenge must be deliberate rather than accidental, but it does not have to be immediate in its delivery. Just as an avenger can wait and bide his or her time in taking revenge, so, too, can nations store up the debts that are owed to them and retaliate when the time is right. Indeed, waiting to take revenge provides its own ancillary punishment, torturous in its own way. The wrongdoer knows his just deserts are coming and must always look over his shoulder to avoid being taken by surprise. Hamlet stumbles around Denmark throughout the entirety of Shakespeare's play alternating between madness and self-doubt. His mother, Gertrude, and his uncle, Claudius, their reign fragile and their deaths all but certain, know that eventually the addled son of the murdered king will do his duty and avenge his father.

All this talk about proportionate retaliation does make one think that the world would be better off if managed by business majors rather than inept politicians and loathsome dictators—at least when it comes to doling out vengeance. Revenge requires a heart full of passion and a head for numbers. It is a moral enterprise, not a political one, and performed not to achieve an advantage but to redeem a debt. Whether in the Bible or on modern day battlefields, it's best when the avenging nation—or the individual who must resort to vengeance—is motivated by math and knows how to keep the books.

Even British rock bands understand this simple accounting principle. The Who, one of the iconic bands of the British invasion of the 1960s and 1970s, sang, "My love is vengeance, That's never free" on its 1971 single, "Behind Blue Eyes."[12] Vengeance is always repayment, even if it is delivered as an act of love. There is nothing arbitrary or reckless about it; you're either owed payback or you're not. A true debtor is never surprised when vengeance arrives. He might ask for one more day, but he never blurts out: "The check is in the mail!"

How much vengeance to take and in what form should it be delivered is, however, a mixture of art and science. Ancient societies never doubted the morality of revenge. All they had to decide was who the authorized avenger would be and whether his manner of taking revenge was properly tailored for the original loss. Neither God nor Jacob was troubled by the moral duty to avenge the rape of Dinah. The Old Testament didn't prohibit the taking of revenge. Cities of refuge were created precisely because avengers were on the loose with rightful claims against wrongdoers. Those who were innocent or merely negligent were permitted sanctuary. But there was no escaping punishment that was justly owed.

What concerned ancient peoples was not vengeance but its excess. Vengeance always carried the risk of an infinite recycling of revenge. Ethnic violence and tribal blood feuds are still traceable to repetitious revenge cycles. They occurred when retribution went too far, when getting even somehow was not enough. Fresh wounds and new debts invite entirely new rounds of payback. It was the fear of voracious vengeance that convinced governments to go into the revenge business for themselves. Individuals were suddenly required to outsource their revenge obligations by handing them over to the state.

Governments believed that as institutions freed of the emotion that causes hatred to run amuck, the state is better suited to tailor punishment than vindictive victims too blinded by rage to take the true measure of what they were owed. Peter French observed that vengeance always concerns proper fit.[13] The act of revenge must always be a well-suited response to the underlying injury. Size matters when it comes to revenge. How much revenge is too much? How little is the bare minimum? The fit must be suitable, the measurements specific, to qualify as moral revenge. Private avengers and robed jurists are both in the same business, and each must be ever mindful of what gives them the authority to avenge, and for whose ultimate benefit justice is being done. No matter the arena, regardless of whether justice is being delivered by the state or by a deputized avenger, moral revenge must possess these four basic elements: (1) there must be a severe moral injury or act of wrongdoing; (2) the avenger, or the court, must have the authority to seek vengeance and communicate to the wrongdoer why vengeance is being taken and on whose behalf justice is being delivered; (3) the wrongdoer must be deserving of punishment; and (4) the punishment must not be disproportionate to the original injury; it must properly address and pay back for the harm.

So what does an eye for an eye actually look like, and how can such complicated measurements be determined?

This is the cornerstone of *lex talionis*, the law of the *talion*—the intellectual and metaphorical birthplace of an eye-for-an-eye. It establishes the ground rules for retaliation and informs the principle of just compensation and the balancing of loss and repayment—"life for life, eye for eye, tooth for tooth, hand for hand." No more, and no less—the basic formulation of equivalence and reciprocity that is codified in the books of Exodus, Leviticus, and Deuteronomy. All the necessary fuss about proportionate revenge derives from the *talion*.

The *talion* is no less fastidious than an audit by the Internal Revenue Service. It establishes an upper limit on how much an avenger can take in response to another's wrong. More crucially, however, it sets forth a lower limit, too, which imposes a moral obligation *to* avenge. Vengeance is not optional; it is obligatory. Some measure of revenge *must* be taken; it cannot simply be forsaken or ignored.[14]

There is no justice in pretending that a moral injury never actually occurred. The moral balance of communities, and the sanity of victims, cannot tolerate the outrage of such casual forgetting. But the fear of igniting blood feuds and gluttonous revenge is moderated by an upper boundary of restraint. Proportionate revenge demands a perfect fit. The prerequisites of an eye for an eye do not permit the substitution of a limb for the taking of a life. As Bonasera came to learn, there is no "a life for a rape."

Or maybe there is. The recent Argentine thriller *The Secret in Their Eyes*, which received the Academy Award for Best Foreign Language film in 2010, puts the lie to Don Corleone's words and introduces a new twist on how to seek vengeance against a rapist who has also committed murder.[15] In the film, a wife is raped and killed in her home. The detective assigned to the case promises the victim's husband that when he is caught, the assailant will be given a life sentence for his crime. The wrongdoer is apprehended, but he is eventually released due to a procedural error and police corruption.

A quarter of a century later, the detective travels to the home of the victim's husband. He wonders how the man has managed to live all these years without the love of his life. Apparently, with great difficulty. The widower appears not to have fared well. But then again, neither has the rapist/murderer. The crime that was never successfully prosecuted was not forgotten, even though no one has seen the accused in years. The police had promised the husband that his wife's murderer would spend his entire life in prison. And so far he has, locked up in a makeshift cell in a small building near the main house where the widower lives. There he has been imprisoned all this time, aging alone, with no one to speak to, not even his bereft jailor, who has fashioned a punishment that mirrors his own emptiness, measure for measure.

Compensation and punishment are not so easily interchangeable. Accuracy is the governing ethos of revenge. Precision is both the avenger's duty and his secret weapon. The avenger who worries about fit is not the avenger who easily loses his head. Revenge is admittedly emotional and personal, but that doesn't mean that it can't also be lucid and clear-headed. Emotion can lead to exactness rather than excess. The avenger who is mindful of suitability is not likely to be accused of taking disproportionate vengeance; proper fit rarely leads to a blood feud.

Similarly, the *talion* has a message for the reluctant avenger. He, or she, is given a mandate of what is at least *minimally* required. Indulging too much constitutes unjustified revenge; partaking in too little—not going far enough—violates a different moral principle. To not satisfy the debt is morally repugnant. The eyes of the community are always watching. And a human being's sense of honor and self-worth will accept no less than proper payback. Hamlet was one such ambivalent avenger, and while it takes two acts of the drama for him to stumble about before doing his duty, he knows that his mother and uncle will have to die in retaliation for his father's murder.

Revenge is not an act of lawless barbarism, although it is understandable how deeply this catchphrase, over time, has shaped our perceptions. Nor is it true that revenge is always animated by anger and rage. If revenge is the antidote to lost honor—if it is indeed the only way to reclaim one's honor—then anger doesn't have to be the guiding principle behind vengeance at all. To that point law professor William Ian Miller asks, "Couldn't [the victim] also be motivated by a sense of grief or duty or love? Perhaps they're desperate to set things right for their loved one. Perhaps they're not motivated by rage but by a grim sense of purpose, or a keen sense of obligation. We demean the wide emotional range of what the avenger might feel."[16]

And we also demean, and fail to comprehend, why vengeance becomes so essential to a feeling of justice. One of the reasons why modern societies have such trouble with revenge is because they have so little appreciation of honor as having its own intrinsic value—of something that is worth fighting to reclaim. We speak of honor abstractly, not as something that can be taken away, its absence painfully felt. A bruised body receives compensatory relief under the law; wounded pride, however, has no equivalent remedy.

Dishonor and disrespect deserve compensation, too, the kind that is not measurable in monetary terms. Instead, we insist that what is unbearable should be internalized and made tolerable—suck it up, walk it off, let it go. But we can't. Steven Pinker points out that sociologists remain puzzled as to why more murders, comparatively speaking, are not perpetrated in connection with robberies or drug deals. Instead, we see homicides linked to insults, humiliation, curses, and the damage done to reputation.[17]

As William Ian Miller has said, "In our Utilitarian, highly sophisticated society, we don't think as clearly as the people in old cultures. They were much better at evaluating things that we think can't be captured in dollars. They knew what a man was worth. Why? Because they measured his honor."[18]

All this suggests that vengeance is never casually undertaken, nor is it necessarily the handiwork of unhinged emotions. There are rules for revenge; and the first rule is that it be justified. Petty slights, imagined insults, and feigned injuries can never give rise to revenge. Lost honor must have arisen from a true act of dishonor. Some material loss, some moral injury, some true deficit must occur, creating a debt owed to the victim that must be repaid. Modern Western cultures tend to value human beings by net material worth. But ancient peoples were better at taking true stock of human beings, and they knew that honor was a more worthy measure of value than money. And when lost, it had to be reclaimed, even if that meant taking justice into one's own hands. But, still, not without guidelines. As one biblical example, the story of the rape of Dinah, illustrated both the moral duty to avenge and the consequences of immoderate revenge.

Yet most people believe that an eye for an eye is a biblical green light in favor of vengeful, dismembering fury. What kind of a person other than a savage would forcefully take out someone's eye? But this misreading, so widely shared, is one of the reasons why revenge labors under so many falsehoods and much societal scorn.

The Old Testament doesn't promote people "going postal". The Old Testament merely recognizes that loss must be repaid to victims and that avengers are the delegated beneficiaries of the payback—it is their task to fulfill. No one has a superior right to redeem the debt. Given the inevitability of revenge, the Bible simply wishes that it be done correctly.

No one is entitled to the repayment of an eye unless they have actually lost one. Evening the score places the avenger in the position of a creditor. But the rules of vengeance ensure that credit limits are always in place. Avengers must act responsibly. An avenger might be angry, and he might have good reasons for that anger, but his vengeance must always take account of the actual debt. There is no such thing as a revenge jackpot, where avengers leverage debts like Wall Street bankers, surpassing getting even by multiples on the way to greater revenge riches. Even with vengeance, the house always wins. No matter how sloppy the avenger is in his life, no matter how poorly his arithmetic, precision must always guide the discharging of the debt.

Think of Shylock in Shakespeare's *The Merchant of Venice* sharpening his knife, checking on the accuracy of his scale, preparing to take his pound of flesh, but being warned by Portia, the judge in drag, that the pound of flesh denominated by the bond does not permit the spilling of any of Antonio's— his debtor's—blood. Shylock wants his revenge. But he can only have what he bargained for, what he is allowed—to take no more than a pound of flesh, measure for measure. One pound of flesh is his upper limit, his full entitlement. Like all acts of vengeance, the satisfaction of this debt demands accuracy. Even if he can carve out an exact pound of Antonio's flesh, how will he stop the blood, which is not part of the original bargain, and will, by necessity, unbalance the scale?[19]

It is the very specificity of this debt that forces Shylock to put away his knife—no matter how deserving Antonio and his friends are of receiving a good old-fashioned dose of biblical revenge. In *The Merchant of Venice*, the law of the *talion*, as much as Portia's clever lawyering, actually limited Shylock's vengeful impulses—the *talion* working both sides of this dispute, supplying the necessary check on revenge even as it required that vengeance be done.

The *talionic* principle always operates in the shadows of moral injury, reminding the avenger that as much as there are obligations *to* avenge, there are also reciprocal limitations *on* revenge. This is precisely what Jacob meant in the book of Genesis when he lamented how poorly his sons had miscalculated the amount of Shechem's debt. The scales were once again uneven; the murder and sacking of Shechem's tribe had now produced a new set of debts that would require another round of repayments—this time with Jacob and his family in the position of debtors rather than as creditors and justified avengers. And the moral lesson within this biblical parable is that standing up for family honor is essential, but taking too much revenge leaves the family vulnerable.

Short of constituting a principle of blind and irrational rage, the *talion* establishes an orderly vision of justice and fairness. And it extended far beyond the ancient peoples of the Bible. It is also found in the Hammurabi Code. The *talion* influenced the medieval tribes of Iceland and Germany. Tribal cultures all over the world adopted similar rules designed to accomplish a variety of retributive and compensatory goals. Each was a mix of punishment and revenge, compensation and satisfaction.

In medieval England, for instance, the loss of a middle finger required the compensation of four shillings; a broken rib was three shillings; the loss of a foot, fifty shillings, thirty for a thumb, a little more than sixty-six for an eye.[20] All of these recoveries for tortious injury were achieved without government intervention, without courtrooms, without prison walls. Present-day workers' compensation laws were long preceded by the law of the *talion*. Everyone understood what an eye was worth—not the literal eye, but something of predetermined, equivalent value. When it came to a life, however, an intentional killing was usually satisfied in only one finite way, although in some cultures a combination of money and services might permit a life to be spared.

With the rise of Christianity and the New Testament, human beings were told to renounce their right of revenge—not because vengeance was too risky, but because it was deemed too unbecoming for the followers of the Prince of Peace. In the New Testament, God declares in the book of Romans (12:19): "Dearly Beloved, avenge not yourselves, but rather give place unto wrath: for it is written: Vengeance is mine; I will repay, saith the Lord."

Once God reserves the right to vengeance only for himself, the moral cause of revenge begins to lose its moral authority. In the book of Luke (10:30–36), Jesus tells the story of the Good Samaritan, which diverts Christians away from justifiable revenge and in the direction of forgiveness, mercy, and compassion. And in the book of Matthew (5:43–48) lies the most disastrous undoing of the equalizing benefits and fundamental morality of revenge. It is here, in Jesus's Sermon on the Mount, where the principle of loving one's enemies first appears. For millions of Christians around the world, what might seem to be an unnatural act of love becomes a true labor of love. But it also forbids avengers from evening the score.

"You have heard that it was said, 'An eye for an eye and a tooth for a tooth.' But I say to you, Do not resist one who is evil. But if any one strikes you on the right cheek, turn to him the other also; and if any one would sue you and take your coat, let him have your cloak as well. . . .

"You have heard that it was said, 'You should love your neighbor and hate your enemy.' But I say to you, Love your enemies and pray for those who persecute you."

With the Old and New Testaments crossing wires when it comes to vengeance, what did biblical people ultimately believe? Christianity favors turning the other cheek and practicing mercy as a salvational response to injury. But even as Christians counsel "to forgive and forget"—backed up by the teachings of modern psychology that anger causes sickness—we all know that these slogans of civil society are difficult to live by. Turning the other cheek is not a natural reflex of the human anatomy. And if forgiving means forgetting, then whatever religious benefits derive from such teachings are surely offset by an even greater moral sin: the act of forgetting, the pretense that a wrong never took place at all.

John Demjanjuk, a Ukrainian who served as a guard at the Sobibor concentration camp in Nazi-occupied Poland, emigrated to America after the war and lived in Ohio for many years as a law-abiding citizen until the Justice Department discovered who he was—or who they thought he was. After being stripped of his citizenship in 1985 for lying about his past, he was extradited to Israel to face trial. But he ended up back in the United States when the Israeli Supreme Court, which had already sentenced him to death in 1993, was forced to overturn his conviction when it learned that the Americans had prosecuted Demjanjuk under the wrong alias. They thought he was the notorious guard at Treblinka, Ivan the Terrible. As it turned out, Demjanjuk was, indeed, a guard, but at Sobibor, not Treblinka, and he wasn't Ivan the Terrible. He was a much lower mass murderer, someone who still participated in the killing of twenty-eight thousand people. Only in the Nazi universe of genocidal excellence would that lofty number not qualify as notorious.

Further legal proceedings lasting nearly twenty years finally resulted in Demjanjuk being deported to Germany in 2009. In May 2011, at age ninety-one, Demjanjuk, who suffered from a number of ailments that forced him to lie on his back throughout the trial, was sentenced to five years in prison. What was the point of prosecuting a sick, ninety-one-year-old man for a crime that took place in 1943? The punishment, which involved many years of prosecutions and jail sentences with the final one assuring that he would die in prison, which he did, less that a year later, took decades and cost millions to achieve, but it was anxiously awaited by Demjanjuk's victims—those dead and alive.

Rudie S. Cortissos survived the Holocaust as a small boy by hiding in Amsterdam. His mother, however, was not so fortunate. She was deported to Sobibor where she ended up as one of Demjanjuk's victims. Costissos, speaking for himself and his mother, testified at the trial. "I had an opportunity to say what I wanted to say for 50 years," Cortissos, now seventy-three, said outside of the courtroom after the verdict was announced. "I'm satisfied. It doesn't mean I can forget; it doesn't mean I can forgive."[21]

Cortissos invoked the word "satisfied" (satisfaction), which embodies the very essence of proportional revenge. Demjanjuk received what he deserved—no more, and no less. And yet Cortissos acknowledged that even though his mother's murderer was finally going to be punished after decades of avoidance, it didn't mean that he could now forget what Demjanjuk had done to her. To leave a crime unavenged is to desecrate the dead. And to forget the wrong is a betrayal of family love. To avenge is to remember, and to act in honor of that memory. Philosopher Berel Lang has written, "Unlike forgiveness which erases the past, revenge preserves it."[22] Hamlet's father, who appears to Hamlet as a ghost in the play's opening scene, doesn't tell his son to avenge his murder. He doesn't have to. He merely says, "Adieu, adieu, adieu. Remember me." For better or worse, Hamlet knows exactly what those words mean and what he must ultimately do to honor his father and heed his final words.[23]

Hamlet's ghost is not alone among the undead who were murdered through treachery and now refuse to rest easy until they are properly re-membered—whether they have their sons honor their memory or they are forced to avenge themselves by returning to haunt the living. All ghost stories and horror films are ultimately tales of revenge—vengeance neces-sitated by the failure to remember.

What's most frightening about horror films such as *I Know What You Did Last Summer* (1997), *The Crow* (1994), and *The Ring* (2002) is not the pres-ence of ghosts and boogiemen, which the rational mind can easily dismiss as being *just* a movie. What can't be ignored, however, what provides the realism and moral urgency for the scary business of horror, is *why* these ghosts haunt in the first place. The avengers may be dead, but they still must have their vengeance. The duty carries over to the grave. The moral lesson that lies underneath all the gore is that the ghosts are not there merely to scare the audience. They serve as reminders that unpunished crimes can't be buried along with the dead.

If justice had been done, if the crimes that resulted in their deaths had been avenged, if the wrongdoers had been justly punished, had their lives been memorialized by acknowledging *how* they had died, then the ghosts would have had no reason to return. Not in the habit of turning the other cheek, ghosts end up turning over in their graves. The failure to avenge can haunt the dreams of those who refuse to do their duty. And wrongdoers, at least in art, can find themselves forever haunted by their dead victims who were denied earthly justice. It might take a lifetime to achieve, but vengeance must occur and, in the mind of the wrongdoer, must always be anticipated. Revenge is looming in the rearview mirror of those who have escaped punishment. It always remains the most crucial piece of unfinished business.

Some societies still practice vengeance. For most other people, revenge simply exists as part of their deepest fantasies. What is certain is that the desire for revenge can't be stopped. Centuries of teachings and prohibitions have failed to make it go away. Whether it was God's declaration that "ven-geance is mine," the Christian prescription to "love thy neighbor," the New Age-y homilies about "letting go" of all anger, the prescribed rules of tribal societies requiring civil payment as compensation for maiming and murder, or the enlightened philosophers who favored the retribution of states over the revenge of individuals, humankind has been relentlessly presented with alternatives but still won't give up on revenge. Most people don't believe that revenge is half the vice it's cracked up to be. What lingers within all human beings is the overwhelming sense of rightness that vengeance evokes in each of us.

Revenge has not been made obsolete with the modern world's reliance on the rule of law. If anything, justice would feel more just if vengeance could better influence the rule of law. The emotional connection that vengeance has with justice is precisely what is most lacking in the state's administration of the legal system. Justice that is stubbornly unconcerned with the honor and dignity of victims will never achieve the satisfaction of revenge. Drawing on this emotional absence as one reason why the legal system suffers from a lack of public legitimacy, Robert C. Solomon has written, "Not that the law and respect for the law are unimportant, of course, but one should not glibly identify these with justice and dismiss the passion for vengeance as something quite different and wholly illegitimate."[24]

Vengeance is not as sinful as we have all been led to believe. Nor does it always invite overindulgence at the revenge table. Avengers are quite able to appreciate the consequence of violating the *talion*. Indeed, there is both poetry and an elegant logic to the Bible's an-eye-for-an-eye formula for measuring revenge. The law of the *talion* is old but not outdated. Vengeance can run its proper course without setting off new and untamable fires of revenge.

Peter French has suggested that it was not so much the fear of recycled revenge that convinced more modern societies to favor a model of institutionalized legal retribution. Payback didn't have to be taken out of the hands of individuals; it wasn't inevitable that the settling of scores could only be confined to legal arenas. Had the state not monopolized revenge, most people would have simply deferred to the *talion*, as they had always done in the past. French identifies several reasons why the private settlement of disputes was forced into retirement. First, having a single entity handle the unpleasant chore of tracking down and punishing wrongdoers proved itself to be far more economically efficient than leaving it up to private avengers. Second, most people are not courageous enough to avenge the wrongs done to them, and society itself is often guilty of moral cowardice, if not squeamishness, when faced with the question of what to do about wrongdoers. All of this was only compounded by the tenets of Christian forgiveness and the willingness to wipe the slate clean rather than hold wrongdoers to account. Over time the necessary backbone that vengeance required collapsed into a puddle of spinelessness. The preservation of honor, which typically sparks the human impulse to avenge, was squelched and forgotten. French writes: "The fact that most of us have so readily turned these important matters over to impersonal, procedurally-structured technologies should not be exhibited as one of our great moral accomplishments."[25]

And, to some degree, and for many individuals, it wasn't even necessary. Few avengers are looking to start a war. Most human beings know when to stop, when the revenge they have taken leaves them satisfied. Robert C. Solomon has written that humankind is not given enough credit for knowing what it means to get even without creating further debts.[26] Most people will satisfy their need for justice by way of a single act of vengeance. Charles K. B. Barton, in *Getting Even: Revenge as a Form of Justice*, writes that in world cultures where acts of personal vengeance are lawful, avengers know not to retaliate beyond measure because otherwise they would become subject to "stiff moral and social disapproval from their communities."[27] Rare is the case, Solomon suggests, when vengeance knows no moderation, when revenge becomes a bottomless pit that can never be filled.

In 1996, William Bonin, Southern California's notorious Freeway Killer, was scheduled to be executed. He had confessed to killing twenty-one boys and young men. The victims were largely hitchhikers he had picked up, raped, and, finally, strangled to death. At his sentencing hearing Bonin not only failed to exhibit any remorse, he placed the parents' of his victims in further agony by withholding information about their sons' deaths. (Clint Eastwood's film *The Changeling* (2008), starring Angelina Jolie, had a similar scene and plotline, based on a true story also set in California about the Wineville Chicken Coop Murders of 1928).

Sandra Miller, the mother of one of the boys who Bonin had raped, tortured, and strangled sixteen years earlier, said that at the moment right before Bonin received the lethal injection she hoped to experience the relief that now "he's finally going to pay." In a letter to Bonin that she wanted him to read right before his execution, she wrote: "You taught me a few things: How to hate, and that I feel I could kill you, little by little, one piece at a time. You'd best get down on your hands and knees and pray to God for forgiveness. I don't know if even He could forgive you. But I hope the Lord can forgive me for how I feel about you"[28]

THREE THE EMOTIONS OF REVENGE

The 2010 Tour de France will be remembered as much for cyclist mishaps and crashes among the riders as for exciting breakneck surges toward the final line. There was even an ungainly fistfight between two riders that served to demonstrate why these athletes depend mostly on their legs and should keep their fists solidly on the handlebars. And, of course, this was yet another year when Lance Armstrong had to swerve away from allegations that several of his earlier Tour de France triumphs may have been enhanced as much by illegal doping as by inhuman pedaling.

During Stage 15 of that year's tour, however, which included a final climb through the Pyrenees, Andy Schleck, from Luxembourg, wearing the yellow jersey signifying that he was the tour leader, looked down from his seat and discovered that his chain had fallen off. The common courtesy in such instances is not to allow the leader of the race to lose time—or for the other riders to take advantage of his misfortune—due to a fall from his bicycle or an equipment failure. Usually, the riders wait until the leader hops back on his bike and resumes the race.

But Alberto Contador, the prior year's tour winner and a personal friend of Schleck, was in second place, thirty-one seconds behind, when Schleck's hands were about to be covered in grease. Contador decided to speed up just as his friend and main competition was slowing down and gained thirty-nine seconds to capture the lead, with Schleck falling to second place overall, eight seconds behind. Contador never surrendered the yellow jersey for the remainder of the tour, which he ultimately won by, ironically, thirty-nine seconds. (In 2012, Contador was stripped of his tour title because he had tested positive for a banned substance, a kind of just-deserts courtesy of the International Cycling Union.) The coincidence of the final times should have only deepened the wound that Schleck felt, but when the tour was finally over he was gracious in defeat. But that was not the case at the finish line of Stage 15.

Regardless of one's appreciation of Tour de France etiquette and whether Contador's sprint while Schleck fiddled with his chain was a breach of decorum rather than the mere luck of the roadway, no one could have faulted Schleck for speaking honestly about his feelings.

"I can tell you, my stomach is full of anger and I want to take my revenge," Schleck said. "I will take my revenge."[1]

Luxembourg may be at least one country where citizens speak honestly about vengeance without fear. Moreover, they apparently don't feel the need to make fine distinctions when it comes to having their revenge. Schleck wanted everyone to know that he was justifiably angry about Stage 15 and that Contador's insult would not go unanswered. The result was more than just a question of Schleck's standing in the race; it was also his standing as a man. Yes, the Tour de France was at stake, but so, too, was his honor.

Even though cycling is a sport that depends on a clock and not a scoreboard, Schleck's first impulse was to even the score. He lost thirty-nine seconds due to Contador's brazen mad dash, and he wanted it back—or its equivalent: "thirty-nine seconds for thirty-nine seconds." Given such a slight margin of victory, had Contador waited for Schleck to slip his chain back on, they might never have traded yellow jerseys and Schleck might have won his first Tour de France.

Nevertheless, at the conclusion of Stage 15, with feelings still raw and the spirit of sportsmanship shattered, Schleck was not a bitter, skinny hothead with massive legs. He was a man with justifiable reasons to feel anger and resentment toward a friend who scampered away from the scene of an accident for his own cynical advantage.

Anger, resentment, and revenge: all words that have a profound connection to justice—and the essential feeling that justice must been done—and yet they are widely regarded as the street talk of lunatics, the behavior of the mentally unstable, the kind of people in need of a Valium. We've heard it all before: no good comes from being angry; resentment can be its own prison; and revenge is an outdated artifact of primitive man.

As much as revenge is about justice, it is also about emotion. There can be no true feeling of justice without emotional satisfaction. They, too, are twinned. Justice cannot be separated from the public's acceptance—in both a moral and emotional sense—that justice was, indeed, done. But since most governments do not allow feelings to be expressed within the institutional settings of a courtroom, true justice either never comes or is entirely wasted in the emotional wasteland of the law.

Robert C. Solomon understood this essential codependency between justice and emotion when he wrote, "To the dangers of vengeance unlimited it must be countered that if punishment no longer satisfies vengeance, if it ignores not only the rights but the *emotional needs* of the victims of crimes, then punishment no longer serves its primary purpose" (emphasis added).[2]

Human beings are deeply aware of when injustice has occurred and when payback is sorely owed. And victims have the moral right to demand satisfaction—in both material terms and with regard to the emotional benefits—even when it is the legal system itself that is the designated dispenser of justice. Revenge responds directly to the human needs of victims, and for all those who are mere witnesses to injustice, that order is restored. The community has its own emotional response to the actions of wrongdoers and an emotional investment in the cause and effect between wrongdoing and just deserts. But if these complicated emotional needs that arise from injustice are granted no admittance inside courtrooms and cannot be expressed through self-help, then where do they go—where should they go?

The ancient Greeks knew the harmful consequences of internalizing emotions that otherwise should be expressed—not simply for reasons of emotional catharsis but also because of moral correctness. Modern man is taught that anger and resentment are unhealthy emotions that reflect poorly on one's character and judgment. And revenge surely should never become the instrument of that anger. The men and women of ancient Greece, however, possessed a far broader appreciation of what these emotions mean, where they come from, and what must be done to satisfy them.

Aristotle, in section 5 of book 4 of his *Nicomachean Ethics*, wrote about anger not as a vice but rather as a virtue. Indeed, those who don't feel or express resentment in response to injustice, insult, and ill treatment are ultimately blameworthy themselves. Moral cowardice is not a thing to be proud of. Resentment is a perfectly natural response to moral injury. In fact, the anger that arises from dishonor can't be ignored without risking further damage to moral character. What kind of a person doesn't stand up for himself? Aristotle would no doubt have responded to the aphorism "don't get mad, get even" by saying that human beings should be expected to experience both sensations—justifiable anger *and* the impulse to avenge.

Peter French points out that Aristotle, along with the Greek playwright Aeschylus, believed that anger can, at times, be a perfect expression of morality—not just in the eyes of the community but also in the soul of the person.[3] Anger is unavoidable, and there is no other substitute for it. Indeed, anger and resentment are key components of human engineering. To fail to experience these sensations as a natural response to moral injury is a design flaw. There are occasions when people should be angry, when they are expected to be angry, when their failure to exhibit an appropriate measure of anger suggests a defect in personal character. Aristotle wrote, "The person who lets himself and his loved ones get trampled on and overlooks it seems like a slave."

Remember Michael Dukakis, another Greek who lived twenty-five hundred years after Aristotle? Dukakis, whose parents were Greek immigrants, was born in America and became the longest serving governor of the state of Massachusetts. It's not clear, however, how much Aristotle he had read along the way. Dukakis is best recalled as the 1988 presidential candidate on the Democratic ticket who lost the election to the first President George Bush. His campaign was not a model of either execution (his opposition to the death penalty didn't help, either) or elocution. In fact, his campaign for the presidency never recovered after one of the presidential debates when he stumbled through this question: "Governor, if Kitty Dukakis (his wife) were raped and murdered, would you favor an irrevocable death penalty for the killer?"

Dukakis, the governor of one of the most liberal states in the nation, replied, "No, I don't, and I think you know that I've opposed the death penalty during all of my life."[4] He took the bait and said what everyone had expected of him. He was a liberal, after all. And a lawyer, too, a profession where emotion is not supposed to affect the even keel of measured, almost mummified dispassion. Yes, he was the governor for all of Massachusetts. And he wanted to lead an entire nation. But he was asked a question that most people felt called on him to respond as a husband whose wife had been raped, not as a political leader. It was the most personal of questions, where the raw emotions of a devoted husband should have trumped any canned stump speech. The question was not a test of his leadership but of his humanity—his very manhood. The public responded negatively and Dukakis lost the election. The country didn't wish to be led by a man who didn't fully appreciate his moral duty as a husband. Where was his anger? How could he have responded so clinically, almost robotically? The people expected to hear moral outrage. Dukakis should have said that as a husband he would have wanted revenge—that his grief and anguish over his wife's murder would have driven him mad with righteous indignation—but as a government official he was accountable to the people and the laws of the state.

Anger doesn't necessarily lead to blind vengeance. One can be angry and decide not to take revenge. It may be too risky, or simply not worth the effort. But the anger itself still should be felt. Moreover, there is nothing blind about vengeance. Just because revenge is driven by emotion doesn't mean that the avenger is unable to see what he is doing. Quite the opposite is true. With revenge comes moral clarity. Blindness comes not from the taking of revenge but from looking the other way in the face of injustice.

Anger as a precursor to revenge is the most familiar route to justice. Those who violate laws, break promises, cause harm, and commit crimes will ignite in each of us the sick feeling of injustice and the reciprocal urgency that justice must be done.

No one who has been victimized can rightly claim any sense of personal worth if he or she registers no reaction, no personal feelings of indignity. Yes, anger can be subordinated to restraint, but to feel nothing when outsiders are appalled is nothing to be proud of.

In speeding up the Pyrenees during the Tour de France, Contador not only took the lead, he rendered his friend Schleck low, leaving him behind in increments far more deflating than the loss of those thirty-nine seconds, as if had let the air out of the tires of Schleck's soul.

In 1992, Lady Sally Graham-Moon was filled with resentment and scorn toward her husband, Sir Peter, when he left their home and moved in with his younger girlfriend. In retaliation she poured more than a gallon of white paint over his prized blue BMW, took a pair of scissors and removed the sleeves of each one of his thirty-two Savile Row suits, and gave away all the priceless wine he had stored in his wine cellar to their neighbors. As anyone who knows anything about the British upper class, the lords and quasi-royals of the United Kingdom are nothing if not decorous and emotionally self-contained. "I'm normally quite in control of my emotions," she said at the time. "In fact I am quite shocked by what I have done."[5]

Elin Nordegren, the ex-wife of Tiger Woods, is not the first woman in a professional golfer's life who found a more interesting and original way to use a golf club. Brenna Cepelak, the former girlfriend of pro golfer, Nick Faldo, took a nine iron and hit a double bogey on his Porsche when he left her for the woman who would become his third wife.[6]

For the ancient Greeks, these retaliatory responses were expected. To do nothing is to send a message to the wrongdoer, and the general public, that the victim has no self-worth and will not marshal the internal resources necessary to reclaim his or her honor. Shattered dignity is not beyond repair, but no elevating and equalizing of dignity can occur without the personal satisfaction of revenge.

Anger and revenge are tied to one another in ways both symbolic and real, it is little wonder that neither is deemed to be socially acceptable behavior. In the extreme, angry people who are not already incarcerated are, instead, encouraged to take anger management courses. No such demands, however, are made on those who suppress their anger, show no emotion—the zombies among us—those who are still capable of causing harm by way of silence and indifference. Passive-aggressive people are not similarly obligated to curb their passivity. There is a dedicated deference to those who are bottled up and in control of their emotions. They are not tarred with the same cultural stigma that is routinely directed against those who default to anger and revenge. The passive are given a pass while the enraged are looked on as if they cannot comport themselves within civil society.

Aristotle and Aeschylus, of course, lived long before Christ. They never considered the salvational benefits that come to those who practice forgiveness. When in Rome do as the Romans do. The Greeks understood the world and the inner life of human beings in a particular way—anger is normal and revenge is expected. In the Western world, however, the motto seems to be: do as good Christians would do or, as Jesus actually said, "Do unto others as you would have them do unto you" (Matt. 7:12).

Does the Golden Rule apply to revenge? Shouldn't victims be expected to retaliate in kind to another's misdeeds? After all, those who do harm are, by their actions, announcing that this is how they wish to be treated. People who do to us what we would never do to them—when they act not with kindness and caring but with violence and disrespect—should expect reciprocal treatment. Christ articulated the path for a good Christian to follow. But not everyone is following the same Golden Rule. Many are doing onto others what they would never tolerate if directed toward them. Reciprocity, obviously, works both ways. But this principle of restraint—whether in turning the other cheek or in doing onto others as one would wish to be treated—is all upended when damage is done and retaliation is withheld. The moral universe collides against notions of Christian charity, resulting in lost honor and wounded pride.

In recognizing this paradox in Christian belief, Peter French wrote that "those that get angry when they or their family or community are attacked, harmed, insulted, treated with disrespect, and so on, and restrain themselves, do nothing in response, are moral failures, not, as Christians would have it, to be praised for 'turning the other cheek.'"[7]

Anger and resentment is the default position that crystallizes in the aftermath of moral injury. To not experience those feelings is unnatural. And having such feelings makes the most moral sense. Forgiveness may be a virtue, but what is so virtuous about being trampled on repeatedly without delivering an appropriate response? Reputations are made equally of honor and cowardice. Forgiveness suppresses the emotional underpinnings and moral imperatives that are most alive in the face of injustice.

Which is why forgiveness is without virtue if it demonstrates to the world that the victim lacks self-respect. As law professor Jeffrie G. Murphy wrote, it is morally essential for victims not to be "doormats" for others because, "if I count morally as much as anyone else (as surely I do), a failure to resent moral injuries done to me is a failure to care about the moral value incarnate in my own person . . . and thus a failure to care about the very rules of morality."[8]

Of course, conversely, to express righteous indignation over moral injury not only contradicts Christian teachings, it also goes against the canon of jurisprudence—the loaded cannon of the legal system—which, for hundreds of years, has blasted human beings for their revenge impulses, demanding that they respond to wrongs by going to their respective corners, cooling off, and then filing a criminal complaint or retaining a lawyer for a civil suit. And so for most people in the Western world, personal vengeance was not an option, and personal satisfaction was surrendered to the rule of law.

So have we, all this time, been cowardly wimps, morally stunted and underdeveloped, unable to stand up for ourselves and all too willing to look to the legal system to retaliate on our behalf—without any emotional involvement? As we recurringly failed in our revenge obligations—either because we were too afraid to do it ourselves or too eager to delegate the responsibility to a dispassionate third party—we salvaged the vicarious thrill of vengeance not by entering courtrooms but by reading novels and watching plays and movies. The suppressed revenge instinct is rather openly and unapologetically displayed in popular culture.

Revenge should have a life outside of aesthetics. Human beings take immense pleasure in cultural depictions of revenge, but their enjoyment is always tempered by the knowledge that revenge dramas are not to be taken seriously because they are, alas, only imaginary. And vengeance can't be taken personally, either, because the feelings that coalesce around justice have been completely depersonalized.

It doesn't only have to be this way with courtroom justice neutered of emotion while movie houses teem with the exhilaration of revenge. The opportunity was always there to invite revenge inside courtrooms. Given its relationship to justice, vengeance should have had a home in courthouses apart from culture. Instead, legal retribution, empty of passion, is what citizens come to understand as justice. As the distinguished jurist, Richard Posner, has written, "law channels rather than eliminates revenge—replaces it as system but *not as feeling*" (emphasis added).[9] The more legal systems have failed to deliver justice, the more people have rushed to read novels and watch revenge films where justice made more sense and appeared to be recognizable, at least morally. The primal feelings so essential to the moral development of humankind gravitated to stories of revenge over legal opinions. There is a deep inner longing to experience the emotional pleasure of vengeance freed from the dryly mechanical, overly technical confines of courtrooms. If not for art, human beings would be completely revenge starved. The emotional absence that victims experience from an unfeeling legal system is roughly equivalent to the emotional investment consumers make in the culture of vengeance.

It's not simply that artists understand the moral necessity of revenge in ways that judges do not.[10] It's that judges simply refuse to see the moral and emotional connection between justice and vengeance. It is not part of a judge's job description to have victims walk away from courtrooms feeling avenged. For artists, vengeance is the most compelling of human dramas. By contrast, judges will do whatever they can to eliminate drama from their courtrooms and allow for as little humanity as possible. This is one of the reasons why dramatic trial scenes in art have no real world counterparts in actual courts of law.[11] Citizens who serve on juries, conditioned by *The Practice* and *Law & Order*, not to mention *Perry Mason* and *Matlock*, often wonder how real trials can seem so boring by comparison.

And it's not just judges. Lawyers, as well, are neither trained to be attuned nor especially sensitive to the complexity of human emotion.[12] This often proves to be a most tragic and ironic deficiency. After all, clients come to lawyers at their most vulnerable. And lawyers are generally obtuse to what their clients have to say. When a client demands a "pound of flesh," most lawyers don't realize that the client isn't serious, that the demand is merely symbolic of a deeper moral wound that cannot easily be appended to a legal complaint.

Moral injury is not the focus of law; indeed, most lawyers have never heard of it. The law is concerned chiefly with bodily injury, property damage or theft, and punishing criminal behavior. For lawyers, legal remedies are limited to settlement checks for civil plaintiffs and jail time for criminal defendants. There is essentially no other relief that the law provides mostly because there is so little imagination among lawyers to envision an array of remedies that would address moral injury. Emotional and spiritual relief is the handiwork of psychologists and the clergy, they would say. Lawyers do not deal with subjective human debris. The fact that there are emotional injuries that the law neither redresses nor heals is of little interest to lawyers who are presumably, and paradoxically, in the business of providing relief from the fallouts of human interaction.

Why emotion is consigned exclusively to clergy and mental health professionals is not always so clear. Doctors and priests do not resolve disputes among those who have suddenly become adversaries. Rabbis and psychologists have no jurisdiction over strangers who cause harm. The clergy can't place criminals in jail, nor can they give victims a public platform to articulate their feelings of loss and indignity and have it memorialized for future generations. Courtrooms should welcome within its precincts all that it means to be human. No other profession can possibly claim as close an affinity with human emotion as the law, and yet no other profession makes such an effort to be so assiduously above it. Doctors and clergy are expected to get their hands dirty with the messiness of humanity; lawyers, by contrast, busy themselves with lifeless case precedents and statutes, which they apply to humanity only as blunt instruments, showing little regard for how anyone feels afterward.

And so it is the artists that are given free reign over revenge. Who else can be trusted with such sensitively raw, emotional material? Artists, after all, are not afraid of the emotional world. Emotion is the muse for artistic inspiration. It is what fills up the silver screen and the blank canvas. It is the language of poets and what comes alive on stage. Revenge is instantly familiar because in the moral universe it is infinitely just. And it crosses all cultures and continents, transcending all languages. Artists illuminate and enrich the human experience with emotional truths, which aren't the same thing as findings of fact in courts of law. When it comes to unpunished wrongdoers, such emotions reflect the human longing for revenge that has been found wanting in the actual delivery of justice.

Perhaps this explains the undeniable influence that revenge stories have had on popular culture—from ancient Greece, to Elizabethan stages, to French novels, and to feature films.[13] Neither the Greek tragedy nor the Hollywood Western would have ever existed were it not for the human impulse to avenge and the larger community's need to witness justice delivered and served in this manner. Revenge sagas—the spectacle of scores being settled and just deserts received—have proven to be the most durable and bankable form of mass entertainment.

Why is revenge such a spectacularly compelling art form? Why are we so hooked on watching it? What's the source of its adrenaline rush?

For one thing, there might be an evolutionary basis for our love affair with the artist's rendering of revenge. Our capacity for altruism may have developed precisely because of our affection for imaginary heroes and in spite of our genetic predisposition for selfishness. William Flesch, a Brandeis English professor, has suggested that fictional heroes, or "altruistic punishers," are popular throughout culture because "nature endows us with a pleasing sense of outrage" at people who do harm and a sense of delight when they are properly punished.[14] Flesch suggests that at very early stages of development human beings realized that they had "an incentive to monitor and ensure cooperation." The altruistic punisher is sending the ultimate moral message: those who do wrong must be punished, even if it has to be performed by someone who has not been victimized and otherwise has no incentive to do so. The hero emerges because his moral conviction has been ignited and he knows what must be done.

Another reason is that with religions and governments having condemned private vengeance, and with legal systems often failing to provide justice that feels morally just, it becomes emotionally necessary that we see revenge played out, even fictionally, in ways that balance the scales. We have to be reassured that it *can* be done even if we see it so rarely performed in our lives. We applaud these heroes because we know they are right and we are relieved to see that wrongs can be righted. And there is the despairing sense that, placed in a similar situation, we, too, would have nowhere else to turn. If the avenger doesn't take justice into his own hands, then justice will not be done, the guilty will not receive their due, and all will be wrong in the moral universe.

We see something of ourselves in the avenger's struggle. Street justice is inherently familiar because most people, at one time or another, have been victimized by the neighborhood bully, the abusive boss, the petty thief, the vulgar thug, the odious merchant, or the adulterous spouse. And the person who did wrong went unpunished. In the vast spreadsheet that itemizes the accounts receivables of revenge, there is simply too much that doesn't add up, too much debt, too much indignity and disrespect, and not enough payback.

Fortunately, the nature of those wrongs seldom rises to the grotesque horrors that are depicted in literature, drama, or film. Many people can live without receiving their satisfaction from the garden variety wrong. But that doesn't mean that the moral injury is any less powerfully felt. Most people can't, or won't, retaliate with the same flair and fury of a Hollywood hero. Surrounded by so many unpunished, unavenged wrongs, is there any wonder why bestselling novels and blockbuster films often depend on stories of revenge to keep pages turning and audiences in their seats? We live vicariously and enjoy the vindication of someone else's sweet vengeance.

Susan Jacoby has observed this phenomenon of the artist's rendering of revenge by writing that "these screen images cannot be dismissed as trash catering to the idle daydreams of bourgeois audiences; their popular appeal is a clear indication that something is askew in the delicate social balance between retribution and compassion. Moreover, there is a profound conflict between the emotions expressed by cheering audiences at *Death Wish* and a public ethic that insists on a justice/revenge dichotomy."[15] The consumers of revenge dramas are no closet barbarians. They are feeling human beings who need to be given some assurance that there is justice in our world, even if it exists largely in art.

There is a rich cultural vocabulary when it comes to revenge. Audiences around the world root for Hamlet, urging him to take revenge against his father's murderer. They grow impatient by his hesitancy. What is rotten in Denmark can only be repaired by revenge; no Danish courtroom will do. Edmond Dantes, the cool and calculating avenger who transforms himself into the Count of Monte Cristo in the eponymous novel by Alexandre Dumas, remains the poster boy for justified revenge. In fact, the novel has influenced an entire genre of revenge-themed feature films that invoke Edmond Dantes as a reminder of the avenger's cause—*V for Vendetta* (2005), *Sleepers*

(1996), and *The Shawshank Redemption* (1994). As a further example of the count's adaptability and appeal to the modern era, a new television drama, *Revenge*, a loosely based retelling of Dumas's story, debuted on ABC in the fall 2011. When audiences hear *The Count of Monte Cristo* mentioned, they know they are about to witness a terrible injustice, the law will fail to punish the wrongdoer, and this tear in the moral universe will call for a righteous avenger to show himself and do what must be done.

Audiences soak up the satisfaction, if not the actual blood that is spilled, in such disparate revenge sagas as *Gladiator* (2000), *The Godfather* (1972), *Death Wish* (1974), both the novel and film version of *A Time to Kill* (1996), and even the grisly musical of splattered capillaries, *Sweeney Todd* (2007). Manohla Dargis, in reviewing the recent remake of *True Grit* (2010) for the *New York Times*, referred to revenge films as an "old-time American religion."[16]

Many of these films are box office blockbusters, others received critical acclaim, and each of them is regarded as a classic of the revenge genre, precisely because they operate on an emotional level, tap into a profound human need, and address an essential moral truth.

Mel Gibson has revealed himself as of late to be an alternately crazed racist and anti-Semitic lunatic, and that's when he's not drinking. His boorish behavior can now reasonably lead to speculation that when it came to some of his iconic films, he wasn't really acting at all—he was merely playing an unhinged version of himself. No wonder he was able to so convincingly apply his lunacy in the service of revenge.

Two of his films, *Braveheart* (1995) and *The Patriot* (2000), in addition to a film version of *Hamlet* (1990), and, of course, his Mad Max oeuvre, are among his most admired performances, and in each Gibson portrayed the avenging hero. The success of the films was due, in part, to their ability to capture the essence of the vengeance genre, the avengers who are easiest to root for and even easier to understand.

The avenger in art is not unlike the prophets in the Bible: neither one wants the job. They'd rather be doing something else. For the revenge seeker, the larger struggle is, initially, not his concern. In *Braveheart*, William Wallace, who will go on to lead the First War of Scottish Independence against England during the fourteenth century, is introduced in the film as someone who merely wants to be a farmer and has no interest in putting an end to the British outrages against the Scots.[17] In *The Patriot*, Benjamin Martin, widower and the father of seven children in South Carolina, decides that his allegiance to his family takes precedence over joining the American Revolution against the British in 1776.[18] In *Mad Max*, Max Rockatansky, a retired policeman living in a dystopian future where the law no longer takes responsibility for punishing the lawless, is forced to avenge the murder of his wife and son when they are ruthlessly killed by a motorcycle gang.[19]

William Wallace, Benjamin Martin, and Max Rockatansky each know that they possess the skills that would make wrongdoers pay mightily if ever faced with the duty to avenge a wrong. But none of them are daredevils and thrill seekers; they are not looking for a fight. As is so often true with revenge, the fight is, instead, brought to them. Wallace's wife is murdered after British soldiers try to rape her, and a Scottish rebellion is suddenly set in motion—led by an avenging husband. One of Martin's sons is murdered and his home is burned down by a ruthless British colonel, and suddenly the Colonials of the Revolutionary War have an avenging father leading a ragtag militia of guerrilla fighters who will make life miserable for General Cornwallis in the American South.

Wallace and Martin would have no doubt preferred that the wrongdoers had picked another victim. But once a wife and a son are murdered with such brutality and callousness, there is no way for Gibson's avengers to turn back.

In contemporary culture, especially in feature films, there is a subgenre of revenge narratives about men whose wives and daughters have been murdered, raped, or both, whose families have been taken away or their children killed, whose property was set on fire and destroyed. And in response to these injustices, the law is either silent, or doesn't exist, or, even worse, is complicit in the crimes.

The classic Western *The Searchers* (1956) and the blockbuster *Gladiator* had these themes in common. In Mel Gibson's *Braveheart* and *The Patriot*, the larger historical claims to freedom as depicted in the fourteenth-century Scottish rebellion for sovereignty and the eighteenth-century American Revolutionary War, respectively, are somehow secondary to the moral obligation to avenge one's family. Audiences, whether in Scotland or in the

United States, recognize the more personal, if not righteous, cause that overlays these historical events. To be sure, the liberation of oppressed peoples is important, but audiences indentify instantly and far more strongly with the grave injustice—experienced on a profoundly personal level—that triggers the duty and unleashes the fury of a man who must now right a terrible wrong.

In art, the killing of a wife or child waits for no jury. The death of a child or the rape and murder of a spouse supplies the avenger with his marching orders, especially if justice cannot be found any other way. Justice is the one moral imperative that can't be negotiated away easily. The avenger must do what is morally necessary because tolerating an injustice is viscerally unbearable. It is not only the avenger who won't be able to sleep until justice is obtained. The same is true of the audience.

Revenge sagas operate in a world of moral absolutes. There are no gray areas—not because the story works best without added complexity, but for a far simpler reason: the bad guy truly *is* bad. He is the "worst of the worst," a subject I will return to later. This idea is often neglected in the politically correct, morally relative times in which we live. We are told that evil is banal. All men are equally flawed. Who is anyone to judge? One person's evil is another's self-righteousness. But in artistic representations of revenge there is no point trying to wish a wrongdoer away, excuse his actions, or give evil a less condemning name. The moral relativism of modern life is rejected in favor of the moral realism that evil does, indeed, exist in the world. We are surrounded by injustice. And guilt that has gone unpunished. Many wrongdoers have not received their just deserts. With the scales so unbalanced, audiences crave stories that are not laced with moral ambiguity, where those who have seen evil will not casually, and cowardly, look the other way.

Revenge narratives have had an enduring influence on worldwide culture. They have inspired the Greek dramatists Aeschylus, Sophocles, and Euripides and the Elizabethan playwright Shakespeare. Vengeance is found in Milton's *Paradise Lost* (1667), Racine's *Phedre* (1677), and Heinrich von Kleist's, *Michael Kohlhaas* (1811), which, in turn, influenced E. L. Doctorow's, *Ragtime* (1975). The Sicilian vigilante sagas received an American makeover with damaged victims transformed into heroic avengers, from Batman to *Death Wish* to Showtime's *Dexter*. And, of course, there was Clint Eastwood's revisionist take on the Hollywood Western, *Unforgiven* (1992), and the infinite offering of horror films that serve as wake-up calls in the middle of the night that the dead demand the justice that doubles as revenge.

Movies such as *A Time to Kill, Kill Bill,* and *Righteous Kill* (2008) have much more in common than merely a certain lyricism about killing. As film titles they are, perhaps, emblematic of the fate of humankind—retaliatory killing is, sometimes, a moral necessity.

No one appreciated this human dilemma better than the ancient Greeks. For them revenge was not only one of the many cruelties of fate that the gods inflict on man. Revenge was also a moral imperative, even without the mischievous intervention of the gods. The gods may have put men and women up to it by placing them in impossible situations, their honor challenged, their sense of fairness tested. However, when faced with the duty to avenge, the people of ancient Greece saw the myths not as mere parables but as instruction manuals for moral survival.

Take the myth of *Oresteia*, dramatized by Aeschylus as a trilogy, which deals with the House of Atreus, the granddaddy of all Greek tragedies and family blood feuds.[20] It starts with Atreus, the King of Argus, who banishes his brother, Thyestes, from the kingdom in retaliation for sleeping with his wife and attempting to trick him out of his throne. Thyestes ultimately returns under religious protection, but Atreus is still in no forgiving mood. Adultery is not easy to forget, especially when combined with a breach of brotherly love. Thyestes had something coming, but what? The same age-old question remained, going back twenty-five hundred years: What constitutes proportionate revenge? Exceed the law of the *talion*, and all hell breaks loose.

Specificity and number crunching is always a tedious and exacting exercise, but ancient audiences to this drama were at least certain as to how much Atreus's vengeance against his brother would violate the *talion*. Atreus would go too far. He concocts a sinister scheme worthy of the most sadistic horror flick. Inviting his brother to a feast, Atreus serves, as a main course, the ground-up remains of Thyestes's own children (except for their hands and heads), who Atreus had killed in final revenge for his brother's betrayal.

What was final for Atreus, however, was far from over. In taking too much in repayment for the debt, in running up the score rather than settling it, Atreus's horrifying actions would invariably invite further vengeance. The House of Atreus had raised the ante on revenge. Now even the children of this family would become fair game. And there can be no proportionate justice when children become the surrogate targets for the crimes committed by their parents. Rather that being killed by his brother, Atreus is, instead, cursed by him. The Oresteian revenge saga is set in motion, taking place over several generations.

Agamemnon, who is best remembered as the victorious king of the Trojan War, is Atreus's son. With the curse fully in place and his fate sealed, Agamemnon should probably never have celebrated his victory—or believed that his life would proceed without tragedy. After all, his father had murdered Agamemnon's cousins and served them up as dinner to his uncle—their father. Surely just deserts would be due. Agamemnon is ultimately murdered by his own wife, Clytemnestra, who took revenge against her husband for sacrificing their daughter, Iphigenia, to the will of the gods. (Agamemnon was warned that unless he killed his daughter the Greek fleet would never reach Troy alive.) Clytemnestra, the aggrieved mother, is assisted by Aegisthius, Thyestes's surviving son (and Agamemnon's cousin), who symbolically, took revenge against Atreus, the uncle who murdered his siblings.

Orestes, Agamemnon's son, flees the country when his mother marries Aegisthius, who has every intention of killing Orestes. Eventually, Orestes returns and, cheered on by his sister Electra, avenges his father's murder by killing his mother, Clytemnestra, and her accomplice, Aegisthus. Wait: there's more to this true Greek tragedy. The Furies, representing human emotions on steroids—vengeance, violence, grief, fear, anger, and hurt feelings—ultimately avenge Clytemnestra's death by driving her murderer (her son) to madness. Is this fair punishment? Even the Gods now begin to wonder whether they have allowed this sadistic saga to spiral out of control. And the best way to create order is to convene a legal proceeding. The God Apollo intervenes and instructs the Goddess Athena to establish a court system within Greek society where Orestes will be placed on trial—the first criminal trial in Greek literature that resembles the administration of law as we know it today.

At this trial, Orestes is exonerated of his crimes when a jury of Athenians is deadlocked and Athena casts the deciding vote in his favor. The Furies, now furious, are legally prevented from carrying out any further vendettas against the House of Atreus. What else should be done with the furious emotions that give meaning to their name? They threaten to unleash a poison onto the land in retaliation for Orestes not being punished for his crime, essentially taking vengeance against the legal system for not doing justice. But Athena convinces them, instead, to become part of the community, participate in future trials, and contribute to the legal system.

Many read this portion of the play, titled *Eumenides*, the third part of Aeschylus's *Oresteia* trilogy, as world culture's first attempt to domesticate vengeance by converting it into a trial of state-supervised, legal retribution. But that's not all it does. *Eumenides* stands for the principle that vengeance and vendettas are officially over, replaced by a legal system. But this legal system is not all machinery; it also has heart. The emotions that animate revenge are not banished from a Greek's conception of justice. By making room for the Furies, the Gods ordained that justice cannot exist without a full outpouring of human emotion. The Furies, and their grab bag of emotions, were given a new assignment. As law professor Paul Gerwitz has written, "Fury is law's partner. . . . Law and passion are inseparable."[21]

Short of exiling emotion from the courtroom, Athena made it possible for the feelings associated with vengeance—all that the Furies bring to bear on revenge—to become a fixture of every legal trial. One implication of *Eumenides* is that victims, and their complicated mix of emotions, cannot be excluded from criminal trials.[22] Those who have suffered the harm, those who are looking to the law to do what's just, represent the deepest repository of emotion in any trial—criminal or civil. The raw emotions that Athena invited back into the courtroom are best typified in the agony and anguish of those who gather in courtrooms in pursuit of justice. If not welcomed inside courtrooms, they will end up unleashed onto the world like the very poison the Furies had threatened and which Athena wisely avoided.[23]

Why then, twenty-five hundred years later, can't courtroom judges display the same wisdom and emotional intelligence of Goddess Athena?

Law can't be limited solely to a strict adherence to a set of rules and procedures without also accounting for the range of emotions that fuel the moral imperatives of revenge. The ancient Greeks understood that perhaps private vengeance would play out better inside courtrooms. But a change of arenas shouldn't shut the door on the human element that would otherwise be on full display in cases of private vengeance. Aeschylus set *Eumenides* outside in a theater in the round hoping perhaps that future avengers would find themselves discharging their fury inside courtrooms—an altogether different kind of theater—where human dramas are real, and the shared morality of the community would have meaning.[24] Courtrooms would welcome every variety of victim who stopped short of becoming an avenger. Indeed, everyone should be encouraged to bring their grievances to the law rather than settling them privately, especially if those grievances are simmering from emotions both unabated and unappeased. As Robert C. Solomon has suggested, "Vengeance deserves its central place in any theory of justice and . . . the desire for revenge must enter into our deliberations along with such emotions as compassion, caring and love. Any system of legal principles that does not take such emotions into account . . . is not . . . a system of justice."[25]

Elle Woods, the fashion-obsessed, dim-witted, legal genius in the film *Legally Blonde* (2001), quotes Aristotle while delivering her Harvard Law School valedictory speech: "The law is reason free of passion."[26] The larger point she makes, however, is that Aristotle was wrong. (Ironically, Aristotle didn't have much of a problem with anger, but he did seem to feel that the legal system could do without passion.) A Hollywood film about a beautiful blonde-haired law student naturally falls on the side of emotion over bloodless legalism. What Elle Woods didn't say is that twenty-five hundred years later, the legal system is still taking its cue from Aristotle in showcasing legal actions devoid of human feeling.

Humankind would have been far better served, however, had another Greek—Aeschylus, not a philosopher but a playwright—left his lasting imprint on the law. Aeschylus understood the role of emotion in revenge and believed that trials couldn't be sanitized, antiseptic affairs. Legal trials may be preferable to blood vengeance, but a court proceeding without emotion is a trial that will not end in justice. Aeschylus was the patron saint of human grief and vulnerability on display inside courtrooms. Without Aeschylus there would be no TV dramas such as *Boston Legal*, *Ally McBeal*, *Judging*

Amy, and surely no classic film such as *12 Angry Men* (1957), perhaps the very best example that the search for justice cannot be achieved without anger being first revealed and then, finally, tempered.

A society that welcomes antagonists inside its courtrooms must respect that an entourage of emotions and hurt feelings will be joining them and will insist on front-row seating. Instead, victims are ushered to the rear, their emotions are stifled while prosecutors and defense attorneys haggle over fine points of law. These very same victims exit courtrooms regretful that they didn't simply take justice into their own hands. Instructing wounded parties to contain their emotions is tantamount to telling them that they were never welcome inside the courtroom in the first place, that the law simply refuses to acknowledge or satisfy their retributive needs. One of the many virtues of courtrooms is that they have the potential to serve as the setting for vicarious vengeance. Unfortunately, the legal system has yet to get behind such possibilities—twenty-five hundred years after *Eumenides* first introduced a way for emotions and justice to coexist within the same legal proceeding.

From betrayal, murder, cannibalism, the murder of one's own child, the murder of a husband, the murder of a mother, the complicity of a sister, to the madness that spills out alongside all that blood, Greek audiences were not surprised by the events described in the *Oresteia* trilogy. Given the horror of the House of Atreus, the *Oresteia* provided a portrait of a doomed family destined to a life of blood vengeance, with overlapping tales of revenge that saw no end until justice and vengeance came to mean the same thing. No family member was safe from another. That's what happens when you kill, cook, and then eat two small children to avenge a single act of adultery. The law of the *talion* is severely transgressed and disproportion becomes a gross understatement. The ancient Greeks saw in the *Oresteia* a cautionary tale about how an unbalanced reprisal inevitably leads to the recycling of revenge.

In still another Greek myth, *Medea*, a scorned wife takes revenge against her husband, and does so in the most ghastly of ways. Medea was a princess in her native land. She betrayed her family and country by saving Jason's life and by also assisting him in his quest to steal the Golden Fleece. For this she was exiled from her homeland, which in those days did not come with a return ticket. Nevertheless, she marries Jason and they travel to his home-land, Corinth, where they have two sons. Not long thereafter Jason falls in love with the king's daughter, who also happens to be a younger woman. As so often happens, these trade-ups for trophy wives end up being terrific career moves—but not so splendid for the abandoned spouse. Especially in this instance, given all that Medea had sacrificed for her husband, Jason's act was a most unbearable betrayal.

Medea is cast aside, discarded without even a good Corinthian divorce lawyer to obtain custody of her children. She now finds herself living alone, in a strange land, no longer a princess or a wife. Everything is lost through no fault of her own. The fact that she bore Jason two sons is suddenly irrel-evant. Corinth permits husbands to abandon their wives without any rights granted to the wife or obligations owed to her. Jason freely remarries this year's model of the local princess, and now he and the sons that Medea gave him stand to inherit the Corinthian throne.

Surely this is not right; this is not just. Something must happen here. The Greeks knew that. Medea couldn't be expected simply to walk away, to pretend that she was neither a wife nor a mother. Some form of justice must exist for wives who were treated so abysmally by their career-savvy husbands. Alas, the justice must come of her own making. Medea takes her revenge by killing not only Jason's new wife, the princess of Corinth, but also her own two children, thus depriving Jason of the royalty and immortality that resulted from his marriage to another.[27]

In the moral universe, what else was Medea to do? Yes, her actions surely made her a candidate for a temporary insanity plea should Athena have convened another trial. Medea's chosen remedy to redeem her shame ex-ceeded any fair measurement of proportion. The murder of her two chil-dren, along with the death of the home wrecker herself, is without balance as retaliation for the crime of adultery. The laws of Corinth had failed her. Medea could not live exiled from her former home while, at the same time, tragically devalued in her new one. But she had gone too far.

The citizens of ancient Greece understood that Medea was deserving of some payback. She had to avenge Jason's betrayal and the shattering of her self-worth. He had it coming, but he could never have seen *this* coming. The Greeks may have been appalled by Medea's methods but not by her retaliatory instincts. There is justice in revenge. But too much revenge can turn the avenger into a metaphor for madness, and diminish his or her claim to justice.

All audiences know this to be true, whether they watched from the open air Theater of Dionysus in ancient Athens, or in Grauman's Chinese Theatre in present-day Los Angeles. Revenge is tantalizing to everyone. This is mostly true because revenge stories are ultimately morality tales. We respond to them emotionally because they serve as object lessons on how to live and on what kind of a world we wish to live in. An injustice needs to be remedied. A victim must be vindicated. A truth has to be told.

Generations of readers have lustily devoured *The Count of Monte Cristo*—not under the covers with flashlights but in plain view. More recently, *The Brave One* (2007), *Reservation Road* (2007), *Taken* (2008), *Inglorious Basterds* (2009), *Death Sentence* (2007), *Red* (2010), *Law Abiding Citizen* (2009), and *Colombiana* (2011) have revived the rich cinematic tradition of vigilante justice in art.

Hundreds of millions of people have purchased tickets to see revenge films where the final curtain really means *The End*. Justice was served, and the justice itself was final. There are no loose ends, ambiguous outcomes, legal acquittals or procedural technicalities by which the guilty are set free. Reasonable doubt is not in doubt, nor can it be so easily manipulated, as it so often is in courts of law. There is nothing quite as morally revolting as someone who gets away with murder. An audience won't sit still for that; and in actual criminal matters, the consequences are far worse: when the guilty go unpunished, the general public loses faith in its institutions.

All debts from moral injury must be settled and satisfied—both in art and in life. When the lights come on in darkened theaters after watching a revenge film, no one feels emotionally deceived. This is perhaps what makes them different from love stories and romantic comedies, where triteness prevails over moral purpose. Revenge movies end with a true sense of resolution, closure in need of no sequel. The guy may not walk away with the beautiful girl, but he does get the wrongdoer, a conquest that is even more universally appreciated.

It is plainly wrong to dismiss the box office receipts of revenge dramas as merely silly fare, the violent fantasies of the savage and bored. Their popular appeal derives from a deep moral conviction about justice and fair play. And they allow the emotions surrounding vengeance to share screen time in ways that are foreclosed in courts of law. The sad truth is that cultural depictions of revenge are far better at dispensing moral lessons than a legal system that releases wrongdoers, shackles the emotions of victims, and disappoints everyone having any contact with it, leaving them frustrated and enraged.

FOUR THE SCIENCE OF MAD

"Revenge is sweeter far than flowing honey," Homer wrote. Lord Byron wrote, "Sweet is revenge." Both of these men were in good company when it came to adopting the sweetness of revenge as a literary metaphor. Recited in so many poems, plays, novels, and screenplays, and given its sugary properties, "revenge is sweet" has by now become the kind of cliché that causes cavities.

Shakespeare, too, saw revenge as synonymous with food. "I will feed the ancient grudge I bear him. . . . If it will feed nothing else, it will feed my revenge," so says Shylock in *The Merchant of Venice*.

"Revenge is a dish best served cold." Or so goes the proverbial maxim that is referenced in the novel *The Godfather* and the films *Kill Bill*, vol. 1, and *Star Trek II: The Wrath of Khan*. It is often attributed to the American writer Dorothy Parker, although its origins date back to an 1841 French novel by Marie-Joseph (Eugène) Sue. Tony Soprano, the Mafia chieftain from *The Sopranos* who was no stranger to food, once mangled the phrase by saying, "Revenge is like serving cold cuts."

Many people say, "I want to taste my revenge" or, even, "I won't be satisfied until I have my revenge," with satisfaction spoken of in the same way as the alleviation of hunger.

What is it with revenge and food? Those who insist on taking too much revenge, who ignore the law of the *talion*, who exceed their entitlement and overfill on revenge beyond the point of satisfaction can be described as revenge gluttons. Alfred Hitchcock once said, "Revenge is sweet and not fattening." That actually may not be so true after all.

Dr. Eddie Harmon-Jones, a neuroscientist at the University of Wisconsin, using sophisticated brain-wave technology, discovered that when people anticipate the taking of revenge after having been insulted or injured, the left prefrontal cortex of their brains is activated in the same manner as when they are about to satisfy their cravings for food.[1] The left prefrontal cortex can't distinguish between food and justice—each sustains life, both are equally anticipated and subject to the same cravings.

So revenge, in fact, is sweet, and buttery, and flavorful, and perhaps even irresistible. A literary metaphor is without meaning if the association it draws on doesn't ring true—or, in this case, taste great. "Revenge is like a baby's sweet smile," or "revenge is like a golden sunrise," or "revenge is like a woman's supple caress"—none of these phrases resonate as recognizable substitutes for revenge. Not even Lord Byron could turn these forced descriptions into poetry. For thousands of years artists have pegged revenge as having the same allure as a special taste. Vengeance and nourishment are like siblings of the soul—both satisfy cravings, both feel so good until taken to excess. Getting sick to one's stomach can arise equally from ravenous food intake as well as the taking of disproportionate revenge.

The visceral connection between vengeance and food has always been obvious, which is why so many poets throughout history and across all cultures mined the same metaphor. With the assistance of modern science, however, we now know that food cravings and vengeance are actually neural roommates, sharing space in the same sector of the human brain. "Revenge is sweet" is both visceral and cognitive. The biological link has always been there. Nature called when it came to vengeance. Human beings always felt it; we just couldn't see it. Intuitively we knew that the revenge impulse was emotional. But that didn't mean that the revenge experience was entirely brainless. The fact is, there is a neurological basis for why revenge is so faithfully associated with comfort food: both are satisfying and are lodged in the same region of the brain where cravings are stored.

And this presents a fundamental problem in the centuries-long crusade against revenge. The one thing that governments and organized religion never counted on was that vengeance might actually be hardwired into the human brain. Revenge is not like a bad habit, something to be licked and overcome. It is as innate to man as breathing, having sex, falling in love, and making war, which is oftentimes represented as vengeance taken against nations. These are not vices but verities. We can't simply wish them away. And this is particularly true of revenge. It is an evolutionary principle, a mainstay of human engineering. And that's why it has never disappeared despite society's considerable efforts to make it go the way of the dinosaurs.

Human beings have had a long history of preserving vengeance in their lives. Revenge is in many ways the cornerstone of our evolutionary history. Why else would we silently applaud vengeance when properly exercised? Why else are vengeful feelings so pronounced when individuals are laid low, or when we witness someone getting away with having committed a wrong? Far from being a human defect, a short circuit of our anatomy, vengeance might actually be one of the clearest expressions of human nature at work. Revenge creates order out of chaos by sending a message as to how one is expected to behave in a civilized society. It also speaks directly to the deep human instinct for fairness. The bond between the evolution of humankind and its reliance on revenge is as inviolable as any other instinct of the human species.

"The urge to take revenge or punish cheaters is not a disease or a toxin or sign that something has gone wrong," says Michael McCullough, a professor of psychology and the author of *Beyond Revenge: The Evolution of the Forgiveness Instinct.* "From the point of view of evolution, it's not a problem but a solution."[2]

Margaret Truman, the daughter of President Harry S. Truman, had been singing professionally since 1947, headlining at such venerable venues as the Hollywood Bowl and Carnegie Hall. She had even signed a recording contract with RCA. In December 1950, Ms. Truman was slated to perform in Constitution Hall, in the nation's capital where her father just happened to be the occupant of the White House. It was going to be a sold-out gig in Washington, DC, in front of her parents and with the considerable advantage of a home-court crowd. Home-court advantage in all ways, except for the *Washington Post.*

Throughout Ms. Truman's fledging career her audiences had generally been quite large and respectful (in the days before the Internet and *TMZ,* how else could citizens keep tabs on presidential offspring except by going to see them in person?), but the critical reception to her performances was usually mixed to mediocre at best. Washington's own media, however, had yet to weigh in on the talents of the nation's first daughter until the day after Ms. Truman performed live at Constitution Hall.

In the next morning's *Washington Post*, Paul Hume, the paper's music critic, wrote that Ms. Truman "cannot sing very well. She was flat a good deal of the time . . ." and had no "professional finish." Ouch!

President Truman, someone who insisted that the buck always stopped at his desk and who never shied away from telling someone how he really felt, wrote Hume a letter, which the flattered critic couldn't resist releasing to the press. He knew that this presidential blowup would make for good copy. The president wrote: "I have just read your lousy review. I have never met you, but if I do, you'll need a new nose." Double ouch or, touché! These words came from a Cold War president, the commander in chief over America's fearsome nuclear arsenal—the man who actually dropped the bomb!—and someone who suddenly showed himself to be an equally combative, defensive father.

When asked about her father's gesture on her behalf, Margaret Truman said, "I'm glad to see that chivalry is not dead." The president's advisers, however, were not similarly amused. In fact, they were furious that the president had now turned a mere music review into such a public fight. In their opinion, this angry, thuggish, undignified letter made Truman appear unpresidential in the eyes of his own people, and equally so in the estimation of world leaders. This was a breakout in hostilities at the lowest possible of levels. If "containment" meant anything in the nomenclature of the Cold War, it should have meant: "Contain your emotions, Harry! Save it for Korea, or Greece and Turkey, for God's sakes."

Surely this was not a great demonstration of the president's judgment. How petty can the leader of the free world be? Truman's advisers feared that the lasting impression from this regrettable piece of musical theater was that such a hotheaded father should never be allowed to have his finger on the atomic bomb. Besides, he already had enough political difficulties without now also appearing to be emotionally unstable. Truman, however, was of a very different mind as to how this was all going to play out with the general

THE SCIENCE OF MAD

public. He reassured his advisers, "Wait till the mail comes in. I'll make you a bet that 80 percent of it is on my side of the argument."

A week later, the president marched his West Wing staff over to the mailroom. On Truman's instructions, the mailroom clerk had stacked up thousands of what were now being called "Hume letters" into two piles— those in favor of their vengeful president and those against. As Truman had predicted, slightly more than 80 percent favored his defense of his daughter. He had, indeed, displayed the highest degree of fatherly chivalry from the grandest of all stages—the Oval Office. Many of these letters, in fact, came from mothers who understood exactly how he felt. They wrote that they, too, would have expected their own husbands to respond the same way, regardless of how others would have perceived it.

The president turned to his advisers and said, "The trouble with you guys is, you don't understand human nature."[3]

In Truman's case, the father who was willing to defend the honor of his daughter played much better on Main Street than his daughter's own singing career would have on Broadway. And his West Wing staff was clearly tone deaf when it came to anticipating public opinion. Truman came across as far more human than if he had instead exhibited the demeanor of a measured, buttoned-up, unemotional Cold War president. Remember how voters reacted to Governor Dukakis's emotionally obtuse response to the hypothetical rape and murder of his wife, discussed in an earlier chapter? The public's expectation is that a true man would stand up for the honor of his wife and make her murderer pay for his crime. A real father would defend his daughter. Dukakis appeared to be a first-class wimp who couldn't get his head out of reciting his campaign's position papers. Truman, in contrast, a true man, was perceived not as a deranged Cold War president but as a righteous father whose daughter had just been publically humiliated.

Perhaps citizens, on certain occasions, prefer to see their leaders more fatherly and less presidential—the real person over the empty suit, the emotionally honest dad over the manufactured wonk, the kind of person who doesn't spend his day reading the polls but actually takes in his surroundings and notices that there are real people who he is morally obligated to protect. It's worth remembering that George Washington is equally regarded as the father of the United States and its first president. And fathers have moral responsibilities to protect the honor of their children. Harry Truman never lived long enough to see this concept immortalized in *The Godfather*. For him it was all instinctual. What's more, he knew that the public would appreciate this singular display of fatherly love.

President Harry Truman correctly assessed the close association between human nature and vengeance. Standing up for oneself—or defending the honor of a child or spouse—is not just a morally righteous act, it is encoded in the DNA of human evolution, programmed into the human brain itself. President Truman may have started out as a haberdasher, but he had the instincts of an evolutionary psychologist when it came to his understanding of revenge and how it relates to humankind.

The assumptions we make about revenge—for instance, that it is innate to our species—is no longer mere uneducated guesswork. Revenge has transcended common sense and has made its way into modern science. Scientists have taken an interest in vengeance and the complicated interplay between emotions and critical thought. From behavioral economics, evolutionary psychology, and neurobiology, recent empirical data— both in the social sciences and in medicine—show that various biological, social, and economic forces can influence the taking of revenge. Social scientists have also found that there are gender, age, income, and cultural differences that determine how people feel about revenge.[4] Perhaps it was a mistake for humankind to have so reflexively surrendered to societal pressure, ignoring feelings of vengeance so indispensable to our mental makeup and so biologically linked to our moral development.

As a species we are profoundly sensitive to injustice and we react viscerally, and cerebrally, to both unfairness and the delivery of just deserts. Fairness and reciprocity are fundamental human concerns. Everyone responds to injustice on some level, and a legal system is not necessary to having such feelings. The human obsession with just deserts long predates courts of law. Children who shout "Hey, that's not fair!" are connecting cerebrally and emotionally with the natural history of the human species. Studies show that children, in particular, are willing to sacrifice their own treats in order to punish other children who have grabbed more than their fair share. "'One for me, two for you' may not be too bad," said Ernst Fehr from the University of Zurich. "But 'one for me, five for you' would not be accepted."[5] Perhaps this study should have served as the scientific rallying cry for the Occupy Wall Street movement.

Nations and cultures also have different levels of tolerance for revenge.

A study published in the British journal *Nature* noted that men experience more personal satisfaction in seeing someone get punished than do women.[6] Men and women were found to be equally outraged by unfair treatment, but men had less empathy for those who were about to be punished and, in fact, took more pleasure from watching the punishment take place.[7] Women express more vengeful attitudes but might ultimately be more squeamish about actually seeing it done, much less doing it themselves.

Yet a recent study published in the National Bureau of Economic Research, involving eighty-nine thousand people in fifty-three countries, concluded that women are, in fact, more vengeful than men; older people are more vengeful than younger people; the poor are more vengeful than the rich; and if someone has been exposed to high crime or has been the victim of a crime, he or she will tend to be the most vengeful of all.[8] Of course, this study only speaks to vengeful dispositions; it doesn't address whether any of the respondents would have actually resorted to revenge if given the chance.

Of course, that's always the problem with polls and surveys. People don't reveal what's actually going on inside their heads; they respond with what they think we want to hear or what's culturally acceptable to say. But now science can actually read minds by taking simultaneous pictures of the brain at work. Peter Sokol-Hessner, from the Center for Brain Imaging at New York University, has explained how magnetic resonance imagining (MRI) machines can reveal the changes that occur in the brain when human beings are placed in certain situations or are forced to react to threats or insults. "As blood pumps through the brain, the oxygen it contains causes small changes in the magnetic field," he says. "The scanner can pick up on that and tell us where the blood is flowing. We get a picture of which parts of the brain are being used."[9] Dominique de Quervain, a neuroscientist from the University of Zurich and the leader of the most important study on altruistic punishment to date, says that "increased blood flow in a certain brain region means oxygen consumption and more brain activity in that region."[10]

All of these recent advances in brain-scan technology finally prove what we always knew to be true in our bones: revenge is very much built into our anatomy and hardwired in our brains.

The prefrontal cortex of the brain is where human beings engage in logical reasoning, cost-benefit analyses, and the performance of critical mental tasks. The parietal cortex and the temporal lobes are involved in decision making, as well. Not surprisingly, these areas of the human brain are much larger than the same areas found in animals. Scientists believe that these sections were the last to develop in human evolution.[11]

In July 2008, the *New York Times*, inspired by the capture of Radovan Karadzic, the former leader of the Bosnian Serbs who was charged with the genocide of nearly eight thousand Muslims, reported on several recent studies showing that there is, among other things, an economic calculation to vengeance.[12] Avengers actually do engage in a cost-benefit analysis before vindicating their loss. Vengeance is not a brainless activity, and revenge is neither as irrational nor as impulsive as we have been led to believe. Avengers are not all Mad Maxes, loose cannons always in a state of half-cocked readiness. On the contrary, avengers are deliberate thinkers and methodical risk takers. And economic theory can be used to quantify revenge and account for those risks.

Below the top of the brain is where the limbic, the orbitofrontal cortex, the right insula cortex, the dorsal striatum, and the caudate nucleus sections are all found. These areas of the brain are believed to have developed first and, along with the amygdala, are involved in the processing of human emotions. Humankind evolved first as emotional beings long before advanced thinking distinguished us from all other life on Earth. During the natural history of our species, our emotional development preceded our facility to reason. An amusing paradox is that rationality was an afterthought in the evolution of the human brain. We pride ourselves on our ability to engage in critical thinking, but our emotions might actually supply the more elegant, if not essential, feature of brain circuitry. The dorsal striatum and the caudate nucleus are especially involved in the processing of rewards (and experiencing delicious tastes) that result from having made a decision or taken some action.[13] This is the region of the brain where feelings that arise from decision making are centered. And it is here where a biological basis for revenge is found, and where the anticipation and taking of revenge generates positive emotions.[14]

One of the reasons why psychologists and economists have joined forces is because the part of the brain that is responsible for rational decision making oftentimes produces irrational results. This phenomenon, so common in everyday life, contradicts the premises of the rational actor model, in which human behavior is always presumed to be rational and predictable. This model, however, seems to work better on paper than it does in practice. The brain is surely capable of consistent rational decision making. But emotional influences keep getting in the way. And the rational actor model has never properly accounted for the psychology of the revenge impulse, where unfairness and injustice bring about a response that is motivated by vengeance and not purely rational thought.[15] Moral outrage cancels out rational choice and still ends up with a decision that makes perfect sense— morally and emotionally. But what's the point of having a highly developed prefrontal cortex if so many people end up making boneheaded decisions? Human beings are, if nothing else, creatures of error. The prefrontal cortex is often grossly underused. Critical thought is suspended and defers to emotional thinking.

People buy feverishly into stock and real estate bubbles. They trust Ponzi schemers even when the methods of these charlatans simply don't add up. They fall victim to addictions, like drugs, alcohol, and gambling, even though the rational mind is fully aware of how ruinous these deviances can be. And when it comes to love, the prefrontal cortex automatically shuts off and the limbic, insula cortex, and striatum sections of the brain, apparently, go into serious party mode. Human beings are fated to fall in love with the wrong people. But if lovers start out as rational actors, why can't they process the clues of a love about to go bad and simply move on to a more suitable mate?

Nonetheless, sociologists, economists, and political scientists are largely guided by, and direct their scholarship toward, the clear-eyed certainties of the rational actor model. Despite so much evidence to the contrary, there remains a presumptive faith that individuals will gravitate toward rational decision making. Revenge, however, is generally understood to be governed by emotional influences and moral rewards. Revenge taps into the spiritual and moral universe; its value is not usually measured in tangible outcomes. This perhaps explains why in a culture where values are measured exclusively in material terms—money and status—the benefits of vengeance can be easily and mistakenly undervalued. The true riches of revenge are experienced internally. They are mainly appreciated as pleasures, in the unreachable, intangible caverns of the soul where honor and duty reside. It's not that the rational actor model fails to properly account for revenge, it's that a very different form of rationality must be accepted in order for the avenger to be properly understood as engaging in rational behavior. In fact, it's perhaps safe to say that the emotions of revenge end up supplanting the steely premises of rationality.

The growing field of behavioral economics, neuroeconomics, and the cognitive neuroscience of social behavior examines the relationship between decision making and irrational conduct. Jonathan Cohen, a neuroscientist and director of Princeton's Center for the Study of the Brain, Mind, and Behavior says, "The key idea in neuroeconomics is that there are multiple systems within the brain. Most of the time these systems cooperate in decision-making, but under some circumstances they compete with one another."[16] It is precisely this competition that explains why revenge is so sweet, and why perhaps, in the mind of the avenger, it might actually be more rational to opt for revenge rather than listen to all the cautionary warnings that play repeatedly inside one's head.

Brain scans, whether from an MRI or from positron emission tomography (PET) machines, which measure blood flow to the brain, show that when people are insulted there is heightened activity in the prefrontal cortex, which is the area of the brain that experiences hunger and cravings.[17] There is also activity in the bilateral anterior insula, which flares up when one is exposed to anger and distress.[18] Justice is neither felt nor experienced by pure reason alone. A strong inner sensation arises that something is either righteously correct or grossly amiss. The heart of the brain, so to speak, where emotions are generated and localized, registers its own reaction.

A craving for chocolate or a feeling of resentment and a desire to strike back in response to the actions of another each causes an immediate increase in blood flow activity to the brain. A revenge fantasy and the need for a chocolate fix can result in the same craving: a desire to be satisfied, whether with temping food or injustice rectified. A dessert of chocolate and just deserts that is witnessed being delivered to a wrongdoer produce similar neural sensations and light up the same regions of the brain.

Given these scientific findings, it's easy to see why revenge has always been referred to as both a pleasure and an addiction. Revenge actually does taste good—even by those who are merely watching from the sidelines. Dramatists always appreciated the sensory power of revenge—and long before anyone ever imagined what a brain driven mad by resentment actually looks like. Even the eighteenth-century Scottish philosopher David Hume would have been unsurprised by these scientific findings. Nearly three hundred years before anyone could have comprehended what an MRI machine looked like, Hume wrote, in his *Treatise on Human Nature*, that the "science of man" didn't necessarily comport with rationality. If anything, reason always takes a back seat to desire, and passion is the most reliable guide to human behavior. To the extent that revenge is animated by desire, Hume would find little difficulty supporting the idea that reason has far less to do with it than does emotion.

The human brain reacts positively when it experiences the satisfaction of getting even. And given that a mind high on revenge looks similar to one undergoing a sugar rush, it is fair to say that the brain has a sweet tooth for vengeance. The increase in blood flow to the dorsal striatum and the caudate nucleus, where the enjoyment of rewards are experienced and where feelings of satisfaction are centralized, suggest that the mind plays no favorites between vengeance and chocolate. Both receive equal billing in the brain. Outside of our heads, however, chocolate is the main course on Valentine's Day. Revenge receives no such indulgence in public enjoyment, and the only date it can get you is one straight to prison. One is accepted in moderation; the other is never tolerated. Of course, these equal levels of neural stimulation are achieved simply by the *anticipation* of satisfaction; one doesn't actually have to consume chocolate or take revenge in order to experience these sensations.

Chocolate isn't the only thing that can disable our critical thinking and activate the emotional spheres of the brain in which the processing of rewards are experienced. Emotions trump pure reason when the brain is exposed to cheaters or sly defectors who craftily manipulate games dealing with money. Scientists who work in the fields of behavioral economics and neuroeconomics have devised a number of experiments that test what happens to the human brain when it is exposed to injustice and unfairness.

Investment games conducted by Jeffrey H. Carpenter and Peter Hans Matthews, both economists at Middlebury College, demonstrate that 10–40 percent of the people they tested would punish someone by docking them money if they were discovered to have played the game unfairly or ungenerously. "The urge to punish seems very strong," Carpenter asserts. "Some people will spend money to punish even if it has no effect on them."[19] Even mere spectators to the game are prone to retaliate. Such is the purview of the altruistic punisher, who is prepared to deliver the punishment or, in the case of the Hollywood hero, take on the role of the crusading avenger at great risk to himself and largely for the benefit of others.

The brain is stimulated not only by resentment but also by the positive emotions that are generated when someone is punished for bad behavior. This offers further credence to the theory that revenge has played, and continues to play, a strong biological role in the human experience. For instance, one Swiss study, conducted in 2004, demonstrated a neural basis for altruistic punishment, and did so by having the participants play the Trust Game.[20]

Volunteers designated as players 1 and 2 were each given $10 and told that they could either keep it or transfer it to another person (player 2). If player 1 chose to turn it over to player 2, the total amount, then in the possession of player 2, was automatically quadrupled to $40, giving him $50 in total. Player 2 was then given the choice to reciprocate and either return half of the $50 to player 1, who, after all was the original source of his newfound wealth, or he could keep the $50 entirely for himself. If player 2 decides to keep all of the money, player 1 has the option to inflict a punishment, for example, taking back $25. It is at the point of anticipating the payback—the inflicting of punishment on player 2 because he behaved so ungraciously—that neuroscientists have observed the most elevated levels of brain activity in the very sectors of the brain that register emotional satisfaction. The study demonstrates that the mere anticipation of revenge can be the source of positive feelings.

The chance to punish player 2, the defector who was more than happy to walk away and hoard his bounty rather than share it, increased the consumption of player 1's oxygen to the striatum, lighting up the same brain circuitry as a visit to a chocolate shop or taking in a revenge movie on a Saturday afternoon. And the same results ensued even when player 1 was advised that there might be a personal cost to seeking revenge. The only difference in that case was that the medial prefrontal cortex, the area of the brain involved in the balancing of costs and benefits, was also activated.

A more recent study, conducted in Germany in 2010, relied on the Dictator Game, in which player 1, the dictator, decides how to split a pie with player 2, who has no means to reject player 1's division, but player 2 is given a chance to punish player 1 at the cost of reducing his own share.[21] The study tested the brain activation of player 2, who is given the opportunity to exercise revenge against player 1, along with the brain activity of a third party, player 3, who merely witnessed and did not derive any material benefit from the exchange. The study concluded that player 2 experienced heightened brain activity associated with altruistic punishment in the dorsolateral prefrontal cortex, the anterior cingulate cortex, and the anterior insula when he chose to involve himself directly in the punishment—meaning, player 2 engages in his own self-help and does not delegate his duty to avenge. As for player 3, she experienced the same brain activation, especially in the limbic regions, such as the insula and the striatum, but only if the punishment had a strong negative effect on player 1—meaning, punishment with real results.

The findings of the German study largely support the conclusions of the Swiss study by establishing, once again, that the reward regions of the brain are activated during altruistic punishment—we like seeing wrongdoers receive their due, even if we have not been personally wronged. And we might even participate in the punishment if called on to do so. The German study included a third player, someone who was merely watching the reciprocity, or lack thereof, between players 1 and 2. She, too, was affected by the witnessing of injustice and received her own neural satisfaction from watching player 1, the dictator, receive his just deserts—even though player 3 had no independent reason to desire revenge, nor would she have been expected to derive a subjective benefit from doing so, and stood to receive no material benefit from the revenge taken by another. As the study surmises, "Observing someone else being treated unfairly could initiate a simulation process which requires the same network as the processing of an unfair offer itself."[22] This study undoubtedly validates a neural basis for why the spectator in the bleachers, or the member of a movie audience, enjoys watching payback when it is deserved and when it results in a true detriment to the wrongdoer.

The witnessing of justice, especially injustice, is not a matter of indifference to most people. It perhaps explains why contemporary culture is so riveted by TV courtrooms, from *The People's Court* to *Judge Alex*. The soap operas that once dominated daytime television have suddenly been replaced by a curious incarnation of reality daytime TV—with storylines entirely focused on parties to a legal dispute. Real cases with actual litigants and real judgments with binding remedies are what now seem to entertain the daytime TV viewer. However, the popular appeal of courtroom-focused TV is not driven entirely by entertainment, or even a desire to learn a moral lesson or see right prevail over wrong. Perhaps, more important, the human brain is simply constructed to enjoy someone receiving a public comeuppance, witnessed by all, each of us sharing in the satisfaction, responding to the inner core of our evolutionary history and neural development.

Another neuroscientific test, the Ultimatum Game—this one dealing with duplicity in matters of dollars and cents—was conducted several years ago by researchers at Princeton University.[23] Two players are handed a total of $10 between them. Player 1 is asked to share the amount with player 2. He can decide to give as much or as little as he wishes; he can divide it up any way he wants. If player 2 refuses the allocation that is offered him, then both players will receive nothing. Both players are aware of the rules beforehand.

The rational actor model would suggest that player 2 should accept any low offer, since rejecting the offer would leave him with nothing. Of course, it would also leave player 1 with nothing. Perhaps player 1 deserves nothing. What if player 1 merely wishes to hand over one dollar, and he gets to keep $9. Surely that's not fair. It isn't like the $10 actually belonged to player 1 or that he had done something special to deserve it. It was a mere fortuity that the money was initially handed to him rather than player 2. He should be punished for his lack of generosity by having player 2 reject the offer, but then player 2 would get nothing out of the deal. Rejecting an insulting offer isn't rational, since one dollar is better than nothing. But then again, perhaps player 2 realizes that he didn't do anything to earn the money, either, so it's better to reject any paltry amount as an act of vindication against the bad behavior of player 1.

The emotion of moral injury is always a game changer when it comes to refuting the rational actor model. A human brain exposed to an insult takes on a very different mindset, one influenced by human nature rather than simple economics. It turns out that most people will reject any offer of $3 or less. And some will turn down any offer that is less than half of the amount player 1 was initially given. Why reject $4, which is essentially free money? John Hibbing, a professor who studies biological connections to social behavior, explained the raw emotions that underlie the Ultimatum Game. "Say it is $20. If I get three or four dollars, I'll say—'Screw you.' I'd rather go away with nothing than see you get most of it."[24]

But what's rational about that? It's certainly not the behavior of a rational actor; it's more like a playground tantrum where the boy excluded from the game just happens to be the owner of the ball. Nursing all kinds of adolescent hurt, he simply decides to go home and take his ball with him. Now, no one gets to play. If he decides to stick around, he might get picked the next time. Everybody wins. Of course, that's what a rational playground actor might do, a kid who doesn't allow his emotions and pride to stand in the way of his long-term interests in schoolyard fun. Of course, any economist who insists that the boy should stay and share his ball obviously hasn't spent much time in and around schoolyards.

In the Ultimatum Game, rejecting the offer spells the end of the game, but player 2 doesn't merely walk away with nothing. Yes, no money changes hands, but player 2 at least receives the satisfaction of not allowing an ingrate to get away with an unjust windfall. The reward is intangible but not altogether immaterial.

And the human brain bears this out. Researchers hooked up volunteers to MRI machines and had them play the Ultimatum Game. When player 2 received a stingy offer from player 1, $3 or less, for example, both the dorsolateral prefrontal cortex (associated with critical reasoning and the balancing of costs and benefits) and the bilateral anterior insula (the limbic region of the brain, which processes anger and distress) were reported as most active. The more personally offended player 2 is from receiving such a disgracefully low offer, the more likely he or she will be to reject it. But the technicians watching from the control room only see brain circuitry lighting up like a starburst as blood flow increases and oxygen is consumed in the limbic region where all those vengeful emotions compete with the rational mind.

A similar study of the Ultimatum Game, this one conducted in the Karolinska Institute's Osher Center in Stockholm, demonstrated that when one player insisted on keeping 80 percent of the money, the amygdala, where outrage is triggered in the brain, and the higher cortical domains, which is associated with introspection and conflict resolution in the upholding of rules, were aroused. Only by giving the participants antianxiety medication could their amygdala responses be suppressed. "This indicates that the act of treating people fairly and implementing justice in society has evolutionary roots. It increases our survival," wrote Katarina Gospic in the journal *PLoS Biology*.[25]

A 2002 study conducted by psychologists at Princeton University examined a thousand people to see how they would punish an assortment of crimes and misdemeanors.[26] Most of the participants carefully tailored their punishment to match the severity of the wrongdoing. They seemed inordinately focused on getting their measurements right, making certain that their sentencing recommendations approximated an eye for an eye. These punishments were given solely to address each offense. The participants were told not to worry about deterring future behavior. The purpose of the exercise was merely to right a wrong, to do what is deserved, regardless of whether it might have an effect on the future. And with that goal in mind, each person went about the tedious business of approximating their punishments, measure for measure.

All of these tests point to the same conclusion: the human brain is wired for justice, and short circuits when exposed to injustice. It is stimulated both by the anticipation of vengeance and the completion of justice. And the brain experiences a particularly intense reaction to unfairness and a compulsive desire to respond to that unfairness—even if it means rooting for revenge from afar or sacrificing something to assure that vengeance ultimately is achieved. And last, the human brain has an inherent understanding that punishment cannot be arbitrary or excessive—that, not unlike the law of the *talion*, punishment must always be subject to proportional limits. Indeed, the enduring legacy of the *talionic* principle must have biological roots, too—the rule simply made infinite sense to ancient peoples. Once again, human emotions, so essential to understanding revenge, play an equal role in the human brain's response to injustice. It becomes emotionally intolerable to watch and, even worse, to experience firsthand.

While the human brain is always on high alert to matters of justice and revenge, the decisions it makes in response to insult and injury are not determined by purely cognitive, logical reasoning. "These findings suggest that when participants reject an unfair offer, it is not the result of a deliberative thought process," writes Cohen, the neuroscientist from Princeton. "Rather, it appears to be the product of a strong (and seemingly negative) emotional response."[27]

Human beings gravitate toward fairness. When they are in the presence of unfairness, or when they are treated unfairly, their minds go mental, and the brain lights up in every section where emotions matter. This heightened neural sensitivity to injustice explains why, when given the chance, human beings will punish the wrongdoer even if it confers no direct personal benefit on them. This is the very essence of "altruistic punishment"—an individual chooses to take on a costly, selfless act for no reason other than that, morally, it must be done. He or she performs this task out of pure altruism and chivalry, even though there may be great risk involved. And, not unlike the human brain's response to cravings, it's the anticipation that always matters most. The idea that justice will be done is more important than how one feels after justice has finally arrived.

Brian Knutson, a psychologist at Stanford University, explained that the absence of self-interest doesn't make altruistic punishment irrational. All it shows is that, "instead of cold calculated reason, it is passion that may plant the seeds of revenge."[28] Ernst Fehr, the director of the Institute for Empirical Research in Economics at the University of Zurich, and a coauthor of the Swiss study, acknowledged that while passion surely plays a role in altruistic punishment, "I do not think that our evidence indicates that passion overrides rationality. In fact, I believe that our evidence shows that people deal quite rationally with their emotions."[29] In the same way that individuals feel personally rewarded by giving to charity, the inclination toward performing a just act is a similarly rational enterprise calculated to produce an intangibly spiritual reward.

When it comes to justice and revenge, one should never underestimate the significance of the emotional sphere of life. But one should also not mistake emotion for misjudgment, for assuming that those who respond emotionally are necessarily without reason. The fact that emotion often drives critical thought doesn't reduce the moral clarity of the decision. Law professor Michael S. Moore has written that "there is . . . a rationality of the emotions that can make them trustworthy guides to moral insight."[30]

In fact, Cohen speculates that these deeply visceral reactions that are lodged in, and instantly uploaded from, the human brain may also have an evolutionary basis. In the days before law enforcement and state-sanctioned retribution, it was important for primitive man never to appear weak or unwilling to retaliate after an attack. "In such an environment," Cohen said, "it makes sense to build a reputation for toughness."[31] One needed to demonstrate that he could not be so easily taken advantage of. Addressing how vital it was for early man to measure up to the societal expectations that force will be met with force, evolutionary psychologists Martin Daly and Margo Wilson observe: "Men are known by their fellows as 'the sort who can be pushed around' and 'the sort who won't take any shit.' . . . In most social milieus, a man's reputation depends in part upon the maintenance of a credible threat of violence."[32]

Offering a similar view that vengeance has an evolutionary basis springing from centuries of human conflict, the anthropologist Lyall Watson speculates that "perhaps our fondness for the idea of just retribution is a sound one, based on long evolutionary experience. It is possible that the satisfaction it brings us, the spiritual fulfillment it seems to bring, despite the pain, is an adaptive response. Revenge makes sense, it feels right, simply because at some level we recognize that it brings long-term stability to competitive rivalries."[33]

Once humankind survived the perils of tribal bullies and nomadic bad asses and realized that not everyone is well suited to a lifetime of vengeance, and after governments stepped in and became the caretakers of justice, why didn't the rational actor simply behave more rationally and recognize the futility of trying to get even? Revenge should have become obsolete, a survival mechanism from an earlier age that now carried unacceptable risks and no longer made sense.

Brain-scan imaging offers an answer to this as well. The neural basis for revenge aligns critical reasoning with emotional satisfaction. Neither necessarily cancels out the other. Achieving moral balance requires a feeling of justice as much as the fulfillment of revenge. So where does that leave the rational actor model or rational choice theory, the brainchild of economists and political scientists, with its complete reliance on reason and rationality? Vengeance isn't irrational for the individual. It is perfectly rational to insist on living in a just society and to assume the task of ensuring that justice will be served. It may, however, be irrational for society to allow individuals to take their own revenge, even if they have wholly rational reasons for doing so. For this reason, in justifying the legal restrictions it places on revenge, society regards revenge as irrational. And it finds itself forever having to make its case against private vengeance. Avengers who act alone and pursuant to their own agenda end up interfering with the state's monopoly over revenge. They get in the way of law enforcement and prosecutorial justice. What is perfectly rational for the avenger can become intolerable for the state.

The rational actor model, however, presumes that human beings are self-guided by the brain and not the heart. And it also assumes that since revenge always carries some risk, a truly rational actor would never willingly place himself in harm's way. Only an irrational person is driven entirely by emotion—the fool who acts first and thinks later. Truly rational actors would never resort to revenge—unless we're not nearly as risk averse to vengeance as we had previously thought.

Brain scans show that the part of the brain that responds to justice is activated by emotional considerations—positive emotional feelings of satisfaction that are generated when a wrongdoer receives his or her due. And these same neural sensations operate without regard to personal risk or the expenditure of personal resources. Human beings apply the risk-reward, cost-benefit calculations to revenge as if there were a mental recipe for vengeance. They don't overlook deliberative judgment. Mental reasoning is not rejected; it is simply added to the emotional mix. Revenge brings emotion and rationality into harmony. And brain scans have demonstrated just how much emotion and reason coexist in the ecosystem of revenge. Human beings are often willing to incur costs if it is in the service of paying back what is justly owed. The precise amount owed is stored in working memory, safely kept and calculated. The brain's recognition of fairness is so acute that in return for more justice, human beings are seemingly prepared to accept more risk. And they do so not out of rash impulse but through measured, critical thought. The avenger knows exactly what he is getting himself into.

Two presumptions about the rational actor model are debunked by these studies; two types of irrationality are exposed. The avenger responds to an insult or injury with a complex interplay of emotional mechanisms and rational considerations. The result might be risky yet still rational. This is especially true in cases of altruistic punishment. A rational actor thrust into the role of selfless avenger is already acting irrationally. Why would anyone punish on behalf of a stranger unless he or she was under the spell of a superhero complex? "Leave the cape and cowl at home, Batman—that's what the police are for." Yet ordinary people are willing to bear the economic cost of making sure that defectors from these economic games, or deviants from society's rules, receive their just deserts, even if there is no material benefit to them. Such impulses are plainly *not* rational, and yet the human brain takes each insult personally, and then rationalizes why something must be done.

Scientific research conducted in 2009 has identified a "warrior gene," monoamine oxidase A (MAOA), suggesting some interplay between behavioral genetics and behavioral economics.[34] There just might be a genetic contribution to altruistic punishment, an evolutionary basis to incur a financial cost simply to punish a wrongdoer without receiving any immediate material reward. The warrior gene responds to resentment and spite, which is similar to the punisher who is motivated by pure altruism.[35] All of this suggests a strong biological and evolutionary basis for revenge and, perhaps, even a Darwinian explanation for the improbable survival of the revenge instinct. The genetic makeup of our species has long factored in the value of vengeance as a survival tool. We have stubbornly held on to it for millennia and have applied it in our lives with the versatility of manna.

We can fake an orgasm, feign sincerity, exaggerate love, contrive all manner of moral outrage, and profess varying degrees of hatred, but the most genuine of all human impulses, the one that is not easily faked or forfeited, is revenge. Love we can live without, or it can be unrequited or experienced from afar. Anger can be managed. Jealousy can be transferred. Fear can be overcome. Hate has a way of fading, and grief dissipates with time. Revenge, however, is not so easily forgotten. It can be delayed, but it can't be ignored. It has a long memory. And the withholding of revenge brings about no inner peace. No other emotion carries the same weight or burden. Unrealized revenge is the great disturber of our sleep and the duty that sometimes summons us from our sleep.

So how to respond to those who maintain that revenge is without reason, that the avenger is the most irrational of men? Legal theorists and philosophers have clearly not been keeping up with the scientific community if they insist that revenge is always irrational and that no reasonable man would ever resort to it. For eight centuries, nation-states have taken it on themselves to track down wrongdoers and administer punishments on behalf of all of society. The revenge impulse, however, is still widely felt and appreciated, if not practiced, on individual levels. And not all people are irrational in their high regard for revenge.

Maybe Harry Truman was right all along: those who make public policy simply don't know enough about human nature. They miss all the signs and mental cues that are vividly captured on a brain scan.

And yet, rational choice proponents see nothing but illogic in revenge. The philosopher Jon Elster wrote that revenge offers only costs and risks and no benefits. "Rational individuals follow the principles of letting bygones be bygones, cutting their losses and ignoring sunk costs. . . . People act in impulsive, unreflective ways, under the sway of emotions too strong to be resisted. . . . Revenge behavior is impulsive."[36]

Judge Richard Posner, one of the leading figures in the field of law and economics, has written that a rational man is fully aware that vengeance "is an extremely clumsy method of maintaining order."[37] Fixated on cost-benefit analysis, the rational actor will come to realize that revenge never truly recoups his losses. Moreover, logically he knows that retaliations raise the stakes on further reprisals.

At the heart of the rational actor model is the clear-eyed, business sense that it is far more costly for society to allow private acts of vengeance than to construct a system of justice charged with maintaining order by way of fines, incarceration, and capital punishment. This argument sounds logical. And it supports many of the premises behind the state's monopoly over revenge. But it misses, if not altogether ignores, the emotional component for why revenge makes perfect rational sense to aggrieved individuals. It isn't always true that the rational actor, focused entirely on cost-benefit calculations, can shut himself off from the way human beings actually experience indignity. Hurt feelings are not so easily neutralized; human beings do not inhabit such sterile zones where risk aversion and logic guides all decisions.

When filtered through the far fuzzier math of the avenger, and the rightness of his cause, a much different set of priorities arises and presumed irrational decisions have a way of making rational sense after all.

Charles Ng, a serial killer, was convicted of murdering eleven people in California in the mid-1980s. He was suspected of killing possibly another fourteen. He was put on trial for killing twelve. There was no finding of guilt, however, with respect to the twelfth victim, Paul Cosner. The jury was deadlocked on that count and so the judge ordered a mistrial. The prosecutors ultimately decided not to retry the case on the twelfth count. After all, the trial had already cost the citizens of California $12 million. Another criminal proceeding would only add to the expense and accomplish little else. Ng was already headed for the electric chair (he still remains on death row in San Quentin State Prison). The murder of eleven people had already gotten him the highest punishment he could receive. What would one more conviction do to change the final disposition of the case?

Paul Cosner's sister Sharon, however, wasn't satisfied with this legal outcome. Yes, Charles Ng would one day be executed for killing eleven victims, but her brother was not included among them. His death was somehow forgotten. There was no record of why and how he died. Without a cause of death, it was as if her brother's life had never existed at all. Ng's execution, should it ever occur, would not vindicate the loss of her brother unless there was a way to connect Paul's death to Ng's act. Sharon Cosner was determined to obtain some official public record signifying that her brother had been killed and that Ng was responsible for his death.

She urged the prosecutors to retry the case, but given the cost and the futility of yet another guilty verdict, they decided against it. It wasn't rational. She then tried a different approach by making a direct appeal to the judge who presided over the case. From him she eventually obtained a one-page, handwritten court order that she used to obtain Paul's death certificate, which now finally listed the true cause of his death. In it the judge wrote: "Paul Steven Cosner went missing in San Francisco on November 2, 1984. He has not been heard of since and it appears the Court finds that he was the victim of murder at the hands of Leonard Lake (a co-conspirator) and Charles Ng."

Sharon Cosner said, "I think it's finally over now. . . . I think this will finally allow us to move on with our lives. . . . Up until Judge Dearman signed this order, there had been no justice, no one held responsible. Now someone has been. . . . [The court order] makes all the difference to me—it really does."[38]

Ng was not found guilty, in a legal sense, of killing Paul Cosner. The judge's order had no legal significance although its emotional, symbolic significance was immense. An official court document, as public record, finally did exist, and proclaimed that Paul Cosner's murder would not be forgotten. Charles Ng would one day pay the ultimate price, and that payment, symbolically, would now be in the service of honoring Paul Cosner's memory as well.

A rational actor in Sharon Cosner's position would have said: "Charles Ng is toast. I know he killed my brother. It's not worth my time and expenditure of emotion, not to mention the state's money, proving something we all know to be true. Ng will ultimately receive a lethal injection, and that's what he deserves." Was it rational for Sharon Cosner to pursue so obsessively some acknowledgment of her brother's death? What was wasteful and irrational for the government was indisputably filled with meaning for the murder victim's anguished sister.

In 2002, Lee Boyd Malvo and John Allen Muhammad, known as the

DC Snipers, terrorized the citizens of six states and Washington, DC by shooting and murdering ten people as part of an Islamic jihad. Because some of the murders were committed in the nation's capital, then attorney general John Ashcroft had the authority to select which jurisdiction would be given the right to conduct this highly visible and emotionally charged capital murder case. Each of the states wished to hold the trial within its own jurisdiction. In fact, they fought over who would get the first crack at prosecuting the DC Snipers with the same ferocity of cities clamoring to host the Super Bowl. The only difference: Super Bowls are moneymakers; high-profile capital murder trials end up rivaling the defense budget of a small country. Economically speaking, murder trials are money losers.

Ashcroft chose Virginia, and the state tried the case in 2003. Muhammad received a death sentence, which was carried out in 2009. Malvo was given a life sentence without parole.

The DC Snipers capital murder trial cost the citizens of Virginia millions of dollars. But the meter continued to run. Immediately after Muhammad and Malvo were sentenced, the five other states insisted that they be given a chance to pursue their own capital murder cases. They wanted these prosecutions held in their own courtrooms, brought on behalf of their own murder victims, and with their own citizens serving as jurors.

Clearly there was no rational reason for doing so. Not only would duplicative trials be wasteful, costly, and redundant, but they also might expose errors or improprieties in the Virginia trial, which could have opened a door for the defense team to undo the earlier verdict. Aside from spending millions of taxpayers' dollars simply to accomplish the same thing as what had already been achieved in Virginia, there was a real risk of prejudicing the outcome. Besides, Muhammad could only be executed once, and Malvo had but one life with which to serve his life sentence. Why not simply take a free ride courtesy of the tax-paying citizens and victorious state prosecutors of Virginia?

The prosecutors of the other states hadn't yet had their shot at the DC Snipers. They wanted their turn. They weren't concerned about wasting taxpayer dollars. In fact, they knew that the citizens of their states weren't worried about the costs either. Holding separate trials in each state had enormous moral and symbolic value that couldn't be measured in money.

What these citizens wanted most was a public reckoning where the crimes committed against their own state residents would be acknowledged. And they were more than willing to pay for it. Muhammad and Malvo had to be punished for violating the laws of each of these states. Yes, a spectacular waste of money, and surely a waste of time. But there was a duty to the dead—a far greater priority than fiscal discipline—that must be publically honored.

One Maryland prosecutor said, "We had six homicide victims here in Montgomery County; none of them has had their day in court. Neither has the community at large had their day in court." A Louisiana prosecutor echoed a similar sentiment, "They murdered a nice Baton Rouge woman.... They have a date with Louisiana justice. I'll do everything I can to make sure that they will make that date."[39]

The evolutionary development of humankind depended on sending a clear message to wrongdoers that no attack or insult will go unanswered. The reciprocity of payback had to be certain and expected. Aside from enforcing a practice of deserved retaliation, it also established an organizing principle of reciprocity—all scores will be settled, and all acts of kindness, friendship, and cooperation will be met, in kind, with similar positive gestures. The former deters misdeeds; the latter produces trust.

The game theory tit for tat demonstrates how this works.[40] A rational man would naturally always gravitate toward reciprocity and mutual advantage, which tit for tat virtually assures so long as both parties are rational and neither chooses to defect from the game. If the first move is positive, the second player will reciprocate—tit for tat. Each reciprocal act of cooperation will invite yet another act of mutual advantage. Once one of the actors does something that requires not an act of cooperation (a defection) but rather an act of retaliation, the second player will respond in kind. At this point, however, it is still possible for the parties to resume cooperation rather than repeated retaliations. The party who defected first must be forgiven. And in order for that to occur, he must respond with a cooperative act. If he does, then order is restored.

Tit for tat mirrors the logic of the Golden Rule: truly do onto others as they actually do unto you—if they are kind, repay with kindness; if they cause harm, then one must reciprocate with harm. Both sides are on notice that the game is always in play. And they know that falling out of line will not be forgotten: "kindness for kindness; evil for evil." Not unlike with revenge, tit for tat is a game of measurement and precision. All rational actors know that it is always best to respond cooperatively, to trade in positive gestures rather than to invite retaliation that benefits no one. And best of all, for those who fear vengeance because retaliation can be excessive and disproportionate, tit for tat ensures that retaliation will never exceed the action that invited the response.

The game breaks down, however, when the first act of retaliation is not forgiven, and the wrongdoer responds with a reciprocal act of revenge. This is where vengeance becomes recycled, where retaliation rather than mutual cooperation begins to define the relationship between the players who, suddenly, are locked in battle that knows no end. The Cold War, with its strategic alliances and diplomatic maneuvers, very much resembled a game of tit for tat—one with, however, annihilating implications. Ongoing hostilities are clearly not mutually beneficial, and the recycling of vengeance is ultimately self-destructive and irrational. The rationality of tit for tat has its own internal logic—you get what you give. The endgame is reciprocity itself—the players are empowered to decide whether the game will be mutually rewarding or infinitely annihilating. Those who cooperate are rewarded; defectors are punished. Without reciprocity there will be open season on whoever develops a reputation for always backing down.

There are still even more refutations of rational choice theory when it comes to revenge. The Prisoner's Dilemma demonstrates how the rational actor might be forced to make a decision that, in the end, doesn't appear to be rational or in anyone's self-interest.[41] Two prisoners are separately interrogated for a crime they jointly committed. If both keep silent and do not implicate the other, the authorities will not have sufficient evidence against either one and they will possibly both be set free. If each blames the other—essentially defecting from the game of mutual trust—then the consequences of the Prisoner's Dilemma are revealed: both will be punished severely, although their cooperation with the authorities will be taken into account. If, however, only one accepts the deal and implicates the other, then the snitch will receive immunity and be set free, while the prisoner who maintained his silence and refused to betray his coconspirator will take the fall and receive the harshest sentence. Since that is the worst outcome of all, the rational prisoner will avoid the trap of the prisoner's dilemma by simply hedging his bets and ratting out the other. That way, at least, he won't be left alone to suffer the consequences of his crime while his duplicitous colleague is set free.

The dilemma that the prisoners must confront is that locked away in separate holding rooms and, in some cases, having no prior social bonds between them, they would have no reason to trust one another. If they had complete trust, then they would both be set free. The absence of trust, however, assures that both will be punished. No one wants to be the only one to take the blame and pay the full price while the other receives the windfall of walking away. Each prisoner rolls the dice that his partner in crime might not defect, in which case the one who does will ultimately go free. For this reason, the most rational choice is also the least optimal one since it requires mistrust and defection. In a world of reciprocal altruism, all prisoners would know to trust one another and always cooperate. No good comes from defection. But rational actors have little faith in altruism and surely know not to count on it. Mutual advantage and trust will set the prisoners free, but they are stuck with the dilemma that rational men and women instinctively know: defectors are more plentiful, and predictable, than cooperators.

Robert C. Solomon has written that games and tactics such as tit for tat and the Prisoner's Dilemma depend on retaliation—both the threat and its occasional delivery—to make cooperation possible. The cheater or defector needs to be reminded that there is a cost to taking liberties with mutual trust. The amount of the cooperation depends on the certainty of retaliation. The lessons of game theory are the same lessons of survival that social animals had to once learn. Humankind would have become an evolutionary failure had it chosen a life of perpetual forgiveness and the tolerance of endless defection. Solomon writes, "Vengeance is not the antagonist to rationality but its natural manifestation."[42]

Once again, however, what is rational for the individual might not be tolerable for society. States can't afford the social costs of never-ending games of tit for tat that are played like duels rather than love fests, where neither party is willing to break the cycle and cooperate. Over time, the game is played to destruction or to one party's disappearance. The ultimate demise of the Soviet Union, which had no tat in response to America's Star Wars program, is one example of this brinksmanship.

But here's another dilemma: if revenge is biologically imprinted in the brain and if the evolutionary history of humankind came to expect both the threat and anticipation of vengeance, and if revenge is ultimately both rational and potentially destructive, then what are we to do with this instinct that can't be stopped, feels so good, and yet demands that we somehow control it?

The answer is neither simple nor hopeful. After all, governments and legal systems do a poor job of acting as surrogates for revenge. Private acts of vengeance carry too many risks. Neuroscience informs us that the human brain cannot tolerate injustice and lights up like a slot machine when it anticipates the delivery of justice. Still, revenge is not a complete panacea, largely because legal retribution is often uneven, private vengeance is hard to measure, and what passes for the rational choice might not lead to the optimal outcome.

And there are those who say that for all its purported sweetness, in the end, revenge is ultimately unsatisfying. Vengeance doesn't actually fulfill its promise of true satisfaction; getting even doesn't make the avenger feel any better.

A study conducted in 2008 and appearing in the *Journal of Personal and Social Psychology*, titled "The Paradoxical Consequences of Revenge," sought to refute the presumption that revenge leads to catharsis and relief, that it produces the necessary closure that is impossible to achieve any other way. Far from delivering closure, the report claims, vengeance actually increases the amount of unsettled aggression that existed before. Those who say "Get it out of your system and go punch a speed bag" would be surprised to learn that punching a bag actually *increases* one's aggression.[43] The anger doesn't actually get out of your system; it stays put right where it was before, but now fully reenergized. The report concludes that people grossly overestimate how much the intensity of their anger and its duration would subside if vengeance was made available to them.

In the 2004 Swiss study led by de Quervain and her colleagues, increased blood flow to the dorsal striatum of the brain, the region closely related to pleasure and satisfaction, was activated one minute *prior* to when the wrongdoer (free rider) was due to be punished—meaning that it measured only the anticipation of punishment and not its aftermath, when vengeance had been taken and the avenger might feel altogether differently. The focus of the study was on the expectation of altruistic punishment—the pleasure that came with its anticipation—and not the actual state of mind of the avenger once the punishment was delivered.

The 2008 study was designed to show the actual experience of witnessing the punishment itself (the brain scans were performed anywhere from one to ten minutes later), which did not match the joy that came from the anticipation of revenge. The avengers were found to be less happy after all. The study found that "people believed that exacting revenge would bring closure, in the sense that they would think less of the free rider, when in fact it had the opposite effect—punishing the free rider made people think about her more, which in turn made them feel worse."[44]

Revenge might feel good as a fantasy, but not in reality. Does this undermine the entire revenge enterprise? Why undertake the time and risk of tracking down and punishing a wrongdoer if the ordeal ends up like that lament in the Rolling Stones' song, where the avenger simply "can't get no satisfaction"? Neuroscientists can prove that the anticipation of revenge activates the blood flow to the brain. But once revenge is finally taken, the blood flow diminishes like a burst balloon. The circuitry lights up for the craving but not the completion.

Revenge is sweet, but sometimes its aftertaste is bittersweet. There is often ambivalence in the aftermath of vengeance. There can be both elation and, then, letdown. And the avenger can become guilt-ridden or remain bereft and without closure. But this neither should come as much of a surprise nor does it rob vengeance of its entwined connection to justice.

In Steven Spielberg's film *Munich*, the Israeli assassins assigned to kill the Palestinians who were responsible for the murder of the Israeli Olympic team in 1972 spend their nights arguing over the moral implications of their task. With each assassination there is seemingly less of a feeling of relief. Doubt enters their conversations. They lavish attention and appetite over their dinners but feel no satisfaction from the vengeance they are feasting on with noteworthy success. Yet they know their duty and what the wrongdoers deserve, and so they forge on avenging the murders committed by Black September—but, again without ever feeling satisfied.[45]

In the films *Braveheart* (1995) and *Gladiator* (2000), the avengers are never given the chance to experience the satisfaction that should otherwise result from their vengeance. In both films the avenger is dead before the score is ultimately settled, or he dies in the process of redeeming the debt. In the classic Hollywood Westerns *The Searchers* (1956) and *Unforgiven* (1992), the avengers complete their task, but there is no happy ending, no realized satisfaction, nothing approximating joyful fulfillment. They simply walk away or return home no happier or accomplished than before.

When it comes to vengeance and justice, it shouldn't really matter how the avenger feels afterward. All that is important is that the emotion is acted on and that the injustice is not ignored—that no moral revulsion comes from the unsettled debt. A happiness quotient is not the standard; satisfaction is achieved by following through with the duty to avenge without regard to whether it puts a smile on the avenger's face. Happiness and satisfaction are two very different endgames. Some avengers will feel satisfied; others will feel ambivalent or won't know exactly how to feel. Revenge is not immune to self-doubt. It is the revenge itself that is obligatory and absolute; the avenger doesn't have to feel elation or relief—he or she merely has to get the job done. What matters is that honor is reclaimed and all debts are redeemed. Everything else is beyond the scope of vengeance or comes merely as an added bonus.

While the avenger doesn't need to be made joyful, it is especially important that the wrongdoer be made apprised of *why*, specifically, he is being made to suffer. Political philosopher Robert Nozick observed that there is a necessary personal tie between the avenger and wrongdoer.[46] They are forever bound by the wrongdoer's deed and the avenger's loss. And this relationship must officially announce itself. After years of toil and then strategic planning, the Count of Monte Cristo let it be known to those who did him wrong that he was actually the betrayed Edmond Dantes, who has finally returned to claim his revenge. Law professor William Ian Miller wondered "what satisfaction could there be in not letting your target know what hit him and for what reason?"[47]

In the 2009 study conducted in Germany, researchers found that participants were satisfied by taking revenge for wrongs done to them, and even more satisfied if the wrongdoer was duly informed why revenge was being taken. The study concludes: "Our findings corroborate the notion that revenge aims at delivering a message between the victim/avenger and the offender, and that revenge is only effective if this message is understood. . . . The message of revenge . . . [is]: 'Never do this to me again.'"[48]

In the film, *The Princess Bride*, Inigo Montoya spends his entire life perfecting his swordsmanship and seeking vengeance against the six-fingered man who murdered his father and scarred both his life and his face. He prepares a speech in anticipation of when he will finally confront his father's killer: "Hello, my name is Inigo Montoya, you killed my father, prepare to die."[49]

The film astutely recognizes that while Montoya might have devoted his entire life to honoring his father by avenging his murder, the final vindication does not have to include his own personal happiness. What's more important is that, in receiving his just deserts, the six-fingered man must also be made aware of the reason *why* his life must now come to an end. Similarly, in *Law Abiding Citizen*, the avenger says to the assailant before killing him, "I know what it feels like to be helpless, just like when I watched you slaughter my whole family."[50] In the Showtime dramatic series *Dexter*, a rogue vigilante prowls sunny South Florida in search of murderers that the Miami legal system has failed to punish. Before ending their lives and avenging the memory of their victims, Dexter surrounds them with the photos of all those they had killed as a symbolic reminder of the scores that are now, finally, being settled.

The satisfaction is in the doing and the enunciation of purpose. The feelings that surface in the aftermath of revenge are not the true measures of vindication. Human beings may experience ambivalence, but that doesn't lessen the moral imperative, which begins with the moral injury and continues until justice is achieved.

On killing the six-fingered man, Montoya acknowledges, "You know, it's very strange. I have been in the revenge business so long, now that it's over, I don't know what to do with the rest of my life."[51]

Revenge isn't supposed to lead to happiness. Revenge won't necessarily bring about catharsis or closure, either. Revenge is not a cure to a sickness or the surrendering to a bad habit. It is a duty to the dead, an obligation to stand up for oneself or for another. Whatever damage was done to the victim won't be repaired if and when the wrongdoer is punished. But that doesn't alter the obligation. W. H. Auden said this about the "Romantic Avenger Hero": "My injury is not an injury to me; it is me. If I cancel it out by succeeding in my vengeance, I shall not know who I am and will have to die. I cannot live without it."[52]

In 2002, during the scandals of the defrocked, pedophile priests throughout Boston, John Geoghan was serving a ten-year sentence for one of 150 accusations of child molestation committed during his time in the priesthood. He sat in jail while many more trials awaited him. But the waiting—of the condemned priest and his tormented victims—came to an end when a fellow prison inmate, Joseph L. Druce, who had been victimized as a child, decided to take vengeance on behalf of the many children who Geoghan had abused. Druce strangled Geoghan in his prison cell, thus ending what would have been years of criminal trials at enormous taxpayer expense, along with endless trauma to those who would have been called to testify.[53]

A most economical final resolution, rationally speaking. The problem was that none of Geoghan's victims felt relief or gratitude for what Druce had done. On the contrary, they were resentful. No one had deputized Druce to give Geoghan his just deserts. The majority of the former priest's victims believed that in being strangled in his cell by a stranger, Geoghan actually got off easy. Worse still, they felt that they had been deprived of their day in court. What they wanted was to be able to speak to their own sense of private violation by confronting this purported man of God who had once molested them. And they wanted the right, which they had earned from their victimization, to ask the court directly to punish Geoghan for what he had done. None of the victims had delegated anyone else to speak or act on their behalf.

After each of their trials had been concluded, many would have been pleased to learn that the priest who still gave them nightmares had been strangled to death. Geoghan surely had to be punished. But it was even more essential for his victims to participate in the process of legal retribution, stating their own cases against the accused. They needed a role and an identity as silent avengers, surrogates of the legal system. They were forever tied to the crime; now they needed to be connected to the punishment. No matter how well intentioned or vicariously vindicating Druce may have been, he was not authorized to serve as judge, jury, and executioner—surely not by the victims he had purportedly sought to benefit.

Addressing the importance of this participatory role, Peter French observed that "the taking of revenge usually produces an emotional or psychological state in the avenger, a feeling of pleasure, a sense of accomplishment, a high. That state cannot fully be experienced if the villain has met his or her end in some natural occurrence, for example, by being buried in an avalanche, unless, of course, the avenger triggered the avalanche with the intent to kill the escaping villain. . . . Unless the avenger is the direct or proximate cause of that ruin, vengeance will not have occurred."[54]

Legal philosophers such as Peter French and Jeffrie G. Murphy have set forth three conditions that must be established before an act of revenge can qualify as justified punishment: it must be deserved; the penalty must be in direct proportion to the harm; and the punishing agent or avenger must have the requisite moral authority to do so.[55] In the case of Geoghan's prison murder, Druce simply did not have the moral authority to inflict this particular punishment. Revenge works best when the victim participates in the judgment and punishment of the wrongdoer—preferably in concert with the legal process or, if absolutely necessary, as a self-appointed avenger.

Victims have preferences. And those preferences challenge the very premises of rational choice theory or the rational actor model. Victims don't worry about costs or fitting in within predictive models. They recognize what a free ride looks like but know enough to wave it away. Having already once been treated as disposable cast-offs, victims want to be players in the vindication that vengeance brings. If revenge was all about punishment, if it was all blood and no brains, why would anyone care who delivered the punishment? But victims do care—care deeply, in fact—and not all avengers are authorized to settle the score, especially when it's not their score to settle. How vengeance is accomplished, and by whom, matters greatly.

At bottom, all victims have an Inigo Montoya speech that they wish to recite. And, in the absence of swashbuckling opportunities for self-help, courtrooms are the ideal settings in which to proclaim publically all of that anguish and rage and to witness justice being done—not in some abstract way, but as a private longing finally fulfilled.

FIVE WHY WE PUNISH

In 1946, Simone de Beauvoir, French existential philosopher, metaphysical novelist, and proto feminist, mostly known for her long-term romantic relationship with Jean Paul Sartre, wrote an essay, *An Eye for an Eye*, which was inspired by the trial and subsequent execution of Robert Brasillach, a Nazi collaborator during Vichy occupied France.[1] Brasillach was one of those despicable intellectuals (every culture has them), the editor-in-chief of a fascist weekly newspaper, *Je suis partout*, which routinely published the names and whereabouts of Jews in hiding. Of course, the Jews who appeared in Brasillach's newspaper were all deported to death camps and never returned to a liberated France. Notoriety in Brasillach's newspaper, for a Jew, was tantamount to a death sentence, the worst possible press coverage imaginable.

This was not lost on the postwar French population who kept score of Nazi henchman of French descent. Many Vichy collaborators received harsh treatment after the war. Some, in fact, were murdered in the streets, strangled to death, shot on the spot. Others, like Brasillach, were tried in courts of law and then executed. There were some people in France, however, who wondered what was the point of all this retribution. After all, the Nazis had been defeated—and resoundingly so. The French Republic had been restored. The Nazis were never going to return, and killing an intellectual like Brasillach—a man who trafficked in newsprint rather than guns, bullets, and gas—is surely not going to deter fascists from trying still another ideological takeover of the world. Brasillach was merely a retail thug, a true middleman, but certainly not a mass murderer.

Many French intellectuals, Beauvoir included, were longtime political liberals who were philosophically opposed to the death penalty. Brain-clouding and barbarian distractions like anger and revenge were thought to be beneath them. Fine minds engaged in deep thoughts don't have time for such low-rent emotions. Revenge is hopelessly messy, undignified, and wasteful of brain cells, they believed. Beauvoir had always regarded herself as one of those sanguine humanists who reflexively opposed hatred, revenge, or the taking of a human life.

Curiously, however, despite the fact that Beauvoir was not a direct victim of Vichy (she was not Jewish and she survived the war unscathed in Paris), she took a deep emotional interest in the trial. And she was surprised at how much her humanitarian impulses had somehow gone on hiatus when it came to her feelings about Brasillach. All of the timeworn liberal justifications for the sanctity of human life had abandoned her, replaced, in this instance, with abject feelings of disgust and hatred. (Of the many French intellectuals who signed a petition seeking clemency for Brasillach, Beauvoir was among those who refused to sign.) Instead, she wrote, "Under the Nazi oppression, faced with traitors who became their accomplices, we saw poisonous sentiments bloom in our hearts. . . . Since June 1940 we have learned rage and hate. We have wished humiliation and death on our enemies."[2]

Why this sudden change? What made Brasillach so special that a hardcore humanist could be so instantly transformed into a champion for capital punishment? Something about this case ignited feelings in Beauvoir she did not have for other murderers, the ordinary kind, those with actual blood on their hands rather than the indirect way an intellectual like Brasillach could be become an accomplice to mass murder.

Still, despite this change of heart, she had no illusions about revenge. Indeed, her support for vengeance was not unqualified. She wrote that the taking of revenge neither restores nor cancels out what was lost. Moreover, she didn't believe that revenge offered the victims of Vichy France any true sense of restitution. And she didn't see how the punishment of Vichy collaborators could possibly be justified on the grounds of social utility. Given the uniqueness of these criminal acts they were unlikely ever to be repeated. And yet Beauvoir concluded that vengeance is surely not irrational, especially in cases of atrocity, where revenge may indeed be an appropriate response to the atrocious.

Not only was Beauvoir unwilling to denounce the taking of revenge, she had her own special reservations about legal retribution—the state monopoly on revenge that governments assume on behalf of all people. Actually, she wondered whether courtroom justice can even be considered a substitute for revenge. Courtrooms, after all, are largely defined by emotional detachment, whereas revenge provides immediate reciprocity between the victim and the wrongdoer—blood for blood. How could a trial—any trial, for that matter—offer the necessary emotional connection that revenge assures if courtrooms are, by definition and common practice, sanitized of emotion? Trials are more like performance pieces, partially scripted, largely ceremonial, even magisterial. They bear little resemblance to one-on-one human encounters where people look each other in the eye and express true feelings of hurt, loss, and shame. For Beauvoir, something is terribly missing when the connection between the act of the wrongdoer and the response of the victim is separated by so much procedural interference and legal static.

The crimes of Vichy made a French philosopher rethink her beliefs about punishment. There was no reason that she should have taken this trial so personally, and yet it affected her in a profoundly human way. Philosophers generally exist in a world of moral abstraction. They don't often worry about living out their own premises about the human condition. What they profess often concerns matters they have never experienced firsthand. And sometimes long-held opinions collapse under the weight of a disobliging reality.

Beauvoir had known Jews who had never returned to France—or anywhere for that matter. She imagined their deaths and, in feeling their absence, realized that Brasillach was no ordinary criminal. However she may have once felt about revenge—or the death penalty—it no longer had the same hold on her. Her philosophy changed; the Holocaust offered its own refinement, one with a sharper more fateful edge. After a lifetime of believing that revenge was wrong and the death penalty pointless, she found herself writing an essay with the most *talionic* of all titles, the biblical phrase instantly emblematic of revenge all over the world. To blankly oppose the death penalty in all instances, to cut oneself off from the natural emotions that are evoked by evil, is to ignore the infinite reasons why punishment of the guilty is so morally mandated and why the failure to punish can result in vengeful lawlessness.

Beauvoir was not, of course, the first philosopher to think broadly about the moral dimensions of punishment. There is a wide variety of philosophical opinion concerning punishment and its relationship to revenge.

John Locke recognized the natural right of every individual to punish wrongdoers, including the right to kill murderers.[3] Plato foreshadowed the more modern theories of rehabilitation, believing that punishment should be in the service of making a wrongdoer an improved person. For Plato, vengeance alone—imposing a penalty in order to make the wrongdoer suffer for the suffering he caused—is not a morally justifiable reason to punish. If the world isn't a better place after the punishment is received, then what's the point? His fellow Greek, Aristotle, however, believed that punishment was an end in itself. There are no other values that can be achieved or that need to be achieved. All that is morally necessary is for the wrongdoer to be punished for the wrong he or she committed. The whole purpose of punishment is to penalize the wrongdoer, not to rehabilitate him.[4]

Jeremy Bentham, the utilitarian philosopher, obviously had Plato in mind in setting forth the basic deterrence rationale for punishment. From the perspective of a utilitarian, the goal of any social policy is to ensure the greatest amount of good that can be achieved for the greatest number of people.[5] Rehabilitation is one such social value, since a truly rehabilitated offender is unlikely to offend again, but so, too, is incapacitation—making certain that the wrongdoer is set apart from, and therefore no longer a threat to, society. Another utilitarian goal of punishment is the deterrence of future crimes. Punishments have the virtue of sending a message to wrongdoers not only that crime does not pay but also that society's payback will be swift and merciless. Wrongdoers who are mindful of society's commitment to punish will surely think twice before taking part in wrongful behavior.

A true utilitarian is always on the lookout for a net social gain. If society is going to the trouble of punishing wrongdoers, the result should benefit everyone. The victim is not the exclusive owner of the injury, which is another way of saying that punishment—both the manner and degree—doesn't belong to him either. This expansive vision of crime and its social implications is precisely why the utilitarian wishes to tailor punishments to maximize social utility. Punishment can't be justified for its own sake or for the sole benefit or satisfaction of the victim. It is never appropriate to harm another human being, even if he deserves it. Without social utility there is no moral basis for punishment—no matter what the misdeed, no matter how severe the wrong.

Utilitarian rationales for punishment are especially well suited to the state's monopoly over revenge. After all, governments step in and standardize what must be done with wrongdoers—whether by criminal statutes or judicial sentencing requirements. The law does not concern itself with customizing justice to satisfy individual needs. The legal system was not created to settle private scores; indeed, it was established to put an end to private vengeance and its public consequence. Justice is for all, which means that individuals are not entitled to justice on their own terms. The rest of us matter, too, utilitarians contend, even those who have no revenge to take and no debts to repay.

Arguably the most valued of all social benefits is the deterrence of future crimes—whether it be from the wrongdoer (known as *specific* deterrence, which discourages a repeat performance) or from criminals in waiting (*general* deterrence, which seeks to neutralize criminal temptation), who will now be deterred given the example that was set by the wrongdoer's mistake. Deterrence is mainly what governments seek to achieve through punishments, ultimately because it makes the job of crime control easier—not in righting a wrong but in keeping the streets safe. A component of this rationale was also practiced by tribal societies—retaliation to reclaim honor *and* to ward off future attacks. The objective was always to deliver a warning to all wrongdoers that society will not overlook criminal acts. The threat that the wrongdoer's actions will not go unanswered is the linchpin of all forms of deterrence, whether established by tribal citizens in more ancient times or maintained through the legal systems of the modern state. As Bentham wrote, "General prevention ought to be the chief end of punishment."[6]

If deterrence occupies the highest rung on the hierarchy of utility, then some crimes will go underpunished simply because they are less likely to be repeated and, therefore, are deemed less dangerous to society. Crimes of passion and white-collar crimes should fall into this category. Crimes with high recidivist rates, such as predatory sex crimes against children, should, under a utilitarian theory, receive the harshest punishment. Indeed, plea bargains aside, the state tends to overpunish sex crimes precisely because keeping violent sexual predators off the streets maximizes the social benefit for all.

Just the same, as any of the victims of Bernard Madoff would attest, the fact that he is neither violent nor likely to bilk clients ever again is not a reason for him to go underpunished based on some "greater good" theory of social utility. Ponzi schemers are, admittedly, a rare breed and generally undeterrable, but they are also lethal. Perhaps this is why Madoff's victims urged Judge Denny Chin to sentence him to the maximum penalty allowable under the law. Social utility was irrelevant to them. What motivated them was pure symbolism and vengeful fury. Madoff's lawyer argued that a sentence of 150 years was a meaningless, mean-spirited punishment, one that placates mob vengeance and offers no other social benefit. Symbolic punishments are retributive by design, with the primary purpose of redressing individual, subjective wounds. A utilitarian, and the state with its monopoly over revenge, has no way to measure the net gain of a symbolic punishment. It is spiritual and emotional in nature and, therefore, beyond the scope of quantifiable, legalistic measurement.

So there are significant limits to utilitarian visions of social justice: in catering exclusively to the net benefits that all of society can enjoy, criminal activity that is widespread will be punished more severely than crimes that affect fewer people; and symbolic punishments that mainly benefit the subjective wishes of a smaller number of victims won't be fully appreciated or strictly enforced.

Utilitarian thinking about punishment arose out of the Enlightenment. Cesare Beccaria, one of the Enlightenment's seminal philosophers, in his 1764 essay *On Crimes and Punishments*, wrote: "It is better to prevent crimes than to punish them. . . . [A] punishment for a crime cannot be deemed truly just . . . unless the laws have adopted the best possible means . . . to prevent the crime."[7]

Of course, part of what it meant to be enlightened in the eighteenth century was to oppose openly the ruthless tyranny so commonly practiced by the kings and queens of Europe. The punishments decreed by kings and sometimes the Catholic Church employed vile instruments of terror and ghastly contraptions that would shock the conscience of mere garden-variety executioners.

The Enlightenment accomplished many things, but chief among them was the outright rejection of sadistic monarchs and grand inquisitors who never hesitated to burn heretics at the stake or stretch the limbs and crush the skulls of those who fell out of favor with the crown. No wonder the philosophers of eighteenth-century Europe had such strong feelings that punishment was always unprincipled and tantamount to torture—perhaps because in their experience it actually was. It's worth noting that the Eighth Amendment to the American Constitution, ratified at the end of the eighteenth century and written by America's own brand of enlightened philosophers, prohibits the government from inflicting "cruel and unusual punishments." The fear of "unusual" punishment was very much on the mind of these men. They seemingly did not doubt, however, the necessity of punishment that was of the more ordinary sort. The Enlightenment introduced the idea that punishment is justified so long as it is predicated on achieving some higher, nobler purpose that can be appreciated by all and is worthy of a civilized society.

Those who ascribe to utilitarian theories of punishment are, at their core, consequentialists. Punishment must result in some favorable consequence that makes everyone better off. Without such consequential benefits, there is no point punishing in the first instance. Consequentialists are forward-looking: the injury or crime has already taken place and there's nothing that can be done that will undo the wrong. Given that it's now all in the past, perhaps some future good can come out of it. The aftermath of a crime presents an opportunity to prevent future harm. In the best of circumstances, punishment might actually lead to some human betterment. The consequentialist aspires to the overall good that punishment might bring. It's a curious form of optimism, indeed, given that it begins with a terrible wrong that sets in motion a chain reaction of social reform and wishful thinking. The punishment hopefully instigates the eventual benefit, like turning lemons into lemonade that will quench the thirst of the collective—regardless of whether the actual victim of the crime ends up feeling satisfied or whether it leaves him with a sour taste in his mouth.

Yet another eighteenth-century philosopher, Immanuel Kant, was also a man of the Enlightenment, but his thoughts about punishment had more in common with Aristotle of ancient Greece. For Kant, punishment is tied to retribution, and retribution is why we punish—plain and simple. Retributivists are, most assuredly, not squeamish about punishment. And they are not plagued by misgivings or doubt. Kant didn't spin around in circles seeking to justify why punishment was obligatory—it simply was. And he certainly wasn't concerned about social utility. It didn't matter to him whether all of society indirectly, fortuitously benefited from a particular punishment.[8] Such a consequence would, in his mind, be an unintended windfall. For Kant, punishment itself is its own reward regardless of any ancillary benefits to the community at large.[9]

And unlike the forward-looking aspirations of consequentialists, retributivists are very much locked in the past; indeed, they are honoring the past by taking care of the unfinished business of the past. They're not so willing to skip ahead to some future benefit that quite possibly may never be achieved. There are more urgent and immediate matters to attend to first. The unpunished crime supersedes all other priorities. In the same way that revenge is related to memory, retribution is fixated on a past event that is forestalling any consideration of the future.

In *Metaphysics of Morals*, Kant wrote that punishment can never be justified for any reason other than that the wrongdoer committed a crime.[10] The wrongdoer is culpable, and therefore he deserves to be punished. Moral blame creates an obligation of just deserts. The consequences of the punishment—to the wrongdoer and to society—are similarly irrelevant. Society doesn't need a reason to punish; the wrongdoer has already supplied the justification. He or she chose to act in a harmful way. He or she wished to be exempted from the laws of society, unilaterally breaking with the state's rules of behavior. Now society is left with little choice but to respond in kind. The moral authority to do so is unimpeachable and nonnegotiable. After all, it was set in motion by the wrongdoer's own misdeed.

Observing the matter-of-fact simplicity of the retributivist's worldview, law professor Michael S. Moore writes, "Retributivism is a very straightforward theory of punishment: We are justified in punishment because and only because offenders deserve it."[11] The decision to commit a crime, freely made, is all society needs to know. And it should make no apologies for what it must do. Surely the wrongdoer realized that some proportionate penalty would be forthcoming. Society cannot excuse the act as if it had never happened. A true Kantian believes that, in imposing a punishment, the state is merely acting on the wishes of a wrongdoer, responding to his lawless behavior with a reciprocated act of retribution. Oddly enough it can be understood as honoring the wrongdoer by giving him what he asked for. Constitutional law and philosophy professor Walter Berns, in his support of capital punishment, expressed this Kantian view in writing that the community's anger over a murder "is an expression of that element of the soul that is connected with the view that there is responsibility in the world; and in holding particular men responsible, it pays them the respect which is due them as men."[12]

Like Aristotle, Kant believed that there was no point searching for a reason to punish when the most obvious one was staring you right in the face: the wrongdoer deserves it; doing anything less would plainly be wrong and surely not just. Indeed, Kant is the father of the just deserts rationale for retribution and, by extension, the patron saint of all avengers, even though he believed that punishment was the province of the state and not the task of a private avenger. Kant may not have trusted ordinary citizens to handle the moral imperative of desert, but he was unequivocal when it came to the state's obligation to punish, and in that way he shared the same common purpose of the duty-bound avenger.

And what about deterrence, the supreme virtue of social utility favored by consequentialists? For Kant, the deterrence rationale is not even worthy as a time waster. Consequentialists overthink this simple dilemma: a person commits a wrong, he or she must be punished; that's what he or she deserves. Deterrence refocuses punishment away from moral criteria and places it in the realm of social policy. Besides, in the end it's not altogether clear whether deterrence works, since undeterred wrongdoers end up being punished anyway.

Steven Pinker has identified a phenomenon known as the "deterrence paradox," which should make consequentialists wonder whether they are all actually closet retributivists. The paradox suggests that everyone, including utilitarians, ultimately believe that wrongdoers should receive their just deserts even if the purported social benefits of punishment prove futile. The paradox of deterrence is that if the wrongdoer knows that he is supposed to be deterred by the threat of punishment and he chooses to commit the wrong anyway, why then does society follow through with the punishment given that it can't achieve the very thing that granted it the right to harm another human being in the first instance?

"Punishment even in the pure sense of just deserts is *ultimately* a policy for deterrence," Pinker writes. "It follows from a paradox inherent to the logic of deterrence: though the *threat* of punishment can deter behavior, if the behavior does take place the punishment serves no purpose other than pure sadism or an illogical desire to make the threat credible retroactively."[13]

The certainty of punishment operates as a threat, a warning to wrongdoers of what awaits them should they commit a crime. When a wrongdoer calls society's bluff, however, choosing to ignore the threat, then the rationale for the punishment collapses, in part because a society that punishes crimes only insofar as to deter them has no real interest in actually inflicting any punishments. The consequentialist's goal is simply to prevent crimes; punishment is not a worthy enterprise on its own. But if wrongdoers still engage in all manner of predation, then the social utility of deterrence ends up without any consequence—other than the commission of yet another crime. Society's threat demonstrably doesn't work, and therefore no net benefit can possibly be gained from actually punishing the wrongdoer.

Nevertheless, with full knowledge that their moral basis for punishment is sometimes nothing but an empty threat, consequentialists, paradoxically, still go through with it. Why? Is it to deter yet some other criminal's behavior, a wrongdoer who is still undecided about his future path to criminality? Scientific data indicate that it is more than likely that nascent wrongdoer's won't be deterred either. Deterrence-based punishment then mirrors the classic definition of insanity: doing something over and over in hopes of achieving a different result.

The deterrence paradox might prove retributivists to be ultimately right: punishment doesn't need to hinge on a social benefit. There are moral reasons to punish without having to scrounge about for a net gain. All society has to do is keep its promise that wrongdoers not be permitted to cheat justice. Yet the fact that crime is not deterred doesn't necessarily mean that the consequentialist is disinterested in punishment for its own sake. The decision to follow through with punishment ends up taking on its own retributive character. Those with a mind for deterrence inevitably flip the switch in favor of just deserts. Failed deterrence nonetheless results in a punished wrongdoer. In the end, retribution is what civilization comes to depend on to bring about social peace and to appease the moral universe.

This paradox was precisely what Simone Beauvoir experienced when she applauded Brasillach's execution. She acknowledged that she saw little purpose in punishing him given that his death had no chance of deterring a future crime. However, she wouldn't allow herself to accept anything less than the most severe punishment of all—this from a woman who didn't believe in capital punishment. Brasillach's despicable deeds were self-condemning and allowed for only one solution. It was through his inhuman actions that Brasillach managed to convert a lifelong humanist into a woman with an impassioned and implacable retributive streak.

If Pinker is correct that seeded within all deterrence rationales lurks the paradox of just deserts, eager to punish without regard to social benefit, then nearly everyone is a retributivist at heart. We arguably all share some affinity for retribution even if we claim otherwise. In a 2003 Gallup Poll, 70 percent of Americans supported the death penalty for wrongdoers convicted of murder. More than half of the respondents, however, explained the reasons for their support by invoking the language of vengeance: 37 percent said "eye for an eye"; 13 percent responded that the guilty deserved to die; 4 percent used the word "justice"; and 3 percent said that it was fair punishment. All of these reasons are ultimately statements that speak to revenge. Only 11 percent, however, regarded deterrence as a credible reason for supporting capital punishment.[14]

Most everyone believes in punishment. When deterrence is shown to be futile, utilitarians don't simply allow wrongdoers to walk away unpunished. And those in favor of the death penalty—society's ultimate punishment— are comfortable framing their support in the language of vengeance. Capital punishment ought to symbolize a powerful deterrent, and yet that's not why death penalty supporters believe in it. Perhaps retributive and consequentialist philosophies are not so different from revenge after all. No matter how they each start out, in the end justice will look a lot like just deserts.

When it comes to payback, which has become the colloquial word of choice for retribution (to retribute), even Kant, the godfather of retributivist thought, didn't see any reason to tinker with the *talion*. He wrote, "Only the law of retribution (*lex talionis*) can determine exactly the kind and degree of punishment."[15] From biblical times to the Enlightenment, proportionate punishment was always and forever mandatory. The ancient law of retaliation has served many different cultures and societies quite well throughout the ages. Curiously, given that the law of the *talion* was always the guiding principle of vengeance, how did it come about that revenge—the feelings it evokes, the measurements it requires—became so irrevocably severed from the general legal theories that justify punishment? All punishment is vengeful to some degree. Punishment, regardless of which theory one abides, is essentially about righting wrongs, settling scores, redeeming debts, honoring memory, and attempting to restore moral balance. As much as justice and revenge, in the moral universe, mean the same thing, so, too, is punishment a stand-in for revenge. The philosophical and emotional reasons why we punish are universally embraced. Nevertheless, the reasons why avengers must emotionally, and mathematically, settle the score are not as similarly appreciated. The retribution of the state is regarded as fundamentally different from the private settlement of disputes, but this is a curious if not altogether forced distinction since vengeance, retribution, and punishment are actually close moral cousins.

According to Kant, retribution is always the business of the state and not the prerogative of individuals. He sets forth a clear qualification between retribution and revenge, as do many philosophers who favor retributive theories of punishment. For example, Robert Nozick sees retribution as being entirely distinct from revenge because the former concerns correcting a wrong while the latter responds merely to an insult.[16] Moreover, for Nozick, retribution allows for limits to be set on the amount of punishment taken, precisely because it is impersonal, whereas revenge draws a profoundly intimate, almost umbilical line between the victim and the avenger—and, in so doing, empowers the avenger to take his vengeance without moderation. This is precisely what Sir Francis Bacon understood vengeance to be when he wrote, "Revenge is a kind of wild justice, which the more man's nature runs to the more ought law to weed it out."[17] Retribution carried out by governments is rational, fully measured and completely unemotional. Revenge, by contrast, boils over with moral righteousness and hotheaded rage, which society simply cannot tolerate.

Many philosophers and legal theorists believe that society has no choice but to seek legal retribution rather than moral revenge. Punishments under the rule of law accomplish several aims. Nozick believes that only retribution reconnects the wrongdoer with moral values he has apparently forgotten.[18] Jean Hampton argues that retribution reaffirms the value of the victim and responds, collectively, to the moral indignation that society feels toward the wrongdoer.[19] She speaks of "moral injury" as the indignation that the victim experiences, caused by a brazen act of diminishment, the symbolic lowering of the victim's rank or value—all perpetrated by the wrongdoer. Moral injury is a wound inflicted to dignity, a stab through the heart of a victim's honor. It is quite different from a physical injury because the violence it creates is an attack on personal pride, to the victim's sense of self-worth. In such cases, Hampton argues, the retributivist is fixated not simply on getting even but, further, on annulling the underlying crime of diminishment, demanding that "the false claim of superiority be corrected."[20]

Similarly, Jeffrie G. Murphy sees a connection between resentment and damaged self-respect. Retribution restores moral balance because, in committing the wrong, the wrongdoer is asserting his superiority over the victim, essentially saying, "I am up here high and you are down there below."[21] Retribution is a way for the victim to channel her resentment and reclaim her self-respect—again, however, only through the apparatus of the law and not by way of self-help.

But if legal retribution is intended to elevate victims and respond to their wish for reclaimed honor, why then does the law operate as if victims are not the intended beneficiaries of the legal system's delivery of just deserts? In defining retribution, Hampton and Murphy borrow the same language of revenge and look to supply victims with the emotional rewards that have always been the lifeline of vengeance. How then did they expect to find it in the one entity—the legal system—which has shown no patience for emotion and no interest in restoring the emotional health of those who come before the law? The burden of punishment remains with the state, but the state has never understood its retributive burden to include victim vindication.

In conjuring the spirit of Kantian, law professor Michael S. Moore believes that retributive punishment is justified for no reason other than that the wrongdoer deserves it.[22] The decision to punish rests entirely on the degree of his moral blameworthiness and desert. Moore notes a paradox similar to what Pinker observed with regard to deterrence: if the retributivist identifies any good or benefit that might arise from punishment, then he cannot truly be a retributivist, since retribution means the equivalent of never having to say you're sorry—you either believe that punishment is always correct because it is simply warranted, or you don't. The tendency of most people, even hardcore retributivists, is to offer up some value that is achieved through punishment, some advantage that is to be gained, whether it be deterrence, incapacitation, or rehabilitation, rather than to accept the absolutist position that no benefit is necessary because moral culpability, alone, is deserving of punishment—period. Nothing further needs to be said; no other value need be identified. Punishment is its own reward.

But here, too, each of these retributive values sounds a lot like revenge, even though retributivists insist that only the state can achieve these values. Whatever benefits there may be to the victim—and all of society, for that matter—they are mere fortuities, incidental to why the state punishes, even as it serves as proxy to whatever claims an individual might have. Perhaps the state, and its citizens, ultimately believes in punishment for the same reason—because the wrongdoer deserves it.

This perspective on retribution would certainly please Kant. Society's obligation to punish is a categorical imperative; the reasons why we punish are universal and absolute; and the decision to punish is not optional. As Kant famously wrote in his "last man on the island" object lesson, "Even if a civil society were to dissolve itself by common agreement of all its members . . . *the last murderer remaining in prison must first be executed*, so that everyone will duly receive what his actions are worth and so the bloodguilt thereof will not be fixed on the people because they failed to insist on carrying out the punishment; for if they fail to do so, they may be regarded as accomplices in this public violation of legal justice" (emphasis added).[23]

Once in the presence of moral blameworthiness, those who stand by and do nothing, turn the other cheek and ignore their duty to punish, end up as "accomplices" to the original crime. The moral character of the community has been defiled by the wrongdoer's deed. Therefore, he must be purged from the community otherwise those who allow him to stay become complicit in bringing about their collective defilement.[24] The last man on the planet is charged with making sure to turn off the lights on the unpunished wrongdoer. It would matter little to a true Kantian that the punishment of the last culpable man or woman on Earth is ultimately senseless, since no tangible, societal benefit can possibly be achieved. On an abandoned planet, no other wrongdoer can be deterred from committing future crimes if no one is left to commit one. And this is particularly true since there are no longer any potential victims either. It matters even less if, after serving his time, the wrongdoer is completely rehabilitated and is no longer a threat to his neighbors. All the neighbors are now gone, and there is no society in existence that can welcome him back.

Yet a true retributivist, and an even truer Kantian, would say that punishment doesn't have to yield an advantage, it simply needs to be morally deserved and carried out. A debt is owed and must be paid back—even if there is neither a society nor an individual who can reap the reward. The moral universe will have its own reckoning, and it will faithfully record the discharging of the debt. The absence of a defined social utility does not dispense with the duty to penalize the wrong. The wrongdoer must be held accountable, and nothing else needs to be taken into account. Just deserts are bindingly tied to only one overriding priority: what is deserved.

The broader point is that there are competing values between legal retribution and moral revenge and between the obligation of the state to serve as the gatekeeper of justice rather than as the enabler of vengeance. Punishment can be used to achieve many different values: deterrence, incapacity, just deserts, righting a wrong, making a public example, reinforcing respect for the law, restoring the moral compass of communities, and, yes, retribution and revenge. But punishment that neither is carried out nor contains the emotional payoff of vengeance won't satisfy victims, instill credibility with the general public, or meet the high standards of the moral universe. There are many such examples in our own legal system of bungled punishments, from the acquittal of the officers in the Rodney King trial in 1992—which resulted in six days of rioting in Los Angeles, totaling fifty-three deaths, 2,382 people injured, and seven thousand fires—to the more recent acquittal of

Casey Anthony in Orlando, Florida, and a nation left stupefied, its collective jaw dropped in utter disbelief, that a mother—whether she was murderous or criminally negligent—could go unpunished and ultimately set free.

The philosophers of the Enlightenment, Beccaria and Voltaire, Locke and Rousseau, never doubted that citizens would voluntarily enter into a social contract with their respective governments. Surely it is better to forfeit some liberty, such as the moral right to seek revenge, in favor of state-imposed punishments that, in theory, serve to benefit all of society and not just the injured party. That, of course, assumes, and should be entirely contingent on, the state actually fulfilling its duty to punish in lieu of a citizen's moral right to do the very same thing. Legal retribution, ultimately, must accomplish the same aim as vengeance, otherwise why would anyone forfeit the right to settle a debt and pay back what is justly owed?

One presumption of the Enlightenment was that the social contract was largely a one-sided agreement—the citizens benefit more than the state. It was more cost efficient, time saving, and mess avoiding to empower the state to assume certain fundamental obligations on behalf of the citizenry. Building roads, bridges, and airports, sanitizing streets, raising standing armies, constructing halls of justice, are all features of the modern state. Collectively we bring such conveniences and necessities about. Nevertheless, governments that collect taxes but fail to deliver on services are no less vulnerable to revolt than despotic monarchs. Vengeance is not easy to give up if justice isn't being provided any other way. The only thing that has changed throughout history is the evolution of the avenger and the varied restrictions imposed by the state. Who should be the proper revenge taker—individuals, families, tribes, God, kings, or governments? The farther away we have moved from the moral right of individuals to seek vindication, the greater the level of injustice and indignity we have forced victims to endure—all in the name of a social contract that purports to protect society from private acts of vengeance.

Certainly it is cleaner for the state to take the lead on revenge. After all, not all avengers want the job, even if they are duty-bound to do so. The state goes to the trouble of erecting a justice and penal system—a vast institutional network dedicated to serving as the revenge proxy for its citizens. But if revenge and retribution are ultimately first cousins in the family tree of punishment, then surely there must be a way to transfer the virtues of revenge into a public setting and still preserve the emotional benefits to victims. Whether they like it or not, the state and its law enforcement agencies function as surrogate revenge takers. They should act like them. A good place to start is in developing strategies and adopting mindsets that place a priority on victim vindication. The government must give people the satisfaction in knowing that justice was, in fact, done. But by surrendering the right of revenge to an entity that is incapable of feeling, it is no surprise that victims end up receiving a depersonalized remedy.

In the film *Unforgiven*, actor-director Clint Eastwood's fresh look on both the cowboy Western and the revenge flick, William Munny, a hired gun, is now a widowed father trying to earn a living as a pig farmer. But the allure of his old profession proves too hard to resist when he learns about a $1,000 reward offered by a group of prostitutes who must avenge the slashed face of one of their own. The sheriff of the town, Little Bill, refuses to arrest and punish the wranglers who were responsible for the brutal assault. Instead, he decides to turn what was an indefensible criminal matter into a simple case of compensatory damages—with the defaced prostitute not even on the receiving end of the compensation. If any damages were owed, Little Bill reasons, it would be to the saloon owner, who is now without the services of one of his prostitutes, all of whom work and live in a brothel above the saloon.

Munny sets off with his friend, Ned Logan, another gunfighter, and they do, ultimately, kill the wranglers. But Munny doesn't accept the reward after he learns that Little Bill had arrested, whipped, and killed Ned—desecrating his friend by posting him outside the saloon wearing a sign. Suddenly, what started out as a professional hit has now become personal for Munny. With the prostitutes fully avenged, Munny must now seek his own vengeance on behalf of Ned. He heads back into town and, like all avengers, announces why he has come and what is about to happen. "I'm here to kill you, Little Bill, for what you did to Ned,"[25] he says on entering the saloon, a solitary figure on a stormy night. And in making good on his obligation to honor his friend, Munny, the washed-up gunman, single-handedly kills five men, including, ultimately, Little Bill. About to fire the final fatal shot, Munny stands over Little Bill.

LITTLE BILL. I don't deserve this, to die like this. I was building a house.

MUNNY. Deserve's got nothing to do with it.

LITTLE BILL. I'll see you in hell, William Munny.

MUNNY, *barely audible*. Yeah.

Little Bill doesn't offer an apology for the whipping and murder of Ned. He merely expresses regret that he won't get a chance to live in his new house. Yet, it wouldn't have made much of a difference to Munny had Little Bill apologized and pleaded for his life. Munny was in no mood for forgiveness. It would not have changed the outcome. What Little Bill did was unforgivable: as the lawman of the town he failed to carry out his duty to punish the wranglers; and he abused his authority in murdering Ned. Munny may have been trained as a killer for hire, but this shootout at the saloon wasn't Munny on the job. He wasn't collecting a reward; he was redeeming a debt in remembrance of a friend. And the wrongdoer isn't likely to apologize in this film since, like its title, he knows he will be unforgiven.

And yet Munny says that desert has nothing to do with why Little Bill must die. We can accept that he believes that he, too, might end up in hell for all of the blood on his hands. But surely he knows that his payback of Little Bill was righteous. Little Bill deserved to die under any theory of punishment. The law of the *talion* would demand nothing less. A hired gun usually doesn't worry about desert, but true avengers can't wake up in the morning without first being reminded of their duty. Is Munny making a statement that punishment is sometimes without principle? The movie audience knows that Little Bill had it coming. While the story takes place on the open frontier during a time of frontier justice, modern audiences, perhaps jaded by their own urban legal systems, still wish to believe in a just world, that those who do wrong will, ultimately, receive their due.

The moral universe loses all alignment with the horizon if wrongdoers escape without first getting what they deserve.

Of course, legal retribution has its moral problems. We all know that even the most steadfast retributive impulses often won't guarantee that a wrongdoer will be paid back. The most frightening defect of constitutional democracy is that guilty people are sometimes set free, acquitted of all legal charges, the unintended beneficiaries of the lapsed judgment or procedural error of law enforcement, or the reasonable doubts placed in the minds of manipulated juries. It is the price we all pay to live in a democratic society. And yet we know that the acquitted wrongdoer is guilty and that the system failed. For better or worse, the Constitution of the United States is far more concerned with the rights of the accused than the heartache of victims. Cynically, it seems as if "criminal justice" means the justice afforded to criminals—the kind of justice that is slippery, avoidant, and exonerating. State and federal prosecutors wield great advantages, of course, with massive subpoena, law enforcement, and prosecutorial powers. But in a very real sense, when it comes to the actual prosecution of criminals, the government oddly operates at a disadvantage. It is often more difficult for the government to prove its case than it is for the defendant to cast reasonable doubt on his or her guilt.

We've all heard the saying: criminals, literally, get away with murder. And sometimes they do.

After all, under our laws, the defendant is always presumed innocent. The legal system rarely acknowledges the implications of this concept. If the defendant is presumed innocent, then his accusers are presumably lying. There is no way—emotionally and logically—of getting around that. At the commencement of a criminal trial, starting fresh and with an open mind, isn't that what a reasonable juror would be guided to think—isn't that the necessary presumption? One can't very well be presumed innocent if his accusers are presumably telling the truth.

Somebody must be lying.

Moreover, the burden of proof is always on the government, and the prosecution must prove its case beyond a reasonable doubt. The defendant is given no such reciprocal burdens. The burden never shifts away from the prosecution, and reasonable doubt has become a nebulous concept, easily misunderstood by jurors and always an invitation to an acquittal. Indeed, jurors are so hopelessly confused about how to apply the legal standard that they end up acquitting otherwise guilty wrongdoers based on doubts that are wholly "unreasonable."

Actually, most of the constitutional amendments are stacked against the government. The Fourth Amendment excludes evidence that may be indisputably incriminating (and possibly true), but unlawfully obtained and therefore inadmissible at trial. The Fifth Amendment protects against self-incrimination and, in doing so, excludes a great deal of truth that might otherwise be supplied by the defendant himself. The accused, arguably the most important person in the courtroom, the one who may possess the most information about the crime—or about his own innocence, whatever the case may be—need not say a word in his defense. The Sixth Amendment turns courtrooms into a blood sport of zealous advocacy where attorneys blow smoke, grandstand, kick obstacles in the way of each other, and discredit witnesses who may be telling the truth so that, by the time the lawyers deliver their summations, the jury has no idea what the truth is or whether it even matters anymore. The Constitution is an enlightened legal document but an imperfect moral one.

Liberal democracy demands a strict adherence to the rule of law and a fidelity to legal procedure. This nation, after all, was founded on a fear of tyranny and the quest for personal freedom. Nothing is more repugnant to Americans than the abuse of power. There is no greater moral outrage than an individual who is made to disappear without due process and equal protection under the law. It is this fear, this nightmare of governmental terror, that accounts for why innocence is always presumed and why the burden rests with the state to prove otherwise.

An article of faith in a liberal society, the frontline excuse for why the legal system is sometimes prone to failure—why injustice is always a possible outcome of the law—can be summed up in the following aphorism, one that all criminal defense attorneys can recite by heart: "It is better for ten guilty people to go free than to punish one innocent person."[26]

But is that really true? It sounds right until one examines its implications. The people who proclaim these wise words rarely come from the pool of citizens who have been victimized by violent crime or who have had loved ones killed by an unpunished criminal. We apparently deem our society to be far more just when we are prepared to sacrifice our own personal safety and moral conviction by setting free large numbers of guilty individuals—all for the sake of guarding against the possibility of imprisoning an innocent man.

Yet we must know that this principle is fundamentally unjust, if not outright suicidal. It is the value judgment that one outcome is preferred over the other that is particularly objectionable. *Better* that ten guilty criminals go free? Why aren't both outcomes equally intolerable and morally unbearable? Innocent people surely should not be punished under the law. But a society that places a lower priority on punishing the guilty—by a factor of 10 to 1, the guilty measured in multiples while the innocent represented by one solitary man—is surely not a society that fears the wrath of the moral universe. Actually, it sounds like a society in love with an exaggerated sense of its own moral superiority, abandoning moral clarity and social peace for a relentless allegiance to legal procedure.

Peter French points out that "a society that is obsessed with an aversion to risking the conviction and punishment of the innocent encourages the guilty to complicate their cases to such an extent that they avoid or indefinitely delay penalties."[27] With procedure valued over truth, it isn't all that difficult to "game" the legal system by clouding the truth and raising the specter of reasonable doubt, all the while playing by the legal system's own rules and beating it at its own game.

It is one thing to demand that the legal system not inadvertently or, even worse, deliberately punish the innocent. It is quite another, in the interest of preventing a gross miscarriage of injustice against one, to unleash the potential for multiple miscarriages by allowing ten wrongdoers to make their return into society—fully acquitted, unpunished, and ready to harm again. What makes society rest easier: the knowledge that unpunished killers are free to kill anew or that every step has been taken to protect one innocent from being unjustly punished? On the scale of horribles, it's not so obvious that the protection of one is morally superior to the unleashing of wholesale violence on the rest.

One sure way to cause the heavens to thunder with outrage is to fail to punish the deserving. Citizens are asked to accept injustice as the price for living in a liberal democracy. But isn't that too much to ask? Isn't the price too costly? The legal system insists that we live with its failure. But it can't have it both ways: prevent citizens from avenging the harms done to them by insisting that retribution is the sole province of the state, while at the same time, chalk up the miscarriages of justice to systemic failure. Systems, unlike actual victims, don't feel the pain of unavenged wrongs. Such situations are tailor made for the aggrieved to take justice into their own hands—measure for measure.

In 2010, the Supreme Court of the United States heard arguments in *Snyder v. Phelps.*[28] The case, which originated in Topeka, Kansas, centered on a civil lawsuit brought by the father of a dead Marine whose funeral was interrupted, if not altogether ruined, by the presence of a church group holding up signs that read, among other things, "God Hates Fags." The Westboro Baptist Church, purportedly, wasn't claiming that Lance Corporal Matthew A. Snyder was gay or that any of their messages were directed at him personally. The members of the church simply wanted to communicate their disapproval of the United States permitting homosexuals to serve in the military. They protested at the funeral in order to express the opinion that God was punishing America's combat forces now that there were gay soldiers among its ranks.

Albert Snyder, the dead marine's father, received an $11 million jury verdict against the church, based on a finding that the protest caused him emotional distress. The church appealed and the appellate court ruled that since the messages were not directed at the marine, they constituted protected political speech under the First Amendment. Not surprisingly, the Supreme Court upheld the appellate ruling, and Chief Justice John Roberts wrote a blistering opinion that amounted to a tutorial on the American values embodied in free speech. The law has always been pretty well settled that the profound sensitivities of the listener cannot preempt the free speech guarantees provided under the Constitution to those who purportedly have something to contribute to the marketplace of ideas.

If America stands for anything, it stands for freedom, and the most cherished of America's freedoms is the right to speak—the right not to be prevented from expressing an idea. The promise that an idea will emerge from speech is of a much higher value than protecting the sensitivities of listeners who might be hurt by the speech. The First Amendment has a long history of privileging speech over pain, which illustrates just how far the Constitution will go in support of personal liberty, unbounded by other values, including human decency.

For instance, courts have ruled that Neo-Nazis can march in a town populated by Holocaust survivors, avowed racists can burn a cross on an African-American's lawn, and a protester can burn the American flag in order to criticize the foreign policy of the United States.[29] All of these indignities are deemed protected speech under the First Amendment. But they are also acts of violence. The vulnerabilities of those who must watch in horror as someone violates them not with their fists but with their hate is of no special concern to the courts. Rather than safeguard the victim from the assault, the government envelopes the speaker in a ring of immunity, ignoring the damage his actions have created.

Albert Snyder summed up his disgust with how the government had enabled a church group to destroy the one moment he had to bury his son, a young man who gave his life for this country. "If the law can't help us and the courts won't do something, someone is going to take this into his own hands."[30]

In 1993, Daniel Driver was on trial for molesting four boys in Northern California. The prosecutors were certain they would prevail in obtaining a conviction. Ellie Nesler, the mother of one of the boys, wasn't so sure. She had only recently learned that the man who sexually abused her son had, a decade earlier, been convicted of molesting another boy. Driver was released from prison for that crime because an expert testified that he was unlikely to ever molest again. Obviously, that expert opinion turned out to be incorrect.

Revolted by this knowledge, Ellie Nesler knew that the legal system had already once failed to protect her son. She decided the law didn't deserve another chance. So when called to the witness stand at a preliminary hearing to decide whether Driver should stand trial for molestation, Nesler demonstrated a mother's love by removing a handgun from her purse and shooting Driver five times in the head and neck, killing him instantly.

Suddenly, in the twisted logic of the criminal justice system, the parameters of the trial had changed. The defendant was now dead. And the mother of the victim would soon become the defendant in her own trial—accused of an even more severe crime than the one she had vindicated by taking her revenge. Nesler was found guilty of manslaughter. (It didn't help that Nesler had a criminal record, and at the time of the shooting there was methamphetamine in her blood.) The judge sentenced her to ten years in prison. In doing so he said, "It was an intentional and intolerable assault on our system of justice. She's proud of what she's done, and if given the chance would do it again."[31] The prosecutor added, "You don't take the law into your own hands, and you don't kill another human being that is vulnerable. And you let the system work."[32]

The "system," however, did not work, and often does not work. If it did, Nesler would not have believed that satisfaction would be possible only through self-help. Tens of thousands of victims, and the families of victims, have found themselves in similar situations faced with the law's failure but lacked either the courage or the conviction to take matters into their own hands. Most people—cautious, law-abiding, willing to take a free ride on the state's judicial system, or simply scared—allow the law to run its course. Most have faith that the legal system will do the right thing, that it will live up to its promises and earn the public's trust. Is this a leap of faith? Is it an example of blind faith? Stripped of the right to avenge, victims stand naked before the law, hopeful that they won't be humiliated any further.

Many come to realize that the law has an equal if not greater chance of failing, and when it does, what remains is a terrible injustice. And injustice, whether because of our evolutionary history or complicated brain circuitry, is the source of great primal pain. To ignore injustice forces all human beings—whether they are direct victims or curious onlookers—to act against human nature. The judge pounds the gavel and decrees a final judgment. She or he instructs victims to return to their homes and accept the law's decision, to wipe from their memories the failed encounter they had with the law, and to reconcile themselves to their loss. And all this from a legal system that proclaims itself to be far more superior at retribution than ordinary citizens are at revenge.

What is not readily acknowledged is that this failure to avenge results in a separate crime—this one, committed by the state.

And that's why Ellie Nesler took the law into her own hands. "What's a mother to do?" her sister asked.[33] After avenging her son Nesler accepted her punishment and began serving her time. But great numbers of citizens across the country did not accept it. Among these people were Oprah Winfrey, Geraldo Rivera, and Charles Kuralt, each of whom called attention to Nesler's plight on their respective television shows. Others hosted fundraisers and spaghetti dinners to help pay for her appeal and to support her children. Lawyers even offered to represent Nesler pro bono.

All of this public fuss on her behalf—this crusading mother, the woman who dared the legal system to treat her as if she was a cold-blooded murderer rather than a righteous avenger—ultimately didn't matter. The molestation of a child and the murder of the molester were separate events. Under the law, these crimes would not cancel each other out. The one did not justify the other. In fact, Nesler ended up committing the greater statutory offense. Nesler broke the law and, even worse, she ignored a prevailing taboo—a taboo older and more reviled than pedophilia. Individuals must not be allowed to become vigilantes. Revenge is primitive; retribution is the purview and prerogative of the state. It is all part of the social contract—the concessions we make, our claim check for signing up with civilization. A central authority will collect the tolls, fight the fires, defend the nation, and punish wrongdoers on behalf of the state without regard to the feelings of victims.

Surely that sounds reasonable, but what happens when the state breaches its part of the social contract it has with the citizenry? It promises to protect and punish, and the promise is broken, the assignment botched. Most assuredly not listed among the Bill of Rights is the right to revenge. Vengeance is not an individual right, but we all feel entitled to justice as a condition of the social contract. Is there a greater good that government can provide?

"Justice for all" means that all individuals are entitled to receive justice. It also means that justice must serve "all"—as in the entire community? We pledge our allegiance to these principles. Naturally we all benefit from having our streets made safer by incarcerating criminals so that they no longer pose a threat to the general public. Justice is available to everyone, but this only means *access* to justice, not the entitlement to a particular remedy. Victims do not have to feel satisfied in order for justice to have been declared done. But by not offering satisfaction and vindication, the legal system oversells what it initially promised and devalues what it ultimately delivers.

Salvatore ("Sammy the Bull") Gravano was a Mafia hit man and underboss for the Gambino crime family in New York. He was responsible for killing at least nineteen people. Government prosecutors, however, offered him a plea bargain and a reduced sentence, along with placement in the Federal

Witness Protection Program, in exchange for testimony against John Gotti. Gotti, at the time, was the putative boss of the Five Families that comprised the Italian crime syndicate in New York City. In 1991, Federal District Judge I. Leo Glasser sentenced Gravano to five years in prison, which was reduced to less than a year because Sammy the Bull had already been in detention for four years.

The families of Gravano's nineteen slain victims were never given a chance to speak in Judge Glasser's courtroom. The court determined that Gravano "no longer poses a threat to this or any other community" and that he had "irrevocably broken with his past."[34] Instead of being punished for murdering nineteen people, Gravano, because of his decision to cooperate with the government, was hailed by at least one law enforcement officer as "the bravest thing [I] had ever seen." After serving the remaining year of his sentence, he and his family were relocated to Arizona. In 2000, he, his wife, and son were arrested and pleaded guilty to operating a multimillion-dollar drug ring. So much for irrevocably breaking with his past. How can people trust the judgment and wisdom of judges if they are so easily duped not by an Einstein, but by a man named Sammy the Bull?

In 2010, a similar case of a Mafia kingpin who participated in eleven murders during his thirty years of service with a crime family ended up spending less than seven years in prison after he agreed to cooperate with the government in convicting fifty-one other mob figures. A federal district judge reduced his sentence to time served. The judge said that the criminal justice system was "dependent on the cooperation of criminals in the prosecution of other criminals. This cooperation does not come without a cost."[35]

Costly, indeed. But are the costs of these bargained down, negotiated pleas simply too much to bear, morally, even though they arguably provide significant value to the criminal justice system by leading to the conviction of other wrongdoers who would otherwise remain at large? Victims get shortchanged, the truth remains buried, wrongdoers triumphantly beat the system, and the dead cry out for justice but can't be heard amid the deaf ears and grinding gears of the law's processing of criminal cases.

Of course, one can certainly argue that the moral sacrifice that comes with leniency results in an overall better legal outcome and a net social benefit. It also serves the interests of legal efficiency as a greater number of wrongdoers are taken off the street without the state having to gather fresh evidence and expend precious resources prosecuting more tenuous cases. In the end, more wrongdoers go to jail by leveraging and reducing the punishment of those who possess valuable, incriminating information.

But in doing so, some wrongdoers end up grossly underpunished. Plea bargains and leniency granted in exchange for testimony achieve the maximizing goals of social utility. But social utility, with its sole focus on the "greater good," rides roughshod over moral balance and just deserts.

Recognizing the moral implications of this dynamic, law professor William Ian Miller wrote, "Today, the state says to the victim: 'We are taking away what, in prior times, was your right to settle this account and we will settle it on your behalf.' Supposedly, we do this for the benefit of the entire society. But if that price is less than what the victim would have gotten in the earlier system, isn't the victim being asked to pay for a wider societal benefit? Doesn't something more need to be done for the person who has been wronged?"[36]

No, it is not better, morally, at least, for ten guilty people to go unpunished in order to ensure that an innocent person is not railroaded through the legal system on account of sloppy or inept law enforcement. Legally we congratulate ourselves for our commitment to procedural rules and for protecting the rights of the accused; meanwhile, we twist and turn at night, unable to fall asleep, knowing that we have allowed known murderers to reintegrate into society—some having never served any jail time at all. Many of our own nightmares are self-inflicted.

And we call avengers outlaws?

The Fourth Amendment and its exclusionary rule is a terrific legal statement that places the burden on the government to make certain that it is arresting the right people and doing so properly. And even when the government identifies genuine wrongdoers, the apprehension and prosecution of those wrongdoers must comport with strict constitutional guidelines. The unquestioned authority of the Fourth Amendment demonstrates just how much the criminal justice system is willing to privilege procedure over truth and how a strict adherence to technical rules can sometimes be used to sabotage justice.

It also suggests that the suspicions of bad faith that the Founding Fathers once attributed to King George III ended up being projected onto America's own law enforcement personnel. Evidence that would otherwise be probative of a crime is ultimately excluded from the trial due to the procedural lapse of a police officer. Without the admission of this evidence a guilty person will be set free. That we are willing to tolerate such an outcome proves how assiduously committed we are to the rule of law. The rights of the accused trump the truth. Isn't the point of criminal justice to serve the truth *and* punish the guilty? The Fourth Amendment sometimes ends up being an impediment to justice, even as it stands as a model of justice.

Surely no one wishes to see an innocent person go to jail. But the cost of ensuring against such a catastrophe can't possibly be equated with ten wrongdoers being set free. As Peter French has written, "It is *not* better that the guilty go unpunished under any circumstances. . . . If we do not punish wrongdoers, they are not going to be punished and that erodes morality. What sort of a society does that adage encourage?"[37]

The net benefit of convicting fifty-one men of the Mafia in exchange for the leniency of time served for one is surely not a moral victory even though the criminal justice system would declare such an outcome to be a singular legal success. But an eye for an eye does not permit the transplant of other organs. The law of the *talion* expects a proportionate retaliation for a specific wrong. The man murdered eleven people! The moral universe recognizes no such trivializing bargains where punishments are substituted and substantially reduced. What we have allowed, what we have enabled, is a social contract written in invisible ink rather than in the blood of wrongdoers who have been underpunished by a legal system that fails to fully appreciate the moral imperatives of desert.

In 1987, in the state of Massachusetts, James Kelley was convicted of two counts of rape and one charge of indecent assault and battery against the victim, Debra Hagen.[38] Ultimately, he was sentenced to two concurrent ten-year sentences for the rape conviction and one concurrent five-year sentence on the assault and battery charge. Kelley filed an immediate motion to stay the execution on his sentence and a motion for a new trial, in which he alleged the ineffective assistance of his counsel. His motion for a stay was granted. It took four years without Kelley having to spend a single day in prison for raping Debra Hagen, but the court finally denied his motion for a new trial. Kelley once more appealed the initial rape conviction and the decision to deny him a new trial. Eight years later his appeal was still pending. Thirteen years had gone by since Debra Hagen was raped, and all that time Kelley walked the streets of Massachusetts a free and unpunished man.

Finally, in 2001, Hagen decided to take matters into her own hands. No, she didn't seek vengeance, although who would have blamed her. Instead, she returned to the courtroom of Massachusetts and appealed to the retributive powers of the state. She filed a motion to revoke the stay of execution of the sentence, essentially asking the court to do what it should have done thirteen years earlier: punish the man who raped her, a man who had already been convicted of his crime and yet still managed to avoid any penalty or punishment.

She could have taken a gun and shot Kelley all by herself. She could have hired a hit man. Instead, she continued to hold up her end of the social contract and deferred to the courts and personally sought leave of those courts. And how did the state of Massachusetts respond to this victim's plea? The lower court dismissed her motion outright, and then an appellate court, in affirming the lower court's decision, ruled that as a mere crime victim, she was without legal standing at all to ask the court to do *anything*. Hagen was merely the victim, the witness for the state with no independent right to rely on the courts for relief.

Under our system of criminal justice, Debra Hagen, who was raped, was deemed insufficiently linked to the crime because she was not a party to the action—she was neither the People of Massachusetts nor the defendant, Kelley. She was only a witness to the crime, not much better than a bystander who might have happened to walk by and watch. Thrown into the machinery of justice merely as a cog and not as a human being, someone with a direct and profoundly personal interest in the outcome, Hagen had been told that she had no standing under the law and no actual business before the court.

No wonder rape victims have little incentive to come forward, press charges, and participate as witnesses on behalf of the state. The state holds itself out as the true and only victim in any criminal proceeding. The actual victims are present merely as lackeys. If the courts won't dignify victims by at least naming them as parties to the action—partners in the search for the truth and the punishment of the guilty—then why should they sit in the back row silently and passively waiting for their chance to testify in connection with a crime to which they were clearly more than mere witnesses? They are the living artifacts of the actual crime scene. Either dignify and empower them, or ask nothing further of them. Better still, grant them the right to seek the justice denied to them, even if that justice looks more like old-school vengeance.

In her book, *Wild Justice*, Susan Jacoby recounts the story of a middle-aged woman speaking on television about the death of her twenty-two-year-old daughter who was murdered by knife point while walking home from a bus stop after a day of college classes. The assailant wanted her purse. She screamed and he took her life. There were witnesses at the scene and so identifying and arresting the murderer was simple. What was complicated, and maddeningly so, was seeing him properly punished by the state, having him receive his just deserts. The wrongdoer pleaded guilty to a reduced charge of manslaughter. In thirty months he was released from prison for good behavior.

The outraged mother said, "I just can't get over this. I will never get over this. To know that the price of my daughter's life was less than three years, that this man is free now to do the same thing to someone else—I can't reconcile myself to it. I can't believe any more that there is such a thing as justice in the world. . . . I felt as though my girl was killed twice—once by that scum, and once by the judge who said, well, you only have to go to jail for a few years. They killed her memory, saying that was all her life was worth."[39]

Such disgraceful outcomes make a mockery of justice and cause us to lose sight of why we punish—because the wrongdoers deserve it. When punishments are so immeasurably uneven, governments become accomplices in the crime. And victims are left with no remedies, no other opportunities for relief. Victims can't file claims of gross negligence against the state, or stop paying their taxes, or join a band of vigilantes. When the legal system fails so miserably, where do the aggrieved go? Where should they go? They are instructed to step aside and defer to the retributive powers of the state. But there is an unspoken truth that officers of the law won't admit: legal systems have butterfingers, courtrooms are filled with witless fumblers, and placing justice in the hands of the law is an invitation to disappointment. The law should always be given the first chance to do what's right. But what happens if it can't, or won't, do what's right—justice in name only, justice that is not just? The victim may have no other option than to resort to self-help. Justice may simply not be achievable any other way.

On some occasions, the legal system will accept a retributive assist from the general public. Men who are thrown into the role of avenger or vigilante are sometimes given more leeway to defend themselves, their property, or their families. Historically, courtrooms have been more welcoming to men who killed their adulterous wives than women who came to realize that the law would not protect them from their violent husbands. The female avenger faces many obstacles, including an apparent double standard. Gender matters in judging citizens out for blood. Women, like Ellie Nesler, are treated less favorably than urban legends like Bernard Goetz who seemed to have arisen from the cutting room floor of a *Death Wish* movie. Unfortunately, avenging women like Raquel Welch in *Hannie Caulder* (1971) and Jodie Foster in *The Brave One* (2007) are aberrational not just because they succeed in getting even but because the law chooses to look the other way in allowing them to do so without any legal consequence.

This imbalance has been especially true for battered women who tried to defend themselves against their physically violent husbands. Wife beating and even child abuse were often deemed "family matters," outside the reach of legal retribution because they were perceived as domestically charged and emotionally messy. As Susan Jacoby has observed, if these acts had involved strangers they would have been classified as crimes. Instead, they were often placed into the category of private settlements—to be worked out in private, between the parties, without the assistance or intrusion of the law.[40]

Judy McBride made repeated calls to the police over a number of months complaining that her husband had beaten her. Each time she was told that the police would not become involved in such a routine matter of domestic violence. With the law refusing to come to her aid, she finally hired someone who would end her misery. It worked. Her abuser was found dead, but she was sentenced to life imprisonment without parole.[41]

The problem is not confined to the United States. Not unlike the case of Ellie Nesler, Marianne Bachmeier, a mother living in West Germany in 1980, walked into a courtroom where the man who had raped and murdered her seven-year-old daughter was on trial. A criminal proceeding convened by a court with a notoriously poor track record of punishing the guilty did not instill in Bachmeier any faith that her emotional need for vengeance would be satisfied. She wanted to make sure that the punishment would be done right and without fail. And, as the mother of the murder victim, she felt morally obligated to participate in the judgment—provided that the judgment was a final one. She fired seven bullets killing the accused and showed West Germany what a speedy trial truly looked like.

Despite her violent, lawless action there was, understandably, great public sympathy for Bachmeier. Even those who reject emotion in courtrooms are not unmoved by such a response to the brutal end to a child's life. No mother should ever have to face such a gruesome tragedy. The West German court ultimately reduced the charge from premeditated murder, which it so obviously was, to manslaughter. Bachmeier was still, however, sentenced to six years in prison.[42]

The state's monopoly on vengeance suffers from the twin bill of its own hypocrisy: it often fails to punish the actual wrongdoer properly and instead punishes the avenger too harshly for bringing about the correct result that the state somehow could not manage to complete on its own. The avenger may be many things—aggrieved, damaged, betrayed, broken—but he or she is *not* a natural, cold-blooded assassin.

Kantian principles clash up against one of Kafka's worst nightmares. The law operates like a machine, but it doesn't always obtain the same consistent, reliable results that modern man expects of his machines. We live with the unsettled sense of two clashing priorities. The demands of legal retribution are often foiled under the strict adherence to constitutional principles. The retributivist who has forsaken private vengeance accepts a legal system rife with imperfection and often indifferent to results. The state holds the franchise on punishment, often squanders it, and, in doing so, unwittingly rekindles the pilot light on the flame that flickers within all avengers.

What sets off the avenger and makes her quest for justice inevitable is quite familiar to anyone who has ever watched a revenge film. In art, the avenger is portrayed as trapped by larger forces that have charted her course. The law tells her: "Put it out of your mind, nothing can be done about it!" Unfortunately, that's not the sort of court decree most victims can accept.

In *The Brave One*, a film that pays homage to the gritty filmmaking of the 1970s where New York City was more often depicted as an urban jungle than as a Wall Street playground, a woman barely survives a brutal beating in Central Park. Her fiancé, however, is not so fortunate. The assailants even walk away with her dog. The police never manage to find and punish the assailants. She is a slight woman who before this tragedy had never handled, much less fired, a gun. But she obtains an illegal weapon and goes on a vigilante rampage throughout the city. The detective assigned to her case grows suspicious that she may be behind these vigilante slayings. Eventually, she locates the men responsible for murdering her fiancé and, of course, settles the score—even reclaiming her dog in the process.[43]

What is most unusual and what makes this an especially arresting vigilante film is that the detective assists the woman in the final killing. The standard storyline in such revenge films is that the law seeks to track down the vigilante, trying to get inside his head in order to get him off the streets, even though he is the only one who seems to care about cleaning them up. The vigilante becomes the hunted even though audiences are rooting for him to stay ahead of the police and right behind the murderer. In *The Brave One*, however, it is the detective who is prepared to take a bullet in order for the vigilante to pull the trigger one final time, which discharges her of her duty and might also release her from some of the pain.

In *A Time to Kill*, an African-American father kills the men (with Klan affiliations) who raped, brutalized, and left for dead his ten-year-old daughter in rural Mississippi. Now, fully unrepentant, he faces first-degree murder charges. The film takes its title seriously: certain crimes are so gruesome and inhuman that only one manner of redress is possible. The jury must decide whether taking the law into one's own hands is always a crime. Sometimes, and under certain circumstances, there is, indeed, a time to kill.[44]

In the Bedroom is a film about a middle-aged New England couple forced to live in the same town as the man who murdered their son. The state prosecutors aren't confident about pursuing the case. The eyewitness didn't actually see the murder; she simply knew the circumstances and only saw the aftermath. The wrongdoer, meanwhile, the son of the town's wealthiest family, is released on bail. What can the bereaved, suddenly childless couple do? How are they expected to live in such a small town, shopping for groceries, running errands, and bumping into the man who received a pass for murder while they remain in their own private prison?[45]

In *Sleepers*, four boys who grew up in the Hell's Kitchen neighborhood of New York City end up in a boy's detention facility where they were repeatedly raped and tormented by the guards. Years later, now grown men and aided by a hardboiled priest and Mafia chieftain, both from the old neighborhood, they reunite to take vengeance against the guards who scarred them into damaged, traumatized adults. While in the detention facility they had become enamored of the novel *The Count of Monte Cristo*. As adults they end up reenacting the novel as they avenge themselves against the men who stole their youth.[46]

So where does that leave the relationship between punishment and revenge? It surfaces sometimes in extraordinary, headline-grabbing cases, and we see it played out much more predictably, and satisfyingly, on movie screens and in narrative fiction. Revenge can look like legal retribution, which, if performed correctly, shares the same uncompromising finality and exactness and offers an emotional component that is unavoidable whenever punishment is based on moral desert. Charles K. B. Barton has observed that "revenge is essentially retributive in character. The core reasons behind revenge are essentially retributive notions of payback, getting even, and ill-desert."[47]

And what about the Christian values of forgiveness and turning the other cheek? If retribution is ultimately vengeful—no matter who exercises it—then Christians must have a hard time reconciling the imperatives of criminal justice with the teachings of the New Testament. But punishing wrongdoers can't possibly be considered un-Christian. After all, how far must a cheek turn?

For many Christians the question always boils down to: What would Jesus do? Curiously, we live in a world where people speculate with such certainty about what Jesus would do in a given situation. But do we really know? Jesus, after all, didn't live during the Holocaust. No relative of his was turned to ash on 9/11. He never experienced the anguish of knowing that his wife or child was brutally murdered. We have no way of imagining what he would have done or whether his Sermon on the Mount would have been amended on account of these tragedies. Yes, it is true that he sacrificed himself, but one hopes that he also believed in justice and would have understood the agony of victims and the moral outrage of forgiveness too casually granted and very much undeserved.

SIX OTHER CULTURES AND REVENGE

It's fair to say that certain cultures around the world sure know how to give revenge a bad name. It certainly hasn't helped that the Western world has for several hundred years poisoned the well against revenge. This is one of the reasons why societies that still practice revenge are blackballed from civilized life, treated as rogue people, not to be taken seriously within the global community. But it's also true that in some cultures the vengeance that passes for justice is no justice at all and, therefore, neither can it be classified as moral revenge.

Certain revenge practices provoke a fair amount of squeamishness. Everyone knows that "eye for an eye" retribution can be gruesome, even if deserved. The very fact that vengeance can bring about a blood feud is an unsavory reminder that revenge is often violent and, from the perspective of Western societies that hold to the rule of law, senseless. But even those who possess only mild sympathies for vengeance, the very ones who love a good revenge movie or silently applaud seeing someone receive his just deserts, nonetheless still shudder when confronted with vengeance in the modern world that has all the markings of a barbaric past. And it is particularly troubling, not to mention confusing, when the vengeance is actually being delivered as judgments in a court of law.

In 2010, a Saudi Arabian judge, operating under strict Islamic law, asked several hospitals whether they would be willing to carry out a very specific, court-ordered punishment—to literally cut the spinal chord of a man who had just been convicted of a crime.

The law of the *talion*'s lineup of symmetrical punishments begins with a "life for a life" and descends to an "eye for an "eye," after which limbs and other human body parts are matched up correspondingly. Ancient peoples surely got the idea of how the rule worked with its easy formula of bodily equivalence. Losses must be reclaimed in kind, measure for measure, the hallmark of equitable retribution. Modern people understand the *talionic* concept, too, but sometimes recoil at the grisly precision—whether it is Shakespeare's "pound of flesh" or, in this case, the Saudi court's ruling of a "spine for a spine."

The Saudi judge wanted a hospital to permanently damage the defendant's spine and render him paralyzed as an equivalent punishment for the defendant having once left a victim paralyzed after attacking him with a cleaver. The victim's brother, Khaled al-Mutairi, said, "We are asking for our legal right under Islamic law. There is no better word than God's word, 'an eye for an eye.'"[1]

In such a case of legal retribution, many Western observers and human rights activists would wonder why depend on a court to mete out justice if it is going to be no more merciful than the most thuggish of biblical avengers. This Islamic court, no doubt, believed that it was exercising restraint and civility by not putting a cleaver in the hands of an avenger. Let a professional handle it. At least the hospital can assure precision in carrying out this especially tailored sentence. Placing the wrongdoer in the same position as his victim undoubtedly has *talionic* appeal, but many would have preferred for the court to impose a stiff jail sentence instead. A less bloodier outcome, for sure, but would it have been equally just? Was the Saudi court taking the *talion* to illogical extremes, or was it spot on? After all, the victim is forever paralyzed. Why should the wrongdoer receive a penalty lesser in degree than the damage he had already inflicted on his victim?

In August 2010, Bibi Aisha, an eighteen-year-old Afghani woman, wound up with her face on the cover of *Time* magazine. She wasn't being featured as a cover girl, although the press attention she received was all on account of her looks. Aisha's face—disfigured and grotesquely missing a nose and ears—brought her unwanted worldwide fame. Living in the Taliban's version of the twenty-first century—a Pashtun tribal society in a remote region of Afghanistan—Aisha, at the age of twelve, and her younger sister, were awarded to the family of a Taliban fighter in settlement of a tribal dispute. Aisha's uncle had killed a relative of the Taliban fighter and, pursuant to the custom known as *baad*, the girls were given over to the victim's family to settle the blood debt.

When Aisha reached puberty she married the Taliban fighter, but since he was off fighting wars against the West, she and her sister were housed with the livestock of her in-laws, routinely beaten, and used as slaves. Eventually they tried to escape, but her husband tracked her down, cut off her nose and both of her ears and left her for dead. In Pashtun culture, a husband who has been shamed by his wife is thought to have lost his nose. The husband was therefore permitted, under religious law, to punish his wife in kind. He carried out a religious custom that would have made even a barbarian blanch—in taking a "nose for a nose."[2]

Of course, Aisha's husband still had his nose. Whatever wounded pride he felt in having a wife, who was being treated no better than a barnyard animal, try to leave him surely could not be the equivalent of cutting off her nose and ears. In the moral universe, and in any sensible reading of the *talion*, wounded pride is not equated with body parts.

Miraculously, Aisha survived this savagery and, aided by the charity of some who were horrified by what had happened to her, traveled to the United States to undergo eight months of reconstructive surgery. Quite unintentionally she emerged as the poster girl for a more complex appreciation of America's war in Afghanistan. In addition to whatever justified vengeance 9/11 had provoked, there was also a pressing human rights concern. Women forced to live under Taliban rule were without legal rights, and virtual death sentences, like the one Aisha had received from the hands of her own husband, were all too commonplace.

Aisha was disfigured and dismembered under color of law, legitimized by the imprimatur of an alleged legal system—the Taliban fighter carried out what the law allowed as his remedy. But color of law in certain societies has no shadings, or the courts are truly colorblind, but only in the most warped and sadistic of ways. The Saudi court that imposed the sentence of a severed spine at least referred to the elegant logic of *talionic* law. The same could not be said for Aisha's husband, whose understanding of proportionate punishment was neither moral revenge nor legal justice.

Afghanistan is also the site where those who commit "social crimes" are frequently sentenced to public executions by way of stoning. In August 2010, a twenty-five-year-old man, Khayyam, and a nineteen-year-old woman, Siddiqa, were sentenced to death for having an illegal sexual relationship. Khayyam was married and had two children and Siddiqa was engaged to marry, but the very idea of his divorce and her breaking off the engagement was impossible under Islamic law. So the couple eloped and ran away. The Ulema Council in the Kunduz Province determined that under Islamic law the proper penalty for such an offense was death by stoning. A spokesman for the Taliban said, "According to Islamic law, if someone commits a crime like that, we have our courts and we deal with such crimes based on Islamic law."[3]

The couple was persuaded to return by their relatives, who also promised to acknowledge their marriage. On their return, however, the Taliban and two hundred villagers, which included Khayyam's father and brother and Siddiqa's brother, captured Khayyam and Siddiqa, and the lovers were stoned to death. One witness reported the crowd as being festive and cheered the stoning as if they were watching a true blood sport with a lethal end. "People were very happy seeing this. The couple did a bad thing."[4] That same month in the Badghis Province, a forty-one-year-old widow who was made pregnant by a man who had promised to marry her was convicted of fornication by a Taliban court. Her punishment: two hundred lashes with a whip followed by being shot to death.[5]

Such penalties under Shariah law are not uncommon throughout the Middle East and Persian Gulf. Many forget that Saddam Hussein ordered the beheading of over two hundred women for alleged acts of adultery, the only evidence coming from their husbands, who were not required to produce any evidence of infidelity. Their uncorroborated word was enough. In 2010, a Saudi Arabian court punished a female journalist, Rozanna al-Yami, with sixty lashes for working on the set of a television program where the male host discussed human sexuality, even going so far as to display sex toys. Rozanna, however, did not appear on camera, only worked as a television program coordinator, and had no involvement at all with the offending episode.[6]

In yet another 2010 case, a Saudi woman who was found sitting in a car with an unmarried man was gang raped by seven men (the man with whom she was sitting in the car was raped as well), and then sentenced to ninety lashes. (Her attackers were sentenced to prison for between ten months and five years.) A strict interpretation of Wahhabi law makes it a crime for a woman to be alone with a man who is not her husband or relative. When her lawyer appealed the decision on the grounds that the penalty was both excessive and nonsensical, the court increased her punishment to two hundred lashes and sentenced her to six months jail time. What's more, the lawyer's license was suspended.[7]

The rule of law can also become a rule of revulsion.

In another Saudi case invoking that same law that prohibited women from mingling with unmarried men who are not their relatives, a seventy-five-year-old widow was sentenced to forty lashes and four months in jail for having two young men bring loaves of bread to her home. One of the men was her nephew, but apparently he wasn't a sufficiently close enough relative to spare her from this punishment.[8]

In Pakistan a woman who is raped will find no justice under the law. Until recently she had to overcome the Hudood ordinance, where, in order to prove rape, a woman was required to produce four witnesses. If she couldn't do so, she was likely to be charged with adultery. The stigma of the rape and the likelihood of a failed prosecution was so great that few women tried.[9] (The attempts to amend the rape laws in 2006 have done little to stem the problem, since rape victims are still too afraid to come forward, and the amended law added a new prosecution for fornication.) Thousands of women had been punished under the Hudood ordinance.

The story of Mukhtar Mai is emblematic of this widespread outrage. In 2002 she was ordered to be gang raped by a village council in retaliation for an alleged wrong committed by her brother. Ever since then she has been an outspoken critic of Pakistan's legal system, calling worldwide attention to the crimes against women under the Hudood ordinance. Along the way she has become a hero to the human rights movement. At enormous personal risk she worked tirelessly to bring the six assailants who raped her to justice. She is still waiting for that justice. Pakistan's highest court upheld the acquittals of five of the six men. Responding to the legal system's outright failure to do justice after all these years, she said, "I am deeply upset by the decision of the Supreme Court. Now I don't have confidence in any court.

The Supreme Court will be responsible if something happens to me or my family."[10]

Another less infamous rape in Pakistan, this one taking place in 2004, involved Ghazala Shaheen, whose uncle eloped with a woman from a higher social caste. The woman's family demanded revenge, and a dozen men raided his niece's home and kidnapped Ghazala and her mother. They were held for eleven days, and Ghazala was raped by two men. The local police made only two arrests and reported the matter as a kidnapping, intimidating Ghazala into not pressing charges for rape.[11]

An Afghani woman, Gulnaz (who only used one name), was imprisoned for adultery after reporting that she had been raped. She was nineteen at the time and was sentenced to three years in prison. When she appealed the decision she was awarded a second trial, which resulted in another guilty verdict and an increase in the sentence to twelve years. While she was in prison she gave birth to the rapist's child. The Afghani government granted her a pardon in 2011, but with the explicit understanding that she would marry the man who raped her. Gulnaz's experience with the justice system of Afghanistan was all under color of law. "My rapist has destroyed my future," she said. "No one will marry me after what he has done to me. So I must marry my rapist for my child's sake. I don't want people to call her a bastard and abuse my brothers. My brothers won't have honor in our society until he marries me."[12]

The loss of honor is invoked all over the world as a legitimate basis for vengeance. And there's a natural coherence between revenge and justice, whether achieved by avengers or courts of law. Nonetheless, these penalties, issued under color of law, feel morally inconsistent with both justice and revenge—satisfying the criteria of neither. In some of these cases, actual judges imposed the sentences in courtroom settings, with lawyers present. Most important, the punishments were supported by actual laws, contained in sacred texts that have been recognized for over a thousand years. But despite the legal formalities, were these cases examples of justice simply because they involved court personnel, invoked codified rules, and were subject to judicial review, or were they acts of mindless revenge that violated the core principles of proportionality?

A court of law doesn't necessary guarantee justice. These rulings were issued in the name of justice, and yet they clearly do not comport with any fundamental understanding of justice as practiced by constitutional democracies. Operating under the guise of law doesn't automatically render the decrees of a court just. The same is true of revenge. Revenge that is unjust or excessive is not revenge, any more than stoning or beheading as a penalty for adultery can be recognized as justice in the moral universe. Private settlements of disputes that lack fairness are no less morally offensive than court orders that bear no relationship to justice—that, indeed, smack of injustice. There are as many examples of unjustified revenge as there are travesties of law. Legal systems are not exempt from moral scrutiny; and no authority can claim the moral high ground when its delivery of justice shocks the conscience and violates the very moral principle that justice must uphold.

Regardless of whether justice takes place in a courtroom or is placed in the hands of an avenger, the goal of vindicating victims is ever present. The pounding of a gavel or the delivery of a court decree cannot override this obligation. A final judgment that leaves victims very much in a state of irresolution can never be final, no matter how it is declared by a court of law. And it won't be honored by those who experienced and witnessed the injustice firsthand. Similarly, any private act of vengeance that ignores the essential, predicate elements of revenge can never be justified. Prosecutors and judges should be held to the same exacting standards as any righteous, deputized avenger. In the cases discussed above, the injustice of the court decrees suffers from the same failing as unjustified revenge: the claimed moral injury did not exist and there was no true wrong that needed to be punished; and even if there was a wrong, the penalties—the removal of a nose and ears; the medieval lashings and stonings conducted by an entire community—were excessively disproportionate.

When discussing the conditions that justify revenge, it always seems to come down to honor, but honor goes both ways: the loss of honor that must be restored to victims; and the honor that compels revenge seekers and justice providers, whether they be private citizens or court officers, to undertake the duty to avenge and to do so honorably. Neither the avenger nor the judge receives an automatic pass in his delivery of justice; both are subject to the oversight and scrutiny of the moral universe. Avengers can go too far—the law of the *talion* becomes transgressed—and they lose their entitlement to take revenge; and courts can be unjust in underpunishing wrongdoers and ignoring the vested interest that victims have in seeing that justice is done. The righteous avenger and the judicious judge each share an inexorable obligation to get it right.

Courts of law are empowered with great responsibility. Whether they like it or not, judges, prosecutors, and the police are morally obligated to carry out their duties with a full appreciation of the stakes that are involved for victims. Blind justice means that the law will not prejudge the parties before the court; it does not mean, and should not mean, that the legal system is blind to the emotional realities of how the parties ended up in court in the first instance.

It can be understandably confusing when honor is invoked so liberally in connection with revenge. Lost honor gives rise to the demand for justice, but are all claims to lost honor the same? To self-servingly purport to have been a victim of a moral injury is not enough. Not all subjective feelings of shame can justify a retaliation. Cultural relativism aside, there is no license to an unqualified green light to seek vengeance for anyone who claims to have suffered an indignity. Moral injury must be held to some objective standard, otherwise every imagined slight, every perceived dis, ends up as a permissible justification for a reprisal.

If revenge must stand the test of entitlement, so, too, must the initial source of moral injury. It, too, has to be objectively reasonable—there must be an *actual* moral injury, otherwise the claimed right to vengeance will not be justified. In order to prevent sham acts of vengeance, the defense of one's honor must be in response to a true loss of honor. Were that not the case, otherwise unprovoked, illegitimate attacks would unjustly cling to the imprimatur of vengeance. Revenge, and its relationship to justice, is subject to rules. Punishment is deserved precisely because the avenger has earned the right to punish.

Bibi Aisha's husband invoked Islamic law in justifying the removal of his wife's nose and ears—all on account of his lost honor. Whether this was accomplished by court order or by self-guided vengeance, the punishment was disproportionate and unjust. Subjective claims to lost honor must not elide the moral authority of revenge and cannot circumvent the rules of vengeance. In civil lawsuits brought in Western courtrooms, frivolous claims are routinely dismissed, with prejudice, and the attorneys who bring them are often sanctioned. The reasonableness of revenge should be held to no less of an objective standard.

What about honor killings and blood feuds? It is estimated that nearly half of the world's peoples once practiced feuding. In many cultures around the world, especially among tribal societies and more remote states, honor killings are still the preferred manner to restore order and reclaim honor. Do these societies have a better handle on revenge and are they more honest about resorting to it, or are they simply stuck in a time warp, living in a forgotten world where civilization had not yet directed its wronged and wounded into modern courthouses?

In Iraq and Kurdistan, between the years 1991 and 2007, more than twelve thousand women were killed in the name of honor. And these honor killings continue. In 2010, Sirwa Hama Amin and Aram Iamal Rassool, two neighbors in northern Iraq, fell in love. But they never told their respective families. Instead, they carried on in secret, professing their love through text messages and e-mail, the only safe haven for those living in repressive societies where star-crossed lovers (along with freedom fighters) would be lost without access to social media.

Sirwa's brother observed her texting Aram, and he, along with other relatives, threatened to drown her. She became both a prisoner of her own home and a battered sister. Eventually, she managed to escape and joined up with Aram. They went to the police and explained that their lives were in danger all because they wished to marry. Instead of finding sanctuary they found themselves arrested. But after appealing to a court they prevailed and were lawfully married—without the approval or consent of their families. Sirwa's family finally agreed that if she and Aram left the village and never returned, they would not be hunted down. For nearly four months they lived but an hour away. One day, however, Aram opened the door and was met by several men, including one of his own brothers and his brother-in-law. Before a greeting was exchanged, seventeen bullets were fired into his chest. Sirwa survived the shootings although she was shot four times in her leg and hip. Today she lives with her young son and doesn't leave the house without an armed escort.

One of Sirwa's brothers said, rhetorically, "Why should she live after she has been that irresponsible about the honor of her family?" A neighbor of both families said, "The girl and the boy should be killed. It's about honor. Honor is more important for us than religion."[13]

Was Amram murdered in an act of justified vengeance for having dishonored the tribal customs of Kurdistan? Or was his death simply yet another tragic and confounding example of moral relativism being used to excuse practices that would be criminal in any other context?

Unjustified, disproportionate killing is killing, which can't be sanitized by calling it revenge and thereby insulating murderous cultural practices from moral scrutiny. The moral purpose that gives rise to justified revenge should not be confused with "honor killings" that are empty of honor and set in motion by those who refuse to mark themselves present in the twenty-first century. These practices fail the basic tenets of the *talion*—they are disproportionate and provoke the recycling of unending blood feuds. Scores remain unsettled. Debts never get redeemed. Instead, the stakes are always raised, which makes peace impossible.

But this isn't true of all societies who resort to vengeance. Some get it right, where honor is invoked honorably. There are locales all throughout the world that are without legal institutions and the rule of law. In spite of that they are, miraculously, not lawless. What they have is a working knowledge of the *talion* and a venerable history of honor killings. In such situations justice and revenge are more strikingly identical because, absent revenge, there would be no justice at all.

As Christopher Boehm pointed out in his classic anthropological study of feuding in Montenegro, "In many respects the morality of several thousand people who are living in a permanently settled tribal territory is unlike our own morality. There is less concern for legalistic maneuvering, and more for personal and clan reputation. There are no specialized police officers or judges, nor are there any prisons. But there are very powerful sanctions that shape behavior, and these operate both directly and indirectly, intentionally and automatically. Feuding was essentially a positively valued institution insofar as the moral system was concerned, in that it involved the upholding of honor. . . . In addition, . . . feuding served as a kind of sanction, because it suppressed certain kinds of immoral behaviors that people knew were likely to start feuds. They also knew that feuds were dangerous, stressful, economically costly, and generally inconvenient from a practical standpoint. . . . Feuding served as a substitute for such authority in that the probability of lethal retaliation and then a costly feud sharply curtailed certain socially disruptive behaviors."[14]

Indeed, social anthropologist Max Gluckman labeled this phenomenon "peace in the feud," the self-regulating principle that, while there are certainly costs and risks associated with defending one's honor through retaliation, the outcome would be far worse in future encounters if the victim decided to remain passive and merely hope for the best.[15] In many cultures around the world, the defense of honor supersedes all other values, including fear. And in cultures where honor killings are customary, there is always the anticipation of vengeance, which operates as its own deterrent. Failing to retaliate when it is expected and deserved only invites further harm. This is exactly the ethos that still governs inner-city drug dealers and Mafia wise guys and was once practiced widely by the highlanders of Scotland, Balkan clansman, Indochinese Mantagnards, Druze and Bedouin tribesman, and the frontiersmen who settled in the Appalachians and in the Wild West.

Each of these cultures adopted the same strategies for survival, in part because they had nowhere else to turn for justice but also because there was no better way to announce to their neighbors that toying with this tribe would be a deadly mistake. Taking matters into the hands of the tribe was not just a matter of honor, it was the only way to survive in otherwise violent, lawless societies. Steven Pinker observed that survival meant "cultivat[ing] a hair trigger for violent retaliation . . . against anyone who would test their resolve by signs of disrespect that could reveal them to be easy pickings."[16]

Once again, such a tribal, tactical survival strategy contradicts the conventional thinking that vengeance, by definition, is always emotional, impulsive, and irrational, that it is a product of momentary rage, that on reflection no rational person would ever resort to it. Like the fallacy of the rational actor model as applied to revenge, here, too, when cultures encourage self-help, refuse to allow wrongdoers to get away with murder, and make it widely known that defending the tribe's honor is a badge of honor and a reputation worth having, the reasons to avenge are just as much steeped in logic as in emotion.

William Ian Miller explained the linguistic origins of the apparent paradox of finding peace in the feud. The Hebrew word "shalom" shares the root for the words "peace" and "pay" with similar words in Indo-European languages. Miller observed that, "'Shalom' means to pay, to make whole, a term that could be equally substituted for 'revenge.' It means to be made whole again, to be paid back in kind, and it's still the modern Hebrew word for 'pay.' It's also the word for 'peace.' Why? Because once you've been adequately compensated, once the balance is even, there can be peace."[17]

Revenge is a way to keep the peace—especially in societies where private citizens must secure their own safety because there are no public peace officers. The more isolated the region, the more insulated it is from the outside world, the more underground it remains from the mainstream, the more likely that vengeance will determine how order is kept and disputes resolved. Repayment must occur; the only question is: *Who* is obligated to do it? This is why no nation, culture, or people on earth are strangers to revenge. Justice must be delivered in some morally recognizable form.

In various corners of the world, revenge that occurs outside of courtrooms and judicial systems is still very much real. For certain tribal societies it wouldn't be possible to fully renounce private vengeance. Doing so would result in chaos, which is ironic since Western societies believe that allowing citizens to take the law into their own hands is the very essence of chaos, a quickstep to moral surrender. And yet the private settlement of disputes still functions as a workable system of justice in many parts of the world.

Actually, for many of these societies, America's outright ban on vengeance is an example of moral confusion, where some rights are valued above others. In the United States, certain liberties, such as speech and religion, are deemed fundamental and inviolable under the Constitution. The rights of victims to have wrongdoers properly punished are not regarded as rights at all, however. In fact, they are sacrificed to other considerations—judicial economy, administrative efficiency, and the general presumption of innocence, which highlights a long list of rights granted the accused. Guilty people are so often set free, and many more will not be punished commensurate with their crimes. What is legally acceptable in the United States can be found to be morally intolerable in other parts of the world. In societies where the repayment of moral debts through vengeance is the very pinnacle of justice, America's judicial system can seem lacking, if not altogether misdirected. After all, the justice that wrongdoers deserve and that victims demand is a right that a moral society should not take so lightly.

In Sicily, not unlike the portrayals of the Mafia in *The Godfather* and *The Sopranos*, no one looks to the law for justice and legal authorities are relied on for neither vengeance nor justice.[18] The core principle of *omerta* obligates Sicilians never to cooperate with the legal system. In Montenegro, it is morally incumbent to retaliate with a revenge homicide following the killing of a member of their society. Christopher Boehm explains that, "after a first killing had occurred, the retaliatory homicide that followed was considered not only to be reasonable and proper but also to be *morally necessary* by traditional Montenegrin standards."[19] Savo Todorovic explained the meaning of *osveta* (vengeance) as "a kind of spiritual fulfillment. You have killed my son, so I killed yours; I have taken revenge for that, so I now sit peacefully in my chair. There you are.'"[20] Milovan Djilas, an avenger from the Balkans, described the emotions generated by revenge as "an overpowering and consuming fire. . . . Vengeance is not hatred, but the wildest, sweetest kind of drunkenness, both for those who must wreak vengeance and for those who wish to be avenged."[21]

And what about the ditherers, the hapless Hamlets and the nervous wrecks? The poor soul who neglects to avenge a father, a murdered relative, or a deceived daughter "can no longer appear in public. Nobody speaks to him; he has to remain silent. If he raises his voice to emit an opinion, people will say to him: avenge yourself first, and then you can state your point of view."[22] In Corsica, the reluctant avenger is exposed to a serious form of public reproach known as *rimbecco*, which takes place either by way of small insults or the moral revulsion of the entire community. To fail to avenge a murdered father essentially makes it impossible to show one's face. The son might spend a lifetime surrounded by a community of cold shoulders and icy stares.

J. Busquet notes that "the *rimbecco* can occur at any moment and under any guise. It does not even need to express itself in words; an ironical smile, a contemptuous turning away of the head, a certain condescending look— there are a thousand small insults which at all times of day remind the unhappy victim of how he has fallen in the esteem of his compatriots."[23]

Similarly, in Albania, a relative who fails to take vengeance against one who harms a family member will face severe social ostracism. So strong is this national norm that those who do not fulfill their obligation fear punishment from the entire community. A bloodied cloth hanging outside of a home is a sign that a son isn't willing to uphold the family's honor. As one researcher has noted, "If you get killed and you are my sister, I have an obligation to take revenge. If I don't take it, I get punished. It has to do with the beliefs of the majority, and what people expect me to do. If everyone expects me to take revenge, I will do it."[24]

This concept sounds so foreign and strange, and it is, but it's not entirely unfamiliar. The recently remade film *True Grit* seems so fanciful and curious to modern-day audiences. As revenge movies go, this one stands out because the putative avenger is a young girl. Generally speaking, it's easy to root for the avenger because his or her quest is so righteous. But not all avengers are equally believable. We can appreciate their heartache and their sense of duty, but we doubt their capacity to accomplish their aim. We believe that Dirty Harry and Rambo are capable of triumphing over impossible odds in order to even the score. But what are we to make of a fourteen-year-old girl, in the Wild West of all places, who insists on avenging her father? What does teenage vindication look like when one is neither a wizard from *Harry Potter* nor a vampire or werewolf from *Twilight*?

Mattie Ross, the heroine from *True Grit*, travels far to make sure that the man who murdered her father is brought to justice.[25] The local sheriff, however, doesn't want the job of tracking down her father's killer. The wrongdoer, Tom Chaney, has already decamped into Indian territory. The sheriff has his own townspeople to protect, and chasing after Chaney will be dangerous and possibly futile. He suggests that the young girl simply go home to her mother and younger siblings. But Mattie can't go home; she won't go home and she will not accept that the justice owed to her father is not achievable. There *is* no going home without Tom Chaney being made to pay the price for the debt owed to her family. In refusing to turn back, Mattie knows that she must find someone of sufficient true grit who will assist her in doing her duty. And she even brings along her own gun just in case she will be called on to settle the score herself, the duty falling squarely on her teenage shoulders.

What else can a daughter do? The law wouldn't fulfill its obligation so the daughter must find her own outsized grit to perform the obligation herself. There is no other place to turn. And she can't simply return home—not because she would be exposed to a cowboy version of a Corsican's *rimbecco* but because her father's memory, and the moral outrage that his killer managed to go unpunished, would forever haunt her. To be worthy of her father's love Mattie must honor his memory and settle his accounts.

The moral and cultural obligation of family members to avenge their murdered loved ones is powerful indeed. It crosses all cultures and applies to all nations. The fictional Hamlet and Mattie Ross lived in different centuries and continents, and they went about avenging their fathers quite differently, but yet they both understood, along with all those who rooted them on, what must be done without having someone remind them. This self-knowledge, this most innate of all intuitions, goes to the very essence of what it means to be human. And it is imbedded in the complicated circuitry of the human brain. Those who choose to ignore the signals and set aside the obligation will be forever plagued by worst kind of Fifth Commandment violation—the dishonoring of an unavenged parent. Spouses and children are deeply mindful of this rule. This is why victims expect so much from police, prosecutors, and judges: they are plainly aware of their duty; they know the absolute importance of what they have delegated to strangers; and they have every reason to insist that justice be done right.

The deep-seated relationship among honor, family obligation, and revenge is the lifeblood of blood feuds and honor killings. In Albania, which has been the setting of blood feuds for more than three thousand years, revenge is codified as the law of the land, the customary law that has been observed for centuries by the northern clans of the Albanian highlands.[26] Not unlike the citizens of Sicily, no Albanian truly believes that the government is a credible or reliable provider of justice. It makes far more sense for the populace to rely on a system based on the canonical past—medieval as it may be. As one Albanian, Sophie Arie Puke, explains it, "Everyone knows the law doesn't work here. You can bribe your way out in no time. . . . The only way to make killers really pay is to take back the blood."[27]

The lesson, time and again and all over the world, is that when the law fails and victims are deprived of the leveling that comes with revenge, the aggrieved will invariably resort to other time-honored methods of making things right—even if it requires resurrecting ancient norms or resorting to street justice.

The *Kanun*, or the canon, is the Albanian code that regulates blood feuds, along with other aspects of human behavior. Humanitarian groups estimate that a thousand Albanians are killed each year from this widely accepted practice of vendetta killings, all mandated under the *Kanun*.[28] It begins with the following principle, Albania's version of an eye for an eye: "Whoever kills will be killed. Blood is avenged with blood." The death of a victim can be avenged only by taking out a vendetta against the killer. In fact, there are 168 rules on how vengeance can properly be undertaken—including the manner of retaliation and the amount that will satisfy the moral debt.[29] Even women are deployed in this ritual, not as revenge takers but as revenge cheerleaders. If the Albanian justice system happens to get to the wrongdoer first, the duty of the family to avenge is not extinguished. When the wrongdoer is finally released from prison he knows that his debt to the victim still survives. Vengeance alone can cancel the debt. One of the victim's relatives, assigned the task of settling the score, will be waiting to greet the wrongdoer on his release.

Such a scene nearly played itself out not in Albania—but in present-day Rhode Island. In 1975, Michael Woodmansee was sentenced to forty years in prison for gruesomely murdering a five-year-old boy, Jason Foreman. (Woodmansee ate the boy's flesh and shellacked his bones.) Rhode Island has an "earned time" law, which permits the early release of prison inmates for good behavior and for having worked prison jobs during their incarceration. Woodmansee, scheduled to be released in August 2011, would have served only twenty-eight years of his negotiated plea. From the moment of sentencing, with the trial aborted for a plea bargain, Woodmansee had already shortchanged the state of Rhode Island and the boy's father, John Foreman, of what he had owed. Now it was measurably worse. On hearing that his son's murderer was soon to be a free man, Foreman said, "If this man is released anywhere in my vicinity, or if I can find him after the fact, I do intend to kill this man."[30]

By sheer coincidence and without any fanfare, a long-standing Albanian custom was almost adopted by an aggrieved Rhode Island father. And whether one is Albanian or not, most people around the country sympathized with Foreman's ordeal and wondered whether he shouldn't have been the first to greet his son's murderer on release from prison, where the debt could finally be redeemed.

With the fall of communism in Albania (the last of the Eastern Bloc countries and perhaps the most oppressive of them), a democratically elected government came to power, along with functioning institutions and a justice system that was supposed to extend throughout the entire country. But corruption has been rampant, and the people who live in the mountainous regions of northern Albania continue to resort to the *Kanun* to resolve their disputes. The government has been ineffective in stopping it. What worked in Albania's medieval past continues to be relied on even into the twenty-first century.

And the reasons are obvious and unsurprising. What all revenge societies have in common is either a nonexistent legal system or an ineffectual one. If not given a meaningful opportunity for justice, the avenger is left with no other choice. The moral imperative of justice, which is cross-cultural and truly global, is never negotiable. Governments may routinely cheapen justice with the discounting formula of plea bargains, but victims know that guilt can't be negotiated downward, that punishment in the moral universe can't be reduced merely to free up a jail cell. If governments truly wish to take vengeance out of the hands of individuals, legal systems will have to become more dependable in delivering justice. The deficiencies and moral corruptions of the law serves notice to individuals that this most vital responsibility of the state might be better trusted to the hands of a truly dedicated avenger.

The irony is that, despite their archaic appearance, revenge cultures have much in common with ardent free-market capitalists. The inefficiencies and incompetence of controlled economies is the best justification for the free hand of laissez-faire. And, here, too, the failure of governments to deliver justice consistently provides a justification for individuals to keep their options open when it comes to revenge. The private enterprise of vengeance becomes a far more reliable dispenser of just deserts. And in some cultures where there isn't even the pretense of a legal system, individuals are forced into the business of handling justice privately. Remember Bonasera's wise words: "For justice, we must go to the Godfather."

In some nations around the world other than the United States, it's even worse.

The villagers of northern Albania have been placed in the unavoidable position of revenge takers, with predictable results. Since the reinstatement of the *Kanun*, twenty-eight hundred feuds have broken out across the Albanian countryside. Families have gone into hiding; boys have stayed home from school, knowing that they are likely targets of retaliatory revenge. Albania is one contemporary example of what happens to an entire nation when the state refuses to take its revenge responsibility seriously.

The pervasiveness and social cost of blood feuds, vendettas, and honor killings is too much for most people to stomach. There are sensible reasons, owing much to our aversion to the ghastly and the gruesome, why we should prefer assigning vengeance to professional authorities. Leaving it up to morally wounded individuals can seem downright savage. As William Ian Miller suggests, "Conventional wisdom conceives of vengeance cultures as barely cultured at all, all id and no superego: big dumb brutes looking for excuses to kill."[31] And as sociologist Roger Gould observes, revenge is the default position for many societies. "What may look like savagery to people accustomed to rational-bureaucratic justice systems," he writes, "is often the only sensible course of action in a context in which disputes are inevitable, third-party intervention is unavailable, and a failure to retaliate might invite further offenses."[32]

Even if we were to accept that these worldwide, time-honored, and time-tested principles of revenge actually work, and even if they achieve a moral clarity that byzantine legal systems never come close to obtaining, how can we allow individuals to go off the prix fixe menu of justice and order up their own revenge à la carte? After all, we still live under a system of laws even if the application of those laws has not always improved on the justice of an earlier age. Our first inclination is to say: This is the system we have; it's surely not perfect, but a system of laws depends on the acceptance and consensus of its citizens to obey those laws and, when necessary, learn to live with its mistakes.

But that's not a natural impulse, especially when the operation of the legal system so often trivializes the plight of victims forced to endure a lifetime knowing that they had abdicated their responsibility and allowed a moral injury to go unanswered. We don't wish to witness barbarism masquerading as vengeance, but neither are we able to tolerate a moral outrage pretending to be justice.

In 2003, in a Bronx, New York, courtroom, Rasool Ashishi, from Brooklyn via Yemen, was convicted of manslaughter in the shooting death of his uncle, Abdullah Hassian. He was sentenced to eighteen years in prison. Ashishi confessed on the night he was arrested that he took a cab from Brooklyn to his uncle's store in the Bronx. When his uncle arrived he called out his name and fired several bullets, fatally wounding him in the neck. Ashishi said that his brother was killed in Yemen by one of his uncles (not Hassian, but a different uncle), and the custom in Yemen obligated him to avenge the death of his brother by killing some other member of the wrongdoer's family.[33] When such cultural customs make their way over to the United States, emigrating with the same adaptability as a suitcase or a music craze, people naturally recoil in horror. Such lawless practices should not be swallowed whole within the melting pot, celebrated like the Feast of San Gennaro or the Chinatown Lunar New Year Festival. Self-help shouldn't be one of those cultural customs that are allowed to pass through Customs.

Dexter Filkins, at the time a reporter for the *New York Times*, is an old-school war correspondent. In his book *The Forever War*, he recounts his experience covering the wars in Iraq and Afghanistan and their devastating implications both within and beyond the Green Zone. His anecdotes of what he witnessed have the same emotional resonance of other wartime reportage, but in Iraq and Afghanistan, there is not just the madness of war but also the conflict of cultures, the sense that what is being seen is not just surreal, but virtually from another planet.

Filkins tells a story about the Sunni Awakening and how at least some of the motivation of the insurgents had less to do with retaking control of the country than with the settling of family debts. Abu Marwa, an insurgent with the Islamic Army of Iraq, killed two Syrian members of al-Qaeda. These two confirmed and strategic kills, however, were only incidentally related to the greater conflict. In addition to fighting al-Qaeda, Marwa sought to avenge the murder of his uncle. And he wasn't satisfied with just restoring his family's honor. Vengeance would not be complete unless he delivered the blood of his uncle's murderers in vials to his widowed aunt. "She drank the blood of the Syrians," Marwa said. "You see. We were for revenge. She was filled with revenge."[34] A reviewer of Filkins's book, Lee H. Hamilton, a former congressman and the cochairman of the Iraq Study Group, wrote ruefully about Marwa's declaration, "These are haunting words amid claims of 'victory' in Iraq." His point seems to be: How could we claim to be winning a war in Iraq if those fighting beside us would drain the blood from our enemies, bottle it up like Coke, and have their aunts drink it down in celebration? Hamilton wondered whether Marwa was an honorable military officer or an insane nephew; what kind of wartime partners are these people?

Clearly, the former congressman rejected any possibility that Marwa's gesture, which seems extreme when viewed through Western eyes, could actually be a rational one—what a man of honor is expected to do in that part of the world. In his review, Hamilton also recalls another of Filkins's anecdotes, this one a 1998 public execution in Kabul, Afghanistan, in which over the loudspeakers one could hear the chant, "In revenge there is life." Hamilton sums up by stating the obvious, "This maxim is . . . foreign to American ears."[35]

Yes, that is true. Given how squeamish and intellectually dishonest Americans are when it comes to vengeance, it is unlikely that in carrying out a death sentence at a state penitentiary, the warden would openly broadcast the words, "in revenge there is life" just before inserting the lethal injection. Preachers from every corner of the country would whip out their books of Matthew and invoke the words of Jesus to "love one's enemies" and "to turn the other cheek." Daytime TV talk shows and talk radio would pronounce this episode of lustful vengeance as still another example of America's moral decline. Others would simply be revolted by such a shameless expression of raw vengeance.

Yet, if the family of a victim whose life was taken by an inmate on death row came to watch the execution and issued the statement, "in this act of justice there is finally closure and the possibility of moving on with our lives"—words not so very different from those that blared through the loudspeakers in a military complex in Kabul—there would have been no public outcry. The cultural context was different, for sure, but the meaning was the same. With justice as the stated value behind the statement, no one would have given it a second thought—the very utterance of the word itself is always self-validating. But the outcome and the motivation of the speaker were identical. In the end all that mattered was that the death was deserved and justice was done. Bear in mind, though, one incident sounded of bloodlust, while the other spoke words of closure and repair, which made the latter acceptable even though both speakers were merely out for the same vindication.

Around the world there are, actually, revenge customs that would be regarded as more civil than what we have just discussed, in part because they mirror the civil remedies offered in American courtrooms. Blood for blood certainly makes many people cringe. However there are other types of exchanges that satisfy the law of the *talion* without insisting on an exact equivalence of body parts. A rough measure sometimes serves equally well and it doesn't require having to open the spigots to a blood bath.

Many cultures allow for blood money to be paid in compensation for loss and in satisfaction of a revenge debt. Icelandic tribes created an elaborate compensatory tort model, establishing valuations for any number of losses and injuries—the earliest known worker's compensation laws or strict liability rules where damages are predetermined.[36] These Icelandic tribes produced a compensatory system that resembled civil remedies in tort. One should not have to receive an *actual* limb to satisfy the avenger's duty to get even, with precision—measure for measure. A monetary value can be placed on every conceivable loss or injury. Taking its cue from ancient Iceland, the tort lawyers of today who deal in bodily injury and worker's compensation can instantly recite the value of an index finger on the right hand of a machinist who is fifty years old and earns $75,000 a year. There are also punitive damages in civil tort cases, where the assigned value is not just to compensate the victim but also to punish the wrongdoer. The objective is to attach a monetary sum of such magnitude that it reciprocates the hurt.

Other cultures refuse to accept money because to do so devalues the debt—precisely because it reduces the injury to money. Money cannot adequately compensate for true loss, and so it cannot be a replacement for a true *talionic* remedy. All monetary remedies in such cases are, by definition, unfavorable discounts, dishonoring the memory of the victim by trivializing his or her experience of being victimized. Many Holocaust survivors, for instance, refused restitution payments from Germany because it would be tantamount to accepting blood money—allowing the Germans to settle their debt to the Jewish people and thereby assuage their collective guilt. Since true compensation in such instances of atrocity is impossible, and the unfortunate German word for these payments was *Wiedergutmachung*, which means "to make whole or well again," many Jews simply wouldn't let the Germans off so easy. After all, "reparations" means to repair, and the consolidated annihilation that was the Holocaust was most definitely beyond repair. The Jewish people would never be "made whole again." If revenge and justice is obligatory, then it can't simply be bought off—it has to be performed and paid back. As one Albanian said: "It's never settled with money. Because it's a shame to settle for money. I have never seen it settled without blood."[37]

Perhaps this is what Quentin Tarantino had in mind in bringing *Inglorious Basterds* to movie screens, or what was behind the recent film *The Debt* (2011), and what motivated the true story depicted in Rich Cohen's seminal book *The Avengers*.

But why should victims stand on ceremony and deny themselves monetary compensation and at least some relief all on account of principle? Why insist on receiving nothing if not blood?

In Iran, the families of victims are offered blood money as compensation, a prescribed payment based on who the victim was—male or female, child or adult. But the wrongdoer still must go to jail. It is a Persian mix of civil and criminal law. Money cannot cancel out a deserved punishment. And the victim's family retains the option to seek a higher level of punishment, which, if he or she chooses, might even include the death penalty.[38] Iran is not a model society of human rights or, for that matter, the rule of law. But oddly enough, when it comes to punishing wrongdoers and satisfying victims, it surely is unique among many nations of the world. Bizarrely, at least with respect to the obligation of the legal system to avenge victims, Iran comes closest to getting it right.

In Iranian criminal courts, the victim is always the centerpiece of a trial—not just Exhibit A, the complaining but emasculated witness, but a full partner in the proceedings. In a case of premeditated murder in which the crime was proven in a court of law, the decision to sentence the wrongdoer to death is made by the victim's family—all under the supervision of a judge. The surviving family might refuse blood money because it would insult the memory of the deceased by cheapening a life and allowing the wrongdoer to avoid punishment with a bribe. In such circumstances, the government will gladly perform the necessary and final act of revenge on the victim's behalf, treating it as a morally legitimate request carried out with the force of law. And all throughout, victims are welcomed as equal participants in the prosecutorial and sentencing phases of criminal justice.

In 2004, Ameneh Bahrami was blinded when a fellow student at the University of Tehran poured a bucket of acid on her face. During the two prior years she had rejected the unwanted advances of Mojid Movahedi, and for this he decided to ruin her life. The attack left her not only blinded but horribly disfigured as well. In 2008, an Iranian court convicted Movahedi of the crime. Bahrami insisted that the court issue a sentence that would force Movahedi to suffer the same fate: a legally supervised blinding with a doctor dropping acid into Movahedi's eyes. "Precisely what he did to me, he should suffer himself," Bahrami said. "That is what I continue to live for."[39] The court agreed with her eye-for-an-eye punishment, finding support for this ruling under Islamic law. When it finally came time to carry out the penalty in 2011, with a physician standing ready to even the score, Bahrami suddenly had a change of heart. "I have drawn back from vengeance," she said, "but perpetrators of crimes should know that this is their true punishment." Movahedi was directed to return to prison where he will remain until he can come up with $200,000 as a restitution payment to the woman who spared his life.[40]

Once again, when we think of revenge, we instantly imagine societies that have not kept pace with the march of time. If we are moving forward and other countries and cultures are standing still—or, even worse, taking a step backward—then their version of vengeance must not be something to emulate. If one accepts as true that justice is simply revenge by another name, then the way vengeance is performed around the world is further proof of the *talion*'s versatility. We're all ultimately committed to the same goal—justice. We just take different paths, even while some of those paths frighten us. Revenge and justice mirror the moral relativism debate. In some cultures revenge is bloodier—hence, blood revenge. But we're all, ultimately, wishing to do what's just. And, yet, we want to believe that a legal system such as ours, flawed though it might be, is superior, in an absolute sense, to any honor culture or revenge society that would empower its people to punish one another—and to do so with such avowedly vindictive enthusiasm.

In Tuscany, a vendetta can be delayed for thirty years in order to drive the wrongdoer mad and to preserve the memorial power of the deed. In Iceland, a severed head was used to inflame the revenge passions of the kinsmen. Similarly, in Corsica, Albania, and Scotland, the victim's bloodied shirt was paraded around to remind the community of what was done and what now must be done in retaliation. One revenge technique that was popular in Sicily was called goating, which involved binding the wrongdoer's feet to a rope that was also attached to his throat.[41] He is then placed inside the trunk of a car. If the unfortunate wrongdoer moves, he strangles himself. But when revenge societies resort to such sadistic methods of obtaining vengeance, those who live in "civil" societies have a hard time not judging the avenger as harshly as the original wrongdoer—sometimes more so. Perhaps there is comfort in knowing that guns still remain the favorite weapon of choice for Sicilian revenge. Goating seems prehistoric and irredeemable by comparison.

And women are not exempt from these practices. Some cultures encourage female dirge singers at funerals. Women in Southern Greece sing lullabies of revenge to the sons of fathers who have been murdered.[42] The songs are intended to insure that the children will always remember how and why they became fatherless. On reaching adulthood they will have been subliminally conditioned to do their duty and to take their revenge. Sicilian mothers would also sing lullabies to their children as a reminder of their duty to honor their dead fathers by redeeming the payback owed to them. Apparently there are no hesitant Hamlets among the Greeks and Sicilians. The idea of inheriting the obligation to avenge was common among many cultures. The practice in Bedouin tribes is still to bequeath grudges to succeeding generations. There is an old proverb: "If a man takes revenge after forty years, he was in a hurry."[43]

Evolutionary psychologists Martin Wilson and Margo Daly have observed how universal these rituals can be. "In societies from every corner of the globe, we can read of vows to avenge a slain father or brother, and of the rituals that sanctify those vows—of a mother raising her son to avenge a father who died in the avenger's infancy, or graveside vows, of drinking the deceased kinsman's blood as a covenant, or keeping his bloody garment as a relic."[44]

Albanians would boil the wrongdoer's blood after the taking of revenge.[45] Montenegrins regarded the boiling of blood as a psychological necessity.[46] In New Zealand, when a rival chieftain was killed during a war, his body would be chopped up, roasted, and eaten by the victorious tribe.[47] Southern Slavic women were known to have their infant children sleep beside the bloodied shirt of a murdered father.[48] In nineteenth-century Corsica, revenge was preceded by a ritual ceremony in which the avenger publically proclaimed his notice of intent to seek revenge.

Cambodians have taken the *talion* and turned it, literally, on its head. In Cambodian culture an eye for an eye is an inappropriate, insufficient standard of measurement in determining what constitutes justifiable revenge. Indeed, Cambodians are firm believers in disproportionate retaliation. Why should the victim only be made even? A victim who is morally obligated to repay shouldn't simply settle the score. He or she should run up the score. Settlements usually mean settling for less—whether it be for love or in revenge. But with revenge, the victim is a casualty of another's wrong. He did not consent to being made part of a revenge story. If there is a revenge debt to be repaid, the honor culture of Cambodia requires that interest be paid along with the principal—tacked on as a bonus, for the trouble of having to undertake the laborious and emotionally wrenching work that is demanded of the avenger. Call it an eye for an eye, plus interest.

Vengeance in Cambodia surpasses the original harm and produces a lopsided measurement—more like a head for an eye, tit for tat with an extra jab for good measure.[49] Victims who must become avengers would never have found themselves in the position of creditor had it not been for the wrongdoer's debt. Cambodians claim a premium for interrupting the life of an otherwise unsuspecting avenger. To be made a victim is always a severe imposition, so getting even can't possibly be enough to settle the score.

It is not at all surprising that Cambodians take their revenge so seriously or have doubled-down on the principle of proportionate punishment. In the aftermath of the Cambodian genocide and the mass murders inflicted by the Khmer Rouge, the sheer massive scale of the crime required an expanded vision of the *talion*, which the culture of Cambodia had already long recognized. Cambodians may not have all availed themselves of this remedy, since most were willing to allow the judicial system to resolve such matters, but most everyone was certain of their entitlement to the full measure of the relief, and then some. More about this later. This quirky take on the *talion*, however, demonstrates once again that the amount of vengeance one is permitted to take is always a subtle undertaking. One person's nominal interest payment is another's highway robbery.

These various examples of how vengeance is practiced in certain cultures, however, can make even the most ardent avenger sprint over to the local courthouse, plead for mercy, and surrender the job. The rule of law, by comparison, even at its most chaotic, always comes across as more sober and sedate. Maybe human beings can't be trusted with revenge on their own terms. "Wild justice," as Sir Francis Bacon once famously wrote about revenge, suggests that even if revenge and justice are the same, vengeance carries with it a native wildness that civilized people abhor.

In spite of all the revulsion, there are certain things constitutional legal systems can learn from the gritty world of honor killings. After all, what makes tribal cultures resort to revenge is precisely the absence of legal authorities that could be depended on to operate just as reliably as righteous avengers. If governments could promise to do it, and do it well, there would never be a need for self-help.

And that's why self-help is typically deployed in urban underworlds and rural frontiers, regions where there is no reliable external and coercive authority that can provide justice. These are places that are beyond the reach of the law, where women and children are vulnerable and where private property can be easily stolen. Without vengeance there would be no limits on bad behavior. And in such places groups resort to their own versions of self-help, known as blood revenge—blood is shed, sometimes vicariously by blood relatives. Yes, where there is vengeance there is also often blood, but not always wasted blood. Justifiable revenge demands only that there be blood for blood; a blood bath is neither required nor allowed. Everyone is on notice that when a moral debt is created, any member of the wrongdoer's family can become a target for retaliation.

Gang-related violence in Los Angeles is one example of this phenomenon. Gang members, by definition, neither are law abiding nor do they expect the law to come to their aid to resolve conflicts with rival gang members. Gangs operate in a shadow world where vengeance is the only justice anyone ever knows. The inner-city ghettos, especially in South Central Los Angeles, are the setting for gang-related warfare among the Crips, Bloods, and Latin Kings. They resemble Wild West frontiers where police protection is nonexistent and street justice is the only way to settle turf battles. The gangsta rap group, Public Enemy, titled one of its songs, "911 Is a Joke."[50]

In each of these instances, whether in tribal societies, urban ghettos, or the blood feuds of Eastern Kentucky, the honor of the group is primarily what is being tested: Will it show itself to be capable of defending its members should one of them come under attack; will it develop a reputation for standing its ground, which is the only way to ensure that its assets won't be stolen?

Some anthropologists, historians, and sociologists, such as Heinrich Brunner and F. W. Maitland, have argued that vengeance was always an irrational and crude method of legal redress.[51] Primitive societies would naturally dispense with revenge once a legal system presented itself as a more viable and civilized alternative. Blood revenge also confounded the rational choice theorists, who reasoned that since vengeance always involved unacceptable risks, no one in their right mind would knowingly engage in such self-defeating behavior—no matter what the governing ethos of the tribe.[52]

Not surprisingly, even in the United States there are wide regional differences in the acceptability of certain practices and in the attitudes of its citizens toward revenge. Steven Pinker has observed that southern states, for instance, have placed fewer restrictions on gun ownership, have allowed homeowners to shoot an assailant or burglar without having to retreat first, are more likely to tolerate spanking and corporeal punishment, tend to be more hawkish on issues of national defense, and, finally, are much more predisposed to execute their homicidal criminals.[53] Moreover, southern states permitted the practice of dueling to a larger degree, and it lasted much later in time, as an honorable, efficient, and low-cost way to resolve the private settlement of disputes.

England and France, of course, experienced a longer history of their citizens reclaiming their honor by way of dueling. Challenging an antagonist to a duel was widely accepted as the preferred blood sport practiced by men of honor. America contributed its own mark to the culture of dueling, and added a political dimension, as well: various political figures, and even one arguable Founding Father, settled their differences with pistols at dawn. President Andrew Jackson won two duels and tried to provoke a third. Up north in New Jersey, the very first treasury secretary of the United Sates, Alexander Hamilton, was not so fortunate. Hamilton was killed in a duel with then Vice President Aaron Burr.[54]

Around the world and across cultures, vengeance served multiple purposes: it kept the peace and restored honor; it provided a sum certainty of justice; it served as the very instrument and measuring stick of justice; it deterred crime and gave necessary pause to evil intention; and it kept memory alive by obligating relatives and tribal clansmen to embrace the moral duty to avenge their dead.

And there was something else, too. Vengeance taught the world about collective responsibility, which is an invaluable lesson for a species so prone to obsessive blame shifting and the avoidance of guilt. One way to keep the peace and discourage bad behavior is to enlarge the circle of intimates who might ultimately become the targets of revenge. Make people responsible not simply for their own misdeeds but also for the criminality, indiscretions, and poor judgment of those, technically, under their watch. In societies that practice blood feuds, maintaining law and order and settling scores are not confined to the wrongdoers who initiated the feud.[55] The deterrent effect was enhanced by imposing a punishment of collective responsibility on the relatives of wrongdoers. The binding of liability, making it self-executing among family members, forced everyone to exercise greater caution and to use better judgment—to think twice before committing crimes. The wrong may have commenced with an individual act that created a debt, but many people might be called on to pay the price for that debt. Everyone was placed on notice that the price of harming another could prove very costly for an entire family.

As Charles K. B. Barton notes, "Any member of the offending group constitutes a legitimate target for revenge because they are all guilty on account of their shared group identity."[56]

Assuming moral responsibility, much less legal guilt, for the actions of others is an alien concept in American jurisprudence. In the United States, as well as in most Western nations, citizens are judged as individuals and liability is assigned and guilt proven based on overt, voluntary actions. Without an affirmative act, no legal duty can be expected of someone who is merely standing around, minding his or her own business. One has to move a muscle, initiate some action, and take a step forward. Only then can his or her actions be counted. We are most certainly not our brother's keeper under American law. We are truly free agents, responsible only for our own voluntary, individual acts. And we cannot be judged unless judgment is based on something we have actually done, and only in connection with our individual deeds. Unless a person chooses to act and her actions are the proximate cause of a crime or results in harm, she cannot be held legally responsible. A conspiracy among confederates who all agree to participate in a crime is typically the only way for an individual to be held culpable for the actions of another. Without an overtly criminal or tortuous act that has a causal connection to a loss or injury, one is unlikely to ever be a defendant in an American courtroom. Guilt is a legal term; responsibility is a moral one, and under the law they have very little to do with one another—the legal basis on which people are judged stands apart from moral concerns.

But this is not true in revenge cultures and feuding societies. By virtue of their self-regulating existence, these societies increase the numbers of people who can be held responsible for committing a wrong. Families and communities are tied to one another not just by blood but also by a broad sense of duty. A community cannot blithely pretend that individuals are free to commit crimes against others without the consequences of those actions being shared by all.

In such societies, moral responsibility is not so easily set apart from legal duty. In fact, in tribal cultures where individuals are permitted if not expected to take the law into their own hands, moral responsibility supersedes legal duty. The boundaries of moral responsibility are enlarged. Legal duty holds too few people ultimately accountable. In revenge cultures, everyone knows that they might become the target of a relative's revenge debt. And for this reason all family members must be kept in line; the deviants must be doubly watched. No one can be permitted to act in complete, reckless disregard of what his harmful actions toward another could mean for the entire group. There is the archetypal account of the kindly uncle who is willing to pay off a loan shark in order to clean up a no-good nephew's gambling habit. The stakes are much higher in revenge cultures. An uncle might have to give up much more of himself to cancel out the consequences of his nephew's poor choices.

This expansive application of vengeance can become the ultimate deterrent: the knowledge that one's family will become equally vulnerable to the righteous claims of the avenger, that the debts of the fathers are collectible against their wives, brothers, sons, and daughters, are powerful incentives to never find oneself in moral debt to another. In revenge societies the target of vengeance might not be the actual person who caused the original loss or injury but, instead, someone in close enough relational proximity to the wrongdoer to be held equally responsible. The family, no matter the composition and character of its individual members, is never presumptively innocent; they all, automatically, become accomplices to the misdeeds of their weakest genetic link.

In Montenegro, the retaliation can be delivered against the wrongdoer or his father or brothers.[57] The Yanomamo Indians of Brazil allow for vengeance to be taken against anyone within the wrongdoer's community.[58] Among the Berbers, the ten closest, most immediate male relatives are deemed "equally culpable."[59] Jibaro Indians of Ecuador and Peru take revenge against any member of the wrongdoer's family because individual actions are inseparable from the whole.[60] The Maori tribesmen of New Zealand insist on *utu*—repayment for an insult. The responsibility for seeking or taking *utu* falls on the entire family of the victim. Any one of them might one day be required to serve as an avenger. Similarly, the responsibility for having caused the injury is enlarged to include the family or group of the wrongdoer. Any member of the wrongdoer's family might become the subject of retaliatory vengeance.[61]

There is both collective responsibility and collective obligation in revenge cultures. Sons avenge their fathers; and sons become revenge targets because of and in place of their fathers. There is always mutuality and codependence. Individual actions reflect back on the group. Payback for harm long since inflicted can be collected against a relative who is otherwise innocent. No one is regarded as having acted alone, and no one can claim that a debt owed to one is not collectable against a wider circle of familial associates.

But the underlying rules of vengeance still apply: the retaliation must be just and proportionate. The only difference is the number of people against whom the penalty can be exacted. The examples discussed earlier of punishments delivered by Islamic courts violate the principle only insofar as stonings, lashings, and dismemberments are without proportion to the originating crime. No *talionic* principle ties the lost honor of an abandoned husband with the severed nose and ears of his fleeing wife. The fact that the moral debt is collectable against an entire family is consistent with the enlarged mandate of collective responsibility, however. But as Jacob realized in the book of Genesis, revenge is never justified if it goes beyond what is deserved.

In China, under the Ming and Qing dynasties, certain acts of revenge were excused under the law.[62] Indeed, vengeance was integrated within traditional notions of Chinese justice, incorporated into the law itself. Doing so created a greater synthesis between justice and revenge. Chinese law recognized that when provocation and moral urgency are great the law shouldn't stand on ceremony and prevent righteous action. For instance, the legal system during that era of Chinese history adopted a rescue/revenge statute, which provided that vengeance can be justified and found excusable in circumstances where a son or a grandson comes to the aid of a parent or grandparent who is being attacked.[63] Regardless of whether the rescuer causes serious injury or even kills the wrongdoer, the law automatically mitigates the punishment. And if the killing arises in the heat of the moment, the rescuer is exonerated or is given the lightest sentence possible under the law. There is no legalistic charade of treating the avenger as if he had committed an independently separate crime divorced from the reality of the situation, which is generally what happens under American law. Nor is there the intellectual dishonesty of requiring the avenger to plead temporary insanity. Instead, Chinese law recognized circumstances where there are moral obligations to avenge, especially when a relative is in harm's way. Even more important, it recognized that vengeance is an act of virtue and not criminality—albeit an act with its own set of complications.

As much as governments have an interest in curbing individual acts of vengeance, they have an equal obligation to protect it—to make it relevant in the lives of its citizens. States need to provide permissible legal pathways through which vengeance can be properly exercised under the law. Maintaining law and order in traditional Chinese culture did not mean that revenge had to be banished from courtrooms and the emotional lives of men and women. Instead, Chinese law embraced revenge and made a place for it in its body of laws, not unlike the ancient Greeks and the role reserved for the Furies in the administration of justice. The Chinese understood that rescue and revenge can take place in the same act. And an act of vengeance is not so far removed from the imperative to do justice. To believe otherwise is to ignore the larger truth that the call for justice and the impulse to avenge share similar features. And for this reason, as the Chinese once proved possible, revenge should be incorporated into the law, with the state playing a necessary supervisory role rather than banishing vengeance from courtrooms and consigning it to the streets.

There is an irony, however, in the way the Chinese associated rescue with its close moral cousin, revenge. Any law student can tell you that in American jurisprudence there is no duty to rescue. To rush to the aid of another in peril may be a moral duty, but it is surely not a legal requirement under common law. In fact, the rescuer is generally held liable in tort for whatever excess injury is caused should his rescue efforts fail—his gallantry notwithstanding, otherwise unappreciated. The message is clear: Don't even consider coming to the aid of another. By not compelling citizens to rescue, the law encourages indifference and neglect, narcissism and selfishness, moral obtuseness and the worst possible kind of legalistic thinking.

Perhaps the best evidence that the American legal system is not guided by moral criteria can be found in the law's bizarre, counterintuitive treatment of rescue and revenge. There is no legal duty under American law to rescue even though there surely is a moral one. Similarly, morally we realize that there are times when vengeance is appropriate, and yet, legally we are cautioned that self-help and private justice are prohibited and will give rise to an independent, perhaps even more severe act of criminality. The moral urgency that naturally attaches to rescue and revenges receive no quarter in American courtrooms, although each is infused with profound moral obligation. Rushing to the aid of another in a time of peril, avenging a horrific crime committed against a loved one—performing these righteous acts is the way most people wish to see themselves. Such heroism is the embodiment of the virtuous life. Yet, the legal system commands us to neither rescue nor avenge. Indeed, those who do so will be punished for their acts of virtue. How can the legal system hope to encourage decent, moral behavior if it actually punishes those who are inclined toward decent, moral behavior?

The law either sanctions moral failure or prevents moral righteousness. Revenge is morally right and the failure to seek vindication is a sign of moral neglect, a dishonoring of the dead, an abandonment of the moral obligation to memorialize loss. There is a moral duty to stand up for oneself and to come to the aid of another. Despite the simple truth behind these principles, rescue is not required under the law; revenge is repudiated under the law— yet both are necessary features of the moral universe.

Traditional Chinese law recognized the moral relationship between rescue and revenge. And by enacting a rescue/revenge statute, it acknowledged the fundamental truth that, morally, the obligation to avenge is not easily avoided, so the law shouldn't label it a crime. The natural impulse to retaliate is itself a form of rescue, because retaliation, by definition, arises in response to the harmful actions of another. If the wrongdoer or tortfeasor had not acted, either criminally or negligently, the avenger/rescuer would never have been motivated to respond.

This reasoning is in many ways no different from a legal claim of self-defense, which justifies actions otherwise criminal but made necessary due to the act of another who created a danger that a reasonable person would naturally have been expected to defend against. In cases of rescue, however, it is the defense of another rather than oneself that is being justified. Coming to the aid of a father or a son, for example, should not be treated differently under the law than defending oneself. The Chinese understood that in such instances, revenge and rescue are the same—driven by the same impulse, motivated by the same imperative. Retaliatory vengeance supplies its own extenuating and mitigating circumstance. The avenger feels obligated to communicate to the wrongdoer why his act of revenge is necessary: "What did you expect me to do, stand by and do nothing?" And these same words should apply for the rescuer, too. There would have been no need to rescue had the victim not been imperiled, no need to avenge had the crime not taken place and had the wrongdoer not acted maliciously, callously, or murderously toward another.

In 2008, a feature article in the *New Yorker* by noted author and biologist Jared Diamond recounted the dramatic story of just one of many tribal honor killings among the New Guinea highlanders.[64] Papua New Guinean Daniel Wemp described a vicious and spiraling cycle of vengeance between the Handa and Ombal clans, resulting in six years of fighting and forty-seven dead—all on account of a pig that had purportedly ruined a garden. When Wemp's uncle, Soll, became one of the casualties of this blood feud, Wemp inherited the duty to avenge his uncle. In the New Guinea Highlands, tribes and clans still observe the ritual that all homicides naturally give rise to a retaliatory revenge killing. From there, however, it escalated into an unappeasable tribal blood feud. Wemp explained that sometimes determining who is to inherit the obligation to avenge is a complicated matter. Whoever is entrusted with the duty eventually becomes the "owner of the fight." Many others are recruited, even from other clans, to join in with what eventually can evolve into a large-scale clan war.

In an explicit rejection of the rational actor model as it applies to vengeance, Wemp, the Handa clansman and nephew who owned the fight—an inheritance of a murdered uncle—explained why he didn't save the time and expense and avoid the risk altogether, by simply letting the law handle the matter: "If I had let the police do it, I wouldn't have felt satisfaction," he said. "I wanted to obtain vengeance myself, even if it were to cost me my own life. . . . The best way to deal with my anger was to exact the vengeance myself."[65]

Diamond unearthed a society organized around the concept of vengeance. No matter how many lives were claimed, or how long it would take for the blood feud to come to some conclusion, personal dignity and social peace were very much dependent on revenge practices that had been in existence for generations and still flourished separate from the official laws of New Guinea. Daniel Wemp's tale had the makings of a great story, which Diamond contrasted with his father-in-law, a Holocaust survivor who never sought retribution for his own losses even when an opportunity presented itself to do so.

One year after the *New Yorker* story first appeared, however, Wemp, and Isum Mandingo, the man who Wemp was purportedly required to kill in their generational stage of the feud, sued Diamond and Advance Publications, Inc., the owner of the *New Yorker*, in the amount of $10 million for defamation.[66] Wemp alleged that the story printed in the *New Yorker* was completely false and caused the men great harm by portraying them as barbarians who resort to such murderous practices.

Diamond and the *New Yorker* stood by the story. They produced notes and recorded conversations that Diamond had had with Wemp in which the Papua New Guinean gave vivid details of how he organized a war of tribal retribution to avenge his uncle's murder. Wemp now claims that he made it all up, and anthropologists have noted that young men of the Papua New Guinea are known to exaggerate their tribal exploits. Diamond's mistake, some have suggested, was an utter failure to fact check what he had been told. Complicating matters further, other anthropologists acknowledged that the Papua New Guinea do, in fact, still engage in blood feuds like the one described in the *New Yorker*. In one province alone, three hundred tribal wars have taken place and claimed the lives of four thousand people since 1991.

The lawsuit was dismissed in July 2010, but the question left unanswered remains: Did Wemp tell the truth but sued Diamond and the *New Yorker* anyway, motivated by the possibility of a windfall settlement? Or did perhaps Wemp avail himself of America's courtrooms out of shame? Once the honor killings of the New Guinea highlanders were exposed to the world in a magazine of such wide reach and renown as the *New Yorker*, perhaps Wemp was simply too embarrassed to have his name associated in the Western world with something as crudely primitive and socially unfashionable as revenge.

SEVEN WHEN SELF-HELP IS PERMISSIBLE

Vengeance and justice are commonly understood as sharing the tortured history of sibling rivals. Justice is the wise child; vengeance is the wicked one. Justice serves the greater good; vengeance only benefits the rogue citizen who refuses to abide by the law. Justice is favored; vengeance abhorred.

Centuries of human history have been dedicated to distinguishing between legal retribution and lawless acts of revenge. The Talmudic hairsplitting and intellectual contortions. All those differences demarcated and distinctions made. The avenger takes his injury or loss too personally, whereas courts of law, governed by the rule of law, are focused not on the harm but on the act itself, not how a wrong wreaks havoc on individuals (and deserves to be punished for that reason alone), but how it diminishes the overall sense of security that is essential to the functioning of a well-ordered society. In medicine they say treat the disease, not the person. Its legalistic equivalent is punish the act not the harm; justice is for all and not for the victim. The morality of vengeance is always subordinated to the legality of retribution.

But the larger truth, the more complete reality, is much more complicated than that. Revenge is not a toxin that modernity left behind, and justice is not the panacea that cures all disputes. Vengeance can actually lead to the just outcome, with the wrongdoer being properly punished and the victim feeling the satisfaction that comes with vindication. At the same time, conventional notions of justice—where victims are consigned to the back row of courtrooms and are silenced from speaking and where wrongdoers are acquitted of all charges or are simply released due to a technicality—can leave citizens feeling bitter and betrayed. There is no justice when the legal system fails, and there is nothing but justice when avengers discharge their duty by paying back what is justly owed.

In actuality, when performed to perfection, vengeance and justice can and should serve the same societal purpose and fulfill the same human need. Each contributes to moral order and community repair; each offers hope that all is right in the moral universe. And they are each present on judgment day; they are not, as so often assumed, separate remedies used independently to address the same wrong. The reason why justice and revenge are treated as if they operate only at cross-purposes from one another is because vengeance is generally misunderstood, while justice is all too often misapplied.

Vengeance is not a social ill if citizens believe that wrongdoers won't otherwise receive their just deserts. And justice cannot take place unless citizens believe that true justice is being offered to them. Justice cannot exist in name alone; it must be morally and emotionally experienced as just, otherwise it is merely an empty pronouncement. Indeed, its public legitimacy depends on a general feeling that it can be relied on as a refuge of first resort rather than as a setting for kangaroo courts and phony show trials. Justice is at its best when citizens believe that just outcomes within the law are possible—which invariably requires wrongdoers to be punished, victims to feel vindicated, and the citizenry to see the legal system as being capable of holding up its end of the bargain in the social contract.

Lamentably, that's not how most people feel. A 2011 poll listed in the *Sourcebook of Criminal Justice* statistics indicated that only 28 percent of respondents in the United States have confidence in the criminal justice system, and only 3 percent think of lawyers very highly.[1] A disturbing poll conducted by the American Bar Association in 2002 showed that 69 percent of respondents believed that lawyers were more interested in making money than in serving their clients, and 57 percent believed that lawyers were more concerned with their own self-promotion than with advancing their client's best interests.[2] Most people are of the opinion that the legal system is not a safe haven and that lawyers and judges are not fair arbiters of truth.

What is the source of this declining confidence in the law, this disconnect between a system of justice operated by emotionally detached practitioners and the promise made by the state that it would be better at delivering justice than would-be avengers acting as independent contractors—a disconnect that has produced a general feeling of injustice experienced by the very people to whom the promise was made? This should not have happened if justice and revenge were not actually rivals but rather mirror images, as I suggest in this book. Their common features would be more apparent, their codependency always on full display whenever a wrong was committed.

That *would* be the case except that states are wrongly invested in a form of justice that ignores the wishes of victims, the very group of citizens who ought to be the focal point of the law's remedial powers. The way to best alleviate their suffering is to incorporate within the law the emotional and moral features that are present in revenge. In joining up with civilization, men and women gained many liberties, but they also forfeited a right to human dignity that was always available to avengers. The lingering question remains: Why can't courtrooms offer up dignity while also dispensing justice?

Under the social contract, that phantom document which, among other things, deprived victims of the right to seek revenge, the rule of man was forever surrendered to the rule of law.[3] Citizens can no more take justice into their own hands than a court of law can shirk its duty to ensure that wrongdoers are punished. The state, with its police, prosecutors, and jurists, must act as the victim's surrogate. And, as any true proxy, the government must stand in the victim's shoes and perform its deputized duty to answer the wrong.

The problem arises because governments do not wish to stand in the shoes of its citizens. What they seek instead is discipline and submission over moral purpose and community consensus. The justice system believes that it has a loftier purpose than merely serving as an avenger, a grander duty of upholding the law without regard to its particular effect on those who have been wronged. Evening the score for individuals is not a priority; setting a standard of conformity is.

Perhaps the best example of this institutional mindset can be seen by how victims are utilized in criminal trials. At no point is empathy for the experience of victimization a valued goal. Not only does the state not wish to stand in the shoes of victims, the victim is deemed to have no standing at all because the state essentially steals the victim's shoes right out from under him. The state purports to *be* the victim while reducing the actual victim to the secondary status of witness on behalf of the state. On the absurdity of this twisted reversal of roles inside courtrooms, law professor Steven Eisenstat comments, "the statement that the community at large, and not the victim of the crime, is the wronged party of a criminal act, is intellectually disingenuous, factually mistaken, and emotional demeaning to victims. It is an example of legal formalism distorting reality, and ought to be recognized as such."[4]

The marginalized victim and the emasculated avenger have no way to express themselves within the law. They are voiceless, peripheral characters in a morality play that isn't very interested in morality. Each has been stripped of purpose and treated without dignity. Yet when it comes to resolving our disputes we are told to always look to the law, to not take it so personally, and to not allow our anger to evolve into revenge. Courtrooms—hallowed like cathedrals and hollow in so many ways that truly matter—lay down welcome mats for antagonists who have been declawed of whatever justifiable anger now brings them before the law.

Courtrooms are convened, if not actually designed, as places of neutral emotion. But harm does not come to the body alone. Human beings are not like dented cars, with fender benders that are easily fixed, leaving no trace of damage. No matter how reparable the bodily injury, there is always the lingering damage done to the spirit. To be victimized is to experience shame, which doesn't disappear like a mere bruise. The human spirit is known for its good memory, but citizens are not permitted an inner life while waiting for justice.

In the film *Eye for an Eye*, a mother whose teenage daughter was raped and murdered by a man that the court system summarily released on a legal technicality is obsessed with having her revenge. An undercover FBI agent warns the grieving mother not to resort to vigilante justice:

KAREN MCCANN: I can't let him go.
FBI AGENT: Let the law deal with this.
KAREN MCCANN: I tried that.

FBI AGENT: OK, let me spell it out for you. It's against the law to kill a person, except in self-defense. They won't care why you did it. You'll spend the rest of your life in prison.[5]

The film *Eye for an Eye* is neither a fictional aberration nor a cynical distortion of the legal system at work. The criminal justice system actually wouldn't *care* why she did it. The murder of her daughter, the moral outrage of her murderer's release, would all become legally irrelevant. She would be treated as if she was a heartless killer, a danger to society, a woman who had murder on her mind and went ahead and acted on it. Yet, the law had failed her in letting her daughter's murderer go free, and she couldn't live with the result. That's why she couldn't simply "let him go."

Emotion is what makes human beings fully human, yet emotional injuries go unaddressed under the law. And the legal system won't permit emotion to be expressed within the confines of the law. In the logic of the law, emotion is always out of order. Emotion expressed by victims is what causes judges to pound their gavels in disgust. Judges are constantly reprimanding people, instructing them how to feel—or how not to feel—about the damage done to them, or how they should comport themselves within courtrooms. Show no emotion and keep your eyes straight ahead. Stand up straight. No slouching. Do not laugh; do not cry.

In one of my earlier books, *The Myth of Moral Justice: Why the Legal System Fails to Do What's Right*, I called attention to the way courtrooms ignore the emotional grievances and moral injuries that underlie most legal actions.[6] What we get are unfeeling "causes of action" that only lawyers can understand. The human dimension gets shredded away—all those indignities, betrayals, and broken promises become whitewashed of emotion, trivialized, treated as a psychological problem and not as a legal one.

People would never have voluntarily surrendered their right to seek self-help had they believed that that the honor they had lost, the suffering they had endured, would become irrelevant to the legal process—regarded more as a nuisance than as the foundational reason for the law's very existence. Citizens still wanted the "self" to be satisfied, and they rightly assumed that the law would supply the "help." They wouldn't have imagined that the social contract meant that the harms done to them could no longer be taken personally. It's one thing for the law to serve as the exclusive punisher. It's quite another to presuppose that individuals no longer claimed an emotional stake in those punishments.

Anger and resentment, however, are present in the human psyche for a reason. No matter what form justice takes, judgment and punishment can't be performed, if they are to have any meaning, without emotion. Justice must always be done; and the feeling of justice must be felt.

Gavels come down hard when judges are presented with human emotion being expressed in their courtrooms. Emotions are always regarded as irrational, which is why they have no place in buildings dedicated to reason alone. The acoustics of courtrooms mute the sounds of human feeling. They are designed with the very worst of emotional intentions. As law professor Samuel H. Pillsbury observes, "Under a retributive system, the effort to suppress all varieties of decision making anger or sympathy is neither morally justified, nor practically feasible. Emotional reactions to penal issues are part of basic human nature. They are also part of our moral experience. . . . We need to discard the traditional opposition of Reason and Emotion and instead distinguish between emotions. In short, we need to distinguish those emotions which are morally appropriate from those which are not."[7]

Citizens are required to come before the law not as themselves but as plaintiffs and defendants from central casting, carbon copies of one another, their individual experiences and heartaches neutered and submerged. The parties to legal actions are even encouraged to all dress alike, their hair parted in the same way, their gazes like zombies, their lips untrembled and demeanor dimmed. The very place where people would be expected to arrive at their most emotionally vulnerable instead becomes monasteries of lifeless, deadened emotion. The emotions associated with getting even and settling the score, which are forbidden in courtrooms, is a large part of the reason why most people know that the legal system will never truly address their needs.

It wasn't always this way. The legal system of the nineteenth century, where individuals served as their own public prosecutors, speaking on their own behalf, featured courtrooms that were, if nothing else, cauldrons of emotion. Law professor Stephanos Bibas notes, "Criminal justice used to be individualized, moral, transparent, and participatory but has become impersonal, amoral, hidden, and insulated from the people. It has thus lost some of its popular democratic legitimacy and support."[8]

With a little fine tuning, courts could be deployed to simulate the experience of revenge, giving people the emotional space to dissipate their anger and discharge their resentment through criminal trials and civil lawsuits. Courtrooms could become places where dignity and respect are regained and reaffirmed rather than squelched. The coldly antiseptic, falsely sanitized presumptions of the legal system at work could surely stand for a human reality check. Anger doesn't have to exist outside of courtrooms alone, permitted only so long as no one chooses to *act* on such feelings.

Paradoxically, however, it is not true that the legal system has entirely given up on the morality of getting even or, for that matter, the expression of human emotion. It does it all the time; it just isn't honest about it. There is an apparent double standard—vengeance through subterfuge—ways for revenge to sneak back into the courthouse and take its seat in the halls of justice. Few barely notice when revenge is so strategically disguised—wrapped up in the law, without the violence yet fully loaded with emotion. Victims, and the families of victims, on certain occasions, are permitted to experience the sensations of revenge without running afoul of the law or inviting the scorn of law-and-order absolutists. What these victims receive is vicarious vengeance. Revenge makes an appearance without announcing itself. Its presence is felt but never referred to by name. Instead, some other presumptively overriding value is being addressed, with vengeance riding sidecar—not as a moral imperative but as a mere by-product of the law.

It isn't as if the legal system takes the gloves off of revenge, setting it free to turn the tables on courtroom decorum. But it does allow certain exceptions where the emotions of revenge are expressed in legal judgments. Victims are given an opportunity to speak to their moral outrage—the vengeful impulse openly and shamelessly revealed.

Remember *Eumenides*, the third part of Aeschylus's *Oresteia* trilogy? A son is driven mad by the Furies for having killed his mother. A trial is convened where the son is ultimately acquitted. The Furies, representing the wide panoply of human emotion, are welcomed inside courtrooms to participate in human judgment.[9] The story makes room for revenge—even within the law. The ancient Greeks were much more honest about vengeance. Inside its courtrooms there was no delineated line where revenge could not cross.

In modern day American courtrooms, however, vengeance straddles the line. There are loopholes in the law, secrete passageways where emotions get taken into account. This is true even though courtrooms purport to be emotion-free zones. These pathways empower the victim emotionally without enabling the closed fist of self-help. Stoic and sterilized legal arenas become showered, temporarily, by the waterworks of grief. Despite all the pretenses and scaffolding of legal justice, some legal outcomes can be made to look a lot like vengeance. These exceptions within the law include capital punishment, victim impact statements, the temporary insanity defense, and general theories of self-defense.

Capital Punishment

No other legal issue is as politically explosive and emotionally charged as capital punishment. A majority of Americans support it; so, too, do a majority of state legislators, certainly in those states where capital punishment is lawful for certain crimes. The Supreme Court has ruled that state laws that permit death sentences for those who commit premeditated murder—and surely for cases involving the worst of the worst—do not violate the Eighth Amendment to the Constitution's prohibition against "cruel and unusual punishment."[10] Nevertheless, despite what the people want, what the wrongdoers deserve, and what the Supreme Court has pronounced, very few murderers on death row end up being executed by the state for their crimes.

So much for democracy in action.

For all the conflict and confusion over the death penalty, it is not as if capital punishment is one of those political issues without a clear moral consensus (for instance, abortion, gay marriage), or where public sentiment varies widely depending on shifting political and moral opinion. On the contrary, all over the world opinion polls show unqualified support for the death penalty—especially in cases of serious crime. In spite of that, most Western nations have outlawed capital punishment.[11] The worldwide public support can't be attributed entirely to a degenerate bloodlust. Something profoundly moral is being suggested in this public sentiment—a longing that those who deserve to be punished should receive their due.

"There is zero evidence that support for the death penalty has gone down," claims Dudley Sharp, an advocate for victims' rights and a death penalty supporter in Houston. "The law on the death penalty has pretty much reached a consensus, too. . . . No one can seriously argue at this point that the death penalty is unconstitutional."[12]

In a recent Gallup Poll Crime Survey, which was reported on November 8, 2010, 64 percent of Americans support the death penalty; 49 percent of those surveyed said that the death penalty is not imposed often enough.[13] These figures have remained consistent for many years. In fact, support for the death penalty in the United States has not fallen below 60 percent since 1972. In an October 2009 Gallup Poll, 65 percent of Americans favored the death penalty; in November 2008, the number was 64 percent.[14] Polling numbers in support of capital punishment were consistently above 70 percent from the mid-1980s through the late 1990s. It reached a high of 80 percent in 1994. In fact, support for capital punishment drops to 50 percent only if Americans are given a somewhat more acceptable alternative to a death sentence, such as life imprisonment with no possibility of parole. What cannot be denied, however, is that when Americans are surveyed about what should be done with the worst of their criminals, just deserts is their guiding principle, not deterrence or rehabilitation.

Supreme Court Justice William Brennan, in *Furman v. Georgia*, the 1972 decision in which capital punishment was first ruled to be unconstitutional under the Eighth Amendment, which at the time effectively placed a moratorium on death sentences in the United States, wrote that "as the history of the punishment of death in this country shows, our society wishes to prevent crime; we have no desire to kill criminals simply to get even with them."[15] And, in a concurring opinion, Justice Thurgood Marshall wrote, "Retaliation, vengeance, and retribution have been roundly condemned as intolerable aspirations for a government in a free society."[16]

Both statements, despite having been written by esteemed and iconic jurists, are demonstrably false, which perhaps accounts for at least part of the reason why four years later the Supreme Court, in *Gregg v. Georgia*, overturned its decision in *Furman*. As discussed in chapter 5, preventing crime is *not* the sole reason to punish criminals. Retribution itself can provide its own justification for punishment—wrongdoers receive what they deserve because of what they have done, regardless of whether it helps prevent a future act. Besides, many crime control experts no longer believe that punishment—whether in the form of incarceration or through capital sentences—actually deters crime.[17] Criminals can't be deterred, but they can be incapacitated—taken out of commission, removed from the general population.

Such is the life of the recidivist—the repeat, career criminal who leaves prison and almost immediately returns to a life of crime. As the distinguished social scientist James Q. Wilson recently suggested in an essay in the *Wall Street Journal* that appeared only a few months before his death, there is at least one explanation for why the crime rate has been falling despite America's recent economic troubles. Many assumed that the crime would have spiked to match the nation's increased levels of economic distress. Wilson, however, observes that, "when prisoners are kept off the street, they can attack only one another, not you or your family."[18] Preventing hardcore criminals from reentering society—whether through incarceration or death—may not influence criminals-in-waiting, but it surely goes a long way toward ensuring that wrongdoers are not given a second chance to commit yet another wrong. So preventing crime, with all due respect to Justice Brennan, is not a convincing reason to punish wrongdoers. We punish them because they deserve it, not because it offers society some tangible future benefit.

It's also not true that the people who make up the society of which Justice Brennan speaks have no desire to kill criminals in order to get even with them. The general public does not make such neat demarcations between crime prevention and vengeance. For most people, all punishment carries with it the implicit, if not openly expressed, desire to get even, to ensure that the wrongdoer receives the poetic justice of just deserts. It is curious that even witnesses to injustice, those not personally harmed, are prepared to give up something of value in order to ensure that the cheater doesn't get away with it, that he gets what's coming to him. Why would they invest in this type of altruism—one that presents no personal gain but nonetheless carries the possibility of risk? Crime prevention has little to do with it. The main draw is always to restore moral balance, to see justice done.

Without hesitation Justice Brennan dismissed revenge as a human value. He discounted the emotional truth that people do, in fact, derive an internal sense of moral satisfaction when wrongdoers are punished. Human beings are invested—personally, emotionally, morally—in just deserts. It is the flipside of the moral revulsion that is felt when innocent people are punished. Both responses are inherently human—the innocent should be found innocent, and the guilty *must* be found guilty.

As for Justice Marshall, what is the source of this condemnation of revenge that he spoke of, these "intolerable aspirations for a government in a free society"? Surely it doesn't come from the general public. The natural history of man and woman is one that made peace with revenge as an organizing principle in their lives. It is not revenge that's "intolerable" to most people but, rather, the moral outrage of unpunished wrongs. That's what keeps people up at night and causes them to shake their heads in disgust when wrongdoers are set free.

Most people are not repulsed by vengeance or capital punishment. How, then, did it happen that death sentences came to be regarded as outside the scope of modern civil societies? One reason is that capital punishment, as a political issue, became co-opted by cultural elites, both in the academy and in the media, who often project a vision of liberal, progressive values that are inconsistent with the opinion of the American mainstream. For many people on the left, capital punishment is just a legalized way to achieve what private avengers have been forbidden to do—take a "life for a life." The fact that the state gets to administer the killing makes it no more acceptable. The very same condemnations against private vengeance are inveighed against judges who impose death sentences. If the taking of a life is wrong in the first instance, and retaliatory vengeance is no less a crime than any other act of violence—neither exempt from the law nor subject to some exception— then any form of killing should be deemed wrong no matter who performs it, regardless of why it was done, or whether the act itself was deserved.

We have all heard the aphorism: "the taking of revenge is wrong because two wrongs don't make a right." Jeffrie G. Murphy astutely notes that the latter is true only if revenge itself is actually wrong.[19] And revenge is surely not always wrong. The taking of a life in retaliation for a cold-blooded murder isn't necessarily wrong, even if the death sentence is not carried out. If vengeance and justice are seeking the same outcome, then in what way is either wrong simply because a murderer receives what he deserves? Confusion over capital punishment has a way of suspending one's critical thinking on the nature of right and wrong. Revenge may be morally correct despite the fact that it is legally forbidden.

Another objection to revenge and its relationship to capital punishment is the idea that revenge forces the avenger to stoop to the same level of the wrongdoer. But it's really the other way around. It is the wrongdoer's act that has devalued the victim, making him low. Vengeance merely brings him back to where he was before the injury led to his descent.[20] Suggesting that vengeance brings the avenger down to the same level of the wrongdoer misses the point entirely. The victim is already in the gutter. Vengeance is the elevator that restores him to his former stature. Revenge is an action of upward mobility with the avowed purpose of making things even again. The avenger is neither debased nor dehumanized; there is nothing downgrading about settling the score. Vengeance is restorative, not diminishing.

Another rap against revenge, and by association, capital punishment, is that it ends up hurting the avengers and society spiritually. It leaves them morally compromised and emotionally scarred. But if there is scarring it comes not from the taking of revenge but in its forbearance. Moral injury arises from the original wrong, and not from the retaliation. Indeed, there are moral consequences to living in a society that shows itself to be indifferent about its obligation to punish wrongdoers. When punishments are trivialized and dismissed, plea bargained and watered down, the morally wounded have no place to take their pain. They are sent home with the nauseating pronouncement that, despite all evidence to the contrary, "justice has been done."

Remember John Foreman, the father from Rhode Island whose five-year-old son Jason was brutally murdered by Michael Woodmansee in 1975? In 2011, he was confronted with a nightmare that he justifiably assumed would not return so soon. Woodmansee had availed himself of Rhode Island's "earned-time" law, which reduced the sentences of those who work during their time of incarceration.[21]

Foreman has threatened to kill Woodmansee "as aggressively and painfully as he killed my son," as soon as Jason's murderer is released from prison.[22] A local neighbor, Walter Campbell, who was among those who searched for Jason when he first went missing several decades earlier, said that he was considering purchasing a gun if Woodmansee is released early. "I think that there are probably a lot of people who would want to kill him if he came back in this town," Mr. Campbell said.[23] Other residents of Rhode Island wondered why the earned-time law should even apply to violent and sadistic offenders and asked the legislature to repeal it. Dale Sherman, who in 1982 was a paperboy whom Woodmansee had drugged and attempted to strangle to death, has asked, "Why is this man still breathing, let alone trying to get out of prison?"[24] Sherman is no doubt mindful each day that he had the good fortune to escape from Woodmansee whereas Jason Foreman was not so lucky.

And who could blame him? Surely this is what first comes to mind when hearing about the tragically grotesque murder of Jason Foreman and the man who, due to a plea arrangement, never served his full sentence even for second-degree murder, which was already a discounted punishment. Far short of representing a life for a life, the Foreman family, and the memory of Jason, have been grossly shortchanged. The phrase "the worst of the worst" applies to Woodmansee like it would apply to no other. His guilt is certain and his evil incalculable. All the same, instead of losing his life for the life he had taken, he bargained for a new punishment, and he received quite a bargain.

So the father of Jason Foreman threatened to accomplish what the state of Rhode Island had failed to achieve though its justice and penal system. And the residents of Rhode Island, where capital punishment is illegal, were also morally outraged and disgusted with this legal outcome. Many were not only rooting Foreman on but were prepared to seek vengeance themselves.

Another recent example of the worst of the worst occurred in Connecticut where all eyes were on the 2010 murder trial of Steven J. Hayes, who, along with an accomplice, Joshua Komisarjevsky, brutally and inhumanly took the life of a mother and her two daughters, and caused many Americans who followed the case to reconsider their feelings about capital punishment. The two men invaded the bucolic home of Dr. William A. Petit Jr., where they beat him unconscious, raped his wife, and strangled her to death, raped his eldest daughter, Hayley, seventeen, and then tied her and her sister, Michaela, eleven, to their beds, poured gasoline around them, and set the house on fire. In November 2010, the jury returned a death penalty verdict for Hayes.[25] (The murder trials were bifurcated. Komisarjevsky, who was also accused of molesting the younger daughter, ultimately received the same sentence.)

When the judge, pursuant to the jury verdict, sentenced Hayes to die, and after Dr. Petit and other family members were given a chance to speak at the sentencing hearing, Hayes's attorney, Thomas J. Ullmann, broke the silence in the courtroom by saying that, despite the admitted gruesomeness of the crime, the death penalty was still immoral. "Today, when the court sentences Steven Hayes to death, every one of us becomes a killer. We all become Steven Hayes."[26]

Actually, we don't. The jury sat through eight days of ghastly testimony—which included photographs of the murdered and violated victims, their ripped clothing, and the charred beds where the girls died of smoke inhalation—and the defense attorney's conclusion is that the jury's verdict, and all those who approved of it, makes them no better than his client. How does everyone "become" Steven Hayes simply by ensuring that he got what he deserves? The defendants were uncommon criminals—only nominally human, at best. This was not a situation where guilt was decided on the basis of flimsy circumstantial evidence or on unreliable testimony. Any reasonable doubt about what had happened on that day had been elevated to an absolute certainty. In fact, there never was any doubt at all. The actions the defendants took in terrorizing and killing these three women were surely not of the same character as a jury verdict that sentenced them to die. The former was monstrous; the latter justice.

Connecticut's governor, M. Jodi Rell, reflected the prevailing mood of her constituents when she vetoed a bill that would have abolished the death penalty and cited the murders of the Petit women as one reason why, in good conscience, she simply could not outlaw capital punishment.[27] (Less than two years later, however, a new Connecticut governor signed a bill to repeal the death penalty.) The defendants offered to plead guilty in exchange for life sentences. The prosecutors rejected the plea deal in this extreme case, demanding that they be prosecuted for having committed capital crimes. Dr. Petit summed up his own support for capital punishment by saying, "My family got the death penalty and you want to give murderers life? That is not justice. . . . I need to stand up for what is just in society and I need to stand up for my family personally."[28]

Sometimes opposition to the death penalty is invoked not by defense counsel but by the prosecutors themselves. In November 2010, roughly the same time as the Hayes verdict in Connecticut was announced, jurors in a courtroom in Denton, Texas—and the aggrieved daughter of a murdered man—were left wondering why they were not permitted to consider the death penalty in the case of Noah Whitehead, who, along with a friend, robbed, stabbed seven times, and slit the throat of a cab driver before burning his body beyond recognition.

When the cab driver's daughter, Lida Vatanpour, asked the district attorney why he was refusing to seek the death penalty for Whitehead, he said, "I just don't feel comfortable." Ms. Vatanpour expressed the feelings of most people in such situations by observing that capital punishment is "not for his comfort zone. It is for justice." She went on to say, "My father was robbed. He had about $108 in his wallet. He was stabbed and hit on the head and he was set on fire. If not this case [for the death penalty], then what case is appropriate?"[29]

The jury ultimately returned a verdict giving Whitehead the maximum prison sentence allowable under the law, which nonetheless shortchanged a daughter's understandable desire for vengeance. Another daughter of Texas, Mattie Ross, albeit fictional, from the novel and film *True Grit*, found herself in a similar situation where lawmen refused to do their job. She ended up having to carry out the punishment herself. Ms. Vatanpour, living in a more tranquil, law-abiding Texas, relied fully on the district attorney's office.

And how did that work out for her—how was her faith in the legal system reciprocated? An assistant district attorney, Jamie Beck, recognizing that the punishment was painfully less than what the Vatanpour family would have expected or desired, said that she hoped the guilty conviction would aid in the family's "healing process."[30] Such patronizing statements are offered by state prosecutors all the time, and nearly always couched in the language of "healing." These platitudes are doled out like consolation prizes. And they are insulting. As Dr. Petit, a physician, someone who is, by profession, in the business of healing, pointed out after Steven Hayes was sentenced to die that whoever came up with the word "closure" as an endgame to capital punishment is "an imbecile." He went on to say, "The hole in your soul is always there."[31]

It is understandable that many people have difficulty confronting the hard but crystalline truth that some people, due to their voluntary actions, simply deserve to die. A strict Kantian knows that it all comes down to desert—what is owed—regardless of how it ends up making victims feel or satisfies what they want. We have an absolute, nondischargeable duty to punish the guilty. But how victims feel shouldn't be so casually dismissed either. When John Allen Muhammad, one of the DC Snipers, was scheduled to die by way of lethal injection in 2009—seven years after he and his teenage accomplice terrorized the nation's capital for three weeks—Nelson M. Rivera, whose wife Lori was killed by a sniper bullet as she vacuumed her van at a gas station, said, "I feel like it's going to be the last chapter of this book and I want to see what his expression on his face is. And I want to see whether he says anything. I want to see his face and see how he likes that—confronting his death."[32]

Rivera's unabashed desire to witness the death of the man who murdered his wife surely troubles some people. But is he wrong? How many of us would feel otherwise if we were confronted with the same loss? How could we even imagine how we might feel? Several of the surviving family members of the 1995 bombing of the federal building in Oklahoma City, which killed 168 people, nineteen of whom were children under the age of six, expressed similar vengeful words during the sentencing of Timothy McVeigh, who was chiefly responsible for the attack. "The sooner [McVeigh] meets his maker the sooner justice will be served," said Darlene Welch, whose four-year-old niece was killed in the blast. Ernie Ross, who was left severely injured after the bombing while working across the street, said, "He will get what he deserved in the afterlife, where he will meet Hitler and Jeffrey Dahmer." Another survivor gruesomely suggested that McVeigh should have one of his legs amputated and then be suspended above sharpened but growing bamboo shoots that would eventually impale him.[33] The court heard this recommendation and decided instead to proceed with the lethal injection. But can we fault a grieving survivor for openly acknowledging such feelings? Isn't that precisely what a capital sentencing hearing should be expected to produce—the grief and rage of those who now look to the law to carry out the punishment that they have been denied from delivering themselves?

Sandra Miller's son Rusty, a fifteen-year-old straight-A student, was abducted at a bus stop, beaten, raped, and then murdered by William Bonin, the notorious California "Freeway Killer," who was eventually convicted of raping, torturing, and murdering fourteen boys. For sixteen years Miller waited until Bonin was finally put to death in 1996. "The rage is unbelievable," she told Bonin in the courtroom. "I loved [Rusty] more than life. I think of how I could torture you. You've brought out feelings in me I didn't know a human being could have."[34]

Who could blame her; who would blame any of them? They've all suffered too much to be judged. In states that provide for capital punishment, these vengeful feelings are invited into the courtroom—or are spoken outside on the courtroom steps—no matter how uncomfortable it makes many feel and no matter how irreconcilable it is with the legal system's standard repudiation of revenge. Victims should not have to pretend that they have no vested interest in seeing those who forever damaged their lives pay for their crimes. The debt paid back to society should be large enough to cover the debt owed, at least equally, to the victim.

Punishment is the cornerstone of a well-functioning and fair criminal justice system. But punishment is not merely what happens to the wrongdoer; punishment must also take into account the effect it will have on the victim. Will the victim feel that the penalty was fair, with full awareness that immoderately vengeful appetites violate the law of the *talion?* The victim's subjective estimation of fairness cannot be divorced from the overall sense of justice. Being impaled by rising bamboo shoots is not what justice allows. The punishment doesn't have to be perfect or ideal, but it must be fair, it must fall somewhere within the *talionic* range between underpayment and excess.

The punishment of a wrongdoer should serve as therapeutic vengeance for the victim, and the failure to recognize that value has most certainly not endeared the legal system to the general public. We think of restorative justice models in the context of the healing and repair of victims. But that's only because we have stripped away from retributive justice the emotional core so central to vengeance. The repair of victims is often directly tied to their sense of vindication. There can be no repair if victims believe that their anguish was never addressed. It is for this reason that, paradoxically, healing and vengeance are not so dissimilar. One can even think about vengeance as a real-world example of restorative justice since the quest to avenge a wrong clears a pathway for victim repair. A victim who insists on having his revenge is taking the necessary affirmative step toward healing. And the legal system should help get her there.

Recognizing how restorative justice for the victim is actually a misnomer unless punishment is delivered to the wrongdoer, law professor Stephen P. Garvey observes that "missing from the restorative agenda . . . is the idea of punishment as moral condemnation. . . . Restorativism cannot achieve the victim's restoration if it refuses to vindicate the victim's worth through punishment. Nor can it restore the offender, who can only atone for his wrong if he willingly submits to punishment. And if neither the victim nor the wrongdoer is restored, then neither is the community of which they are a part."[35]

The focus on capital punishment is always on the wrongdoer whose life will come to an end by the hands of the state. Rarely do we discuss the desire of victims who placed their trust in the law rather than take matters into their own hands. For most victims of violent crime, capital punishment offers the vindication they cannot achieve any other way. It restores the emotional, personalized component of justice and gives victims a voice. Society doesn't maintain ledgers on the debts that are to be repaid by wrongdoers. Most people aren't keeping score unless it is their duty to redeem those debts, when they themselves have become victimized. Actual victims are always keeping score. And they are entitled to feel that something was being done to even that score.

In 1993, seven-year-old Ashley Estell was kidnapped from a park playground while her parents were watching her older brother play in a soccer game. A previously convicted sex offender, Michael Blair, raped and murdered her. He was convicted and given a death sentence. After a number of appeals he was finally put to death. Ashley's father, Richard said, "For me, it's partly closure and partly the focus on personal revenge. I want to see him gone. I can't get it out of my mind what my daughter must have felt."[36] All throughout history fathers have agonized over the damage done to their daughters. And they felt duty-bound—as a matter of honor and as true men—to see that justice was done. Neither the biblical Jacob nor the fictional Bonasera from *The Godfather* was alone in their grief and obligation.

Despite this allowance that the legal system offers them through capital punishment, victims who openly proclaim their desire to watch the death penalty carried out are often treated with scorn. In Houston, Texas, in 1996, the man who murdered Linda Kelley's two children was executed, and she became the first victim in that state permitted to witness the death of a capital defendant. "My family and I have been characterized as hatemongers for wanting to watch him," she said. "We are not hatemongers. If we were really bent on revenge, we would have gotten him ourselves at the trial. We are law-abiding citizens."[37]

And Kelley is correct. She did exactly what the social contract requires—let justice runs its course and place her faith in the legal system. She obligingly did not take justice into her own hands. But when she wished to experience some personal satisfaction in watching the man who murdered her two children pay the ultimate price for his crime—a mere taste of vicarious vengeance—she was made to feel like a heathen with blood trickling from her mouth.

In 1979, when Brooks Douglass was a teenager living in a farmhouse in Oklahoma, two drifters invaded his family's home, hogtied his parents and him and forced them to listen as they raped his twelve-year-old sister. After they were finished they sat down and ate the dinner that the family had prepared before their lives all but ended with such torment. The men then shot all four Douglasses in the back, then walked away with the weddings rings of the parents and $43 in cash. Brooks and his sister miraculously survived. It took seventeen years and multiple trials and appeals before the Douglass children—more than half their lives squandered in the search for justice—lived to see the execution of one of the men who terrorized their family.

Brooks Douglass eventually became an Oklahoma state senator and sponsored a victims' rights bill, which, controversially for its time, allowed victims to witness the execution of those who had turned them into victims.

"I was criticized for fostering revenge," Douglass said. "So what? Who are we to question what a person's feelings are when they go view an execution? There is no other party that has more to benefit from seeing the killer executed than a family member."[38]

Critics of capital punishment point out that executions do not actually bring relief to victims. Some victims report feeling no better at all. This same argument has been offered against the taking of revenge, with Inigo Montoya, the master swordsmen and faithful son from *The Princess Bride*, perhaps the best fictional example of an avenger with decidedly mixed post-vengeance feelings. But should that matter? The obligation to avenge is not contingent on making the victim happy but, rather, on restoring honor to the victim and serving the memory of the dead. Happiness is not an expected outcome nor is joy necessary for revenge to be justified. All that is required is satisfaction, which is not about happiness but, instead, a sense of liberation. The avenger can still feel miserable afterward, but that doesn't affect the duty or alter the responsibility to settle the debt.

Society can justify taking a life for a life without having to simultaneously relieve victims of their heartache and pain. Vengeance is not a guarantor of closure. Revenge comes with no warranties. It is only the score that gets settled, not the agony of the aggrieved. Opponents of capital punishment use this very lack of closure as a reason why society should not assume the role of designated avenger and kill in the name of another. After all, if the death of the wrongdoer won't bring relief to victims, then why should states undertake the logistical and moral burden of performing executions and making capital punishment lawful?

"Taking a life doesn't fill that void, but it's generally not until after the execution [that the families] realize this," said Lula Redmond, a psychotherapist who works with families who have lost loved ones through violent crime. "Not too many people will honestly [say] publicly that it didn't do much, though, because they've spent most of their lives trying to get someone to the death chamber."[39]

But that, too, misses the point. In cases of capital punishment, victims may not feel completely unburdened by the wrongdoer's death, but few ever doubt the righteousness of the remedy. If anything, they regret only that the wrongdoer didn't die sooner, that he managed to drag it out and live longer, that the lethal injection was not sufficiently harmful because it failed to produce the kind of equivalent suffering that the wrongdoer had inflicted on another. After all, the "cruel and unusual punishment" clause of the US Constitution works in only one direction: to protect the guilty, to place limits on what can be done to them. It isn't concerned with the cruelty of the wrongdoer's act, whether the manner and method of his torment was unusual in any way and therefore deserving of a reciprocally cruel and unusual penalty. Punishment in American courtrooms isn't tailored in accordance with the cruelty of the initial act. The law of the *talion* requires that the retaliation be inflicted measure for measure. But in all instances, humanitarian concerns will override just deserts.

Actually, surviving family members of murdered crime victims are not nearly that naïve. Most realize beforehand that the carrying out of a death sentence by the state—or even by their own hands, for that matter—will not free them from their own private prisons of torment in which life sentences are served without bars. There is no panacea in simply witnessing an execution; crime victims are not released from their pain the instant the wrongdoer is deprived of a pulse. As discussed earlier, revenge is sweet in its anticipation, largely because there are emotional and moral imperatives at work and because vengeance is mandated by brain circuitry and human evolution. Nevertheless, the sweetness of vengeance will, for some, eventually give way to a bitter aftertaste. Ambivalent feelings set in, but they don't result in second-guessing. The wrongdoer deserved what he got and the victim is left satisfied. Hollywood revenge movies remind us that happy endings are for the audience to savor, and not for the avenger, who is often not around at the end to celebrate.

To be sure there are always surviving family members of violent crime who are opposed to the death penalty based on religious grounds or for reasons having to do with their own moral code. The tenets of their faith, and the convictions of their moral belief system, don't allow them to accept the taking of a life—for any reason and under any circumstances. They believe in compassion, mercy, and forgiveness and see very little personal or moral value in achieving *talionic* justice. Given that this book is, if nothing else, dedicated to calling attention to the sensitivities of victims and the rights denied to them once they relented to the rule of law, no one can begrudge them a remedy that ignores the moral imperatives of just deserts—if that's what they want. A victim may choose to forgo justice in favor of some other spiritual reward. No one should tell victims how to feel about, or respond to, the losses they have suffered. There is no greater disrespect to a victim than to dictate the terms of his or her repair.

But the state has its own interest in seeing that justice is done, and victims cannot trump those interests either. Victim satisfaction must be balanced against the government's obligation to punish—all according to the moral blameworthiness of the wrongdoer. The problem in the ordinary course of criminal justice system is underpunishment, where victims are left un-avenged and wrongdoers do not receive the punishment they deserve. That is the moral dilemma this book seeks to address: the feeling that justice is not served and victims are left shortchanged. Victims who surrender to their faith or, through their own force of will, are satisfied with incomplete justice have less to complain about when the legal system fails to punish. But surely those victims are not representative of the majority of citizens who are appalled at the assembly line of botched prosecutions and plea-bargained sentences, which leave behind not residual feelings of forgiveness but rather rueful feelings of unconsummated vengeance.

The emotional satisfaction that is a by-product of revenge and that in-heres to the victim should never trump the interests of society in seeing justice done—for its own account. Even if the victim would feel no satisfac-tion at all from settling the score, society still would have an obligation to seek legal retribution against the wrongdoer. The victim's wish not to receive repayment does not in any way cancel the debt owed to the state. If this were not the case, wrongdoers would have the incentive to preselect their victims only among pacifists, whose family members may be similarly inclined to-ward leniency. Surely those wishes could not control the fate of a murderer and his destiny with just deserts.

Walter Rodgers, a former senior international correspondent for CNN, wrote an essay for the *Christian Science Monitor* in connection with the sen-tencing of Steven Hayes, one of the two men who were convicted of triple murder in the Connecticut home invasion of the Petit family. Rodgers was apparently shocked when a friend of his, an "educated physician," no less, admitted that he wanted to see the two assailants receive the death penalty. How could this man, a healer by trade, possibly be in favor of vengeance, the cold-hearted wish to take the lives of the Connecticut killers? Rodgers wrote, "People may have strong feelings about the need for Connecticut to execute Hayes for murder, but let's be honest: Capital punishment is itself about killing. It is a conjoined twin of vengeance, which is blatantly immoral."[40]

Of course capital punishment is about killing, but not all killing is wrong—legally or morally. Wars are fought for righteous reasons and they are not made any less righteous because they result in casualties of war. Indeed, it is in the killing that wars are won and how they come to an end. Surely one can be against all wars, but pacifists and conscientious objectors are not the final authorities on whether the fighting of a war is just and necessary. Moreover, as discussed earlier, the title of the John Grisham novel *A Time to Kill*, which was adapted into a feature film, is not just catchy, it's also correct. There are times when it is necessary to kill; even those who otherwise object to killing come to learn this sad but unavoidable truth. To say that capital punishment is killing is hardly a revelation unless Rodgers is also saying that all killing is wrong and that capital punishment is simply a legalized way of accomplishing that same wrong.

Surely this doesn't require much elaboration, but there is a world of difference between a killing and a murder. Murder is unlawful; killing, however, is not necessarily against the law. The biblical "thou shall not kill" applies to the wrongdoers; it is a preemptive, prescriptive warning that they rethink their evil inclinations. It does not apply to *talionic* retaliators. The wrongdoer's deed now leaves them without choice. There are many forms of killing that all nations and peoples accept as appropriate—whether in self-defense or in the case of just wars. States that execute their worst-of-the-worst criminals are not committing acts of murder; they are simply carrying out deserved punishments against those who have already taken a life and must, due to their own moral blameworthiness, be punished commensurate with that wrong.

Moreover, when Rodgers writes that capital punishment is the "conjoined twin of vengeance," he completely misapprehends the meaning of vengeance. Revenge is a remedy to a wrong; it has no independent existence without that initial wrong. And, yes, capital punishment is related to vengeance, but it is equally related to justice. It is the wrongdoer himself who chooses his weapon and, thereby, sets the stage for his ultimate undoing. As sociologist Ernest van den Haag has written, "By committing the crime, the criminal volunteered to assume the risk of receiving a legal punishment that he could have avoided by not committing the crime."[41] Capital punishment and vengeance are "twinned" only because a wrongdoer has made it so. Neither are necessary unless and until a wrongdoer undertakes a fatal decision that requires a proportionate response in the form of a capital sentence.

And with equally condemning fervor, Rodgers writes that vengeance is "blatantly immoral." How does he come to that conclusion so emphatically and absolutely? If anything, vengeance is patently moral. The reason for its presence in human evolution and its lodgment in the human brain constitutes the very essence of moral development. It is not an outlier in human evolution, like a bad smoking habit that humankind managed to pick up along the way, foreign and corrupting to the human cell structure and enterprise. Vengeance sits comfortably and nobly within the select inventory of human instincts. It needs no invitation to join the club. Revenge, when properly exercised, is plainly moral; it supplies its own justification.

Love and sex, for instance, require no moral justification for human beings to act on those feelings. Nor do honor and duty depend on some independent moral permission slip. Governments won't admit that revenge is as much a divine right as liberty and the pursuit of happiness. Religions would prefer that their foundational texts had never raised the subject in the first instance; the *talion's* eye for an eye, as civilization evolved, became a poke in the eye. But revenge is in no danger of forfeiting its moral gravitas merely because there are those who refuse to acknowledge how indispensable it is and what purpose it serves. The emotional benefits of vengeance are not so easily disentangled from the delivery of justice, especially in the case of capital punishment, where the linkage between justice and revenge are so starkly clear.

Yet, resistance remains great to the simple truth that there are, indeed, occasions where a death sentence is precisely what justice demands. In cases of capital murder, victims are repeatedly denied, if not outright mocked, for wishing to free ride on a legal punishment that they have every right to expect. What victims want, and what murderers deserve, is not legally prohibited. So why not use it more often?

In the Oklahoma City bombing case, US District Judge Richard Matsch limited the number of survivors who were permitted to speak in court during the sentencing phase of the trial. Many more wished to do so. He chose to minimize the list because he didn't want to turn the hearing into "some kind of lynching." He went on to say, "We're not here to seek revenge of Timothy McVeigh."[42]

Once again, who, exactly, is he speaking for? Surely, and understandably, vengeance was on the minds of those who lost loved ones to McVeigh. What kind of relatives would they be if they didn't feel justified in having those feelings and wishing to express them, in open court, as a way of remembering those who can no longer speak for themselves? They had no other way to vindicate this crime. McVeigh was sentenced to die for many reasons: certainly because he deserved it but also because it satisfied the wishes of his victims. And this is why so many of them wanted to speak at his sentencing hearing. Very few, if any, would have expressed ambivalence or shame. The surviving families of McVeigh's grotesque act of domestic terrorism wanted to experience, at least vicariously, the emotional benefits of revenge. Enabling McVeigh's victims to take part in the process that would determine his punishment was the least the legal system could do.

In 2010, soon after retiring from the Supreme Court, Justice John Paul Stevens wrote in the *New York Review of Books*, "An execution may provide revenge and therapeutic benefits. But important as that may be, it cannot alone justify death sentences."[43]

It doesn't have to be the only reason. Moral outrage can take many forms—from the mandate to set a public example to a state's legitimate interest in crime control. But certainly one reason why capital punishment should be utilized with greater frequency is quite simply because that's what crime victims want and that's what they need.

Courts do not impose death sentences for armed robbers and rapists or even embezzlers on the scale of a Bernard Madoff. Capital punishment is reserved for capital crimes. The penalty is triggered by the wrongdoer's deed rather than the victim's need. But if it's true that murderers decide the punishment they will receive by making the choice to commit a particular crime, then death sentences can be viewed as simply statutory punishments, established by the state, automatically applied and fully depersonalized—and neutered of all emotion. The victim's feelings are incidental to the penalty. Vengeance is commonly regarded as emotional, primal, and uncontrollable. But capital punishment, if performed without end-zone celebrations, only incidentally resembles the vengeance that societies traditionally deplore.

Nevertheless, issues surrounding the death penalty are confusing precisely because they are tainted by their association with revenge. Governments admonish citizens not to resort to self-help because vengeance is unlawful and plainly wrong. But when the state imposes death sentences for capital crimes, isn't that the most "vengeful" penalty of all? Obviously revenge can't be all that bad if the state allows itself the privilege but denies it to its citizens—those who actually suffered the harms and have the true moral authority to avenge. Why is the government a more appropriate executioner than the actual victim, or his or her delegated surrogate?

Intrinsic to the law of any state that permits capital punishment lies a deceitful double standard. Crime victims are desperate for personal vindication whereas the state has no emotional investment at all in whether the wrongdoer lives or dies. States can be indifferent to a choice between capital punishment and life imprisonment with no possibility of parole. As long as the wrongdoer has been removed from society permanently, the state can, theoretically, accept either remedy. Crime victims, however, often cannot.

A life sentence without parole for a grieving family member can feel as if the wrongdoer truly did get away with murder. Victims are left to wonder why the *talion* should be so trivialized; why should the taking of a life result in a penalty so out of proportion with the seriousness and consequences of the crime? A state, however, stripped of any emotional involvement, can regard a life sentence as perfectly proportionate. Deterrence and crime control serve as core values of criminal justice. Death sentences and life imprisonment are alternative strategies to enforce law-abiding behavior and maintain safe streets. Once emotion is introduced into the decision, however, there is a world of difference between them. Capital punishment is not supposed to be about helping victims achieve some individual catharsis or closure. But it invariably does because it gives victims what they want—even though the legal system insists that the emotional benefits of revenge is not something citizens are entitled to enjoy.

In its 1976 decision in *Gregg v. Georgia*, the Supreme Court overturned its earlier decision in *Furman* and ruled that state legislatures were once again free to decide whether to put its most violent criminals to death based on the interests of the state in fighting crime and the values of the state in ensuring justice—provided that certain guidelines were met consistent with evolving standards of decency in American society. The court wanted to make certain that, in restoring the death penalty as the highest price a murderous criminal defendant could pay in the United States, no one should confuse capital punishment with the barbaric punishments that once existed in Europe before the Enlightenment.

Justice Potter Stewart wrote for the majority, "The decision that capital punishment may be the appropriate sanction in extreme cases is an expression of the community's belief that certain crimes are themselves so grievous an affront to humanity that the only adequate response may be the penalty of death. . . . Capital punishment is an expression of society's *moral outrage* at particularly offensive conduct" (emphasis added).[44]

Justice Stewart invoked the concept of moral outrage as a primary value in the constitutionality of capital punishment. Most people in the legal profession do not speak of moral outrage, and when they do, they don't usually ascribe any legal significance to the term, as opposed to more obscure, even Latinized terms, such as *stare decisis* or the "rule of law." Moral outrage has its own plain meaning—the disgust and revulsion of the community—and it *should* be a relevant consideration in determining how a wrongdoer is to be punished. Indeed, there might not actually be a more worthy reason to punish. As Walter Berns has written, "Punishment arises out of the demand for justice, and justice is demanded by angry, morally indignant men; its purpose is to satisfy that moral indignation."[45]

The community should have a voice in denouncing certain crimes so odious that no reentry into civilized society can ever be possible again. And the community's moral outrage should also supply the moral basis for why a murderer must be expected to forfeit his own life. By linking capital punishment with the "community's belief"—its moral outrage—Justice Stewart provided a legal explanation for introducing moral and emotional elements into sentencing decisions. The death penalty takes the coldness of legal retribution and infuses it with the rich emotional life force that is the very embodiment of moral outrage.

Writing further in *Gregg*, Justice Stewart acknowledged that the rationale in support of capital punishment, one that depended on society's revulsion, "may be unappealing to many, but it is essential in an ordered society that asks its citizens to rely on legal processes rather than self-help to vindicate wrongs."[46] He goes on to quote Lord Justice Denning, writing in an earlier time but also in a common law court, as a reminder that the rule of law, deriving from the social contract, carries with it an obligation that the state has to its citizens that "in order to maintain respect for the law, it is essential that the punishment inflicted for grave crimes should adequately reflect the revulsion felt by the great majority of citizens for them."[47]

There can be no better way to describe the duty owed to citizens under the social contract. In recognition that citizens surrendered their right of revenge, and in order to earn their respect, the legal system must punish wrongdoers in a manner that reflects the revulsion and common opinion of the people. The Supreme Court, in *Gregg*, drew a legal connection between two retributive values that guide the obligation of states to punish criminals: just deserts and moral outrage. By accounting for the denunciation of the community, the court soared above stacks of law books and entered the domain of the moral universe. And when emotion is introduced into sentencing decisions, the dry concept of legal retribution begins to beat with the quickening pulse of moral revenge. In cases of capital punishment, revenge is given a ringside seat in the courtroom alongside other values under the rule of law. Ironically, it is through death sentences that revenge is given a legal life.

Accepting moral revulsion as a reason to punish is tantamount to taking the blindfold off Lady Justice and outfitting her with x-ray vision. The Supreme Court implicitly ruled that, when it comes to capital punishment, the vengeful feelings of the community are placed on equal footing with the retributive objectives of the state. For thirty-five years *Gregg* has validated vengefulness and acknowledged that the community has the right to be emotionally invested in the nexus between justice and punishment. Sentencing decisions cannot ignore the emotional commitments that the public has in seeing that the legal system is meaningfully interested in achieving moral balance and just deserts.

In the summer of 2011, a Florida jury acquitted Casey Anthony of charges of first-degree murder, aggravated manslaughter, and aggravated child abuse in the death of her toddler daughter, Caylee. During a month-long period when Caylee had purportedly gone missing, Anthony moved in with her boyfriend, got a new tattoo and a liberated life, partied nightly and shamelessly with her friends—and even entered a hot-body contest at an Orlando club. Only at a later date did she report that her daughter had died accidentally. The wealth of prejudicial, yet circumstantial evidence apparently did not disabuse the jury of their reasonable doubt that this negligent mother may have also been a murderous one. Had Anthony been convicted she would have received the death penalty.

In the days following the verdict, however, there was widespread disbelief over the outcome. A number of states immediately proposed enacting a law in honor of Caylee, making it a felony to wait more than one day to report a missing child. Casey Anthony was released from prison and remained in an undisclosed location. Legal justice had run its course, but the more vengeful variety, typified by vigilante justice, was heating up. The drumbeat of moral outrage carried through the rest of the summer.[48] One could say that the masses outside of the courtroom and around the country were nothing more than an ignorant lynch mob who had long since overdosed on the media circus that surrounded the trial and were in desperate need of a civics lesson on the judicial branch. What did they know anyway? Wasn't it better that twelve citizens had been empanelled as a jury of peers and spent months examining the evidence, ultimately concluding that there was reasonable doubt that Casey Anthony had committed an aggravated crime? Wasn't it equally possible that this was a case where a death sentence imposed on a young, innocent mother had been mercifully avoided by a legal system that took its time to evaluate the evidence and conclude that it was insufficient to convict?[49]

What can't be denied, however, is that the community, and much of the country, were thoroughly invested in this outcome. And the fixation wasn't based entirely on the salacious, sordid events and cover-ups that accompanied the death of this little girl. There was a profound sense of incompletion, of justice denied, of obliterated faith in the jury system, of moral failure in the face of smug legal proceduralism.

Justice Stewart was correct in leaving room for the moral outrage of the community to become a factor in sentencing decisions for capital cases. The people who root for the avenger inside darkened theaters while watching feature films are the same ones left mystified by the law's failure when they reenter the light of day and glimpse travesties of justice that can't be corrected—either by caped crusaders or Legal Aid lawyers.

The legalization of capital punishment, and the overwhelming majorities that are in favor of the death penalty, is an explicit acknowledgment that, in the minds of ordinary citizens, the law of the *talion* is not a mere artifact from the Bible with no contemporary relevance. Justice can be blind, but citizens are not expected to have blind faith in the legal system. The community's faith depends on the legal system's own fidelity, if not outright assurance, that evil will be punished. Faith in the law requires the legal system to honestly judge itself worthy of that trust. And one way to earn that trust is by making sure that victims are not denied the vicarious pleasure of knowing that a debt owed has finally been repaid. Walter Berns wrote that, by invoking the language of retribution in *Gregg*, the Supreme Court "recognized, at least implicitly, that the American people are entitled *as a people* to demand that criminals be paid back, and that the worst of them be made to pay back with their lives."[50]

Presently there are 3,261 prisoners on death row, with California having the largest number, 697. Acting on the authority of *Gregg*, thirty-four states now allow for the death penalty, but only forty-six people were executed in 2010, a 12 percent drop from the previous year.[51]

A majority of the states allow for it, and a clear majority of citizens wish to see it carried out—and yet so few executions actually take place. Some of the decline is related, no doubt, to the publicity surrounding cases where DNA evidence is later discovered that leads to the exoneration of a formerly condemned man. New advances in forensic science and the various iterations of the *CSI* franchise, which has turned ordinary beat cops into chemistry geeks, have made everyone aware that DNA can live even underneath a shoe, lodged within a keyhole, and scattered microscopically on bathroom floor tiling. We have all been led to believe that invisible yet fully incriminating or exonerating evidence is littered all over a crime scene, provided that the PhDs on *Bones* and *NCIS* will simply show up and retrieve a sample.

We also live with the knowledge that trials are sometimes sketchy, highly inexact presentations of what took place at the scene of the crime. A criminal trial can get it all wrong; an innocent person may be placed in jail or, worse, ultimately lose his life. (And when it comes to the death penalty population, 98.2% are men.)[52] Sometimes the truth is not reliably uncovered until long after the judge's gavel has pounded and the accused is already taken away, incarcerated, or standing in the condemned queue of death row. In such situations there are those with an incentive to keep the truth concealed, to not own up to their mistake. And far too many death penalty cases result in convictions based entirely on weak presentations of circumstantial evidence.

Capital punishment, when imposed on an innocent man, magnifies the moral consequences of making a mistake and inflames the moral outrage of those who oppose, on principle, the state taking a life. Understandably, there is a growing sentiment that capital punishment is too final and irreversible a remedy to impose given the uncertainty that exists and the improprieties that take place in many murder convictions.

In Justice Stevens's recent commentary on the subject, written as a former justice on the Supreme Court, he pointed out that 130 death row inmates have been exonerated since 1973, largely due to DNA evidence.[53] Tragically, some innocent people—falsely accused and misidentified—have been put to death. Sociologist Ernest van den Haag estimates that of the seven thousand people executed in the United States from 1900 to 1985, twenty-five were innocent of a capital crime. Included in that ill-fated group are Ethel and Julius Rosenberg, as well as Sacco and Vanzetti.[54]

Surely the execution of an innocent man or woman is the ultimate moral failure of the legal system. But the worst of the worst are never among the innocent. The worst of the worst receive this label precisely because they stand out among the accused—their crimes are more deplorable, their guilt unquestionably established.[55] These are the men whose crimes shake the conscience and shatter our faith in humanity. They are never wrongly executed for reasons of mistake. One may disagree with capital punishment on moral grounds, but when it comes to the worst of the worst, the objection can't be that they may be innocent after all. The monstrousness of their mayhem, the proficiency of their crimes, and the verifiability of their guilt were actually never in doubt.

Moreover, in such cases, there is no exclusive reliance on shaky circumstantial evidence, no mishandled evidence, no mistaken witnesses, no exonerating DNA, no false confessions owing to coercion or duress—nothing but unequivocal guilt. When absolute certainty exists, when the evidence of guilt is direct and conclusive, or where the confession is voluntary and resolute, there is no fear that the legal system has convicted the wrong man. No other truth will one day present itself that will contradict the finding that the wrongdoer was guilty. When dealing with the worst of the worst, why not more regularly apply the highest penalty under the law and provide victims of capital crimes with the emotional satisfaction of having their revenge? A murder conviction on the basis of inconclusive circumstantial evidence should never receive the death penalty. But the worst of the worst, by definition, is a special category where guilt beyond a reasonable doubt is established beyond any doubt at all.[56]

The moral appeal of the death penalty is greatest in situations of the worst of the worst precisely because, as a former prosecutor and now law professor, Bob Grant, has said, "it is the expression of society's ultimate outrage."[57] Heinous acts deserve death because no other punishment is appropriate. Grant prosecuted the only man to have been executed in Colorado since the 1960s. In 1986, Gary Davis kidnapped, tortured, sexually assaulted, and then finally murdered a young mother. There was no doubt about his guilt. The evidence that he committed the crime was overwhelming. Why shouldn't he have paid the ultimate price, the only penalty that came even close to approximating what he had done to his victim?

In 2011, a prosecutor in Orange County, California, vowed to seek the death penalty against Scott Dekraai, who, dressed in body armor and armed with three handguns, entered a hair salon and shot nine people, murdering eight, including his wife. The prosecutor, Tony Rackauckas, spent little time considering whether there were any mitigating and extenuating circumstances that would warrant a lesser penalty than death. "There are some cases that are so depraved, so callous and so malignant that there is only one punishment that might have any chance of fitting the crime,"[58] he said.

It's not just the United States where governments are reluctant to execute its worst criminals despite the wishes of victims and the general public. The implementation of the death penalty has been in decline all throughout the Western world and in Latin America, even though a majority of the world's peoples support it, and a majority of those people live in countries that allow for capital punishment: China, India, and the United States.[59] In capping the ultimate punishment for criminals as something short of death, governments purport to know more about what is morally right than the people they govern. But shouldn't representative democracy matter—at least in democratic nations? The will of the people is that those who commit the worst of crimes will be made to suffer the worst of penalties. Jeffrie G. Murphy asks, "For what is a democracy except a form of government in which the majority gets to have its dominant preferences enacted into law—even if those preferences are condemned by a refined and condescending elite?"[60]

The reasons why death sentences are all too infrequently carried out extend from the humanitarian to the utilitarian to the theological. Since state executions have proven ineffective in deterring future crime, there is no utility—no net benefit—to taking the lives of criminals. Courts are not in the business of executing criminals merely to satisfy aggrieved, vengeful victims. Prosecutors are not given the mandate to represent both the interests of the state in crime control and the wishes of victims to feel avenged.

A humanitarian reason to oppose capital punishment is even more perplexing. Human rights groups have conflated the cause of capital inmates with the victims of torture and genocide—two groups of people who have nothing in common. Under this twisted reasoning, the taking of a human life is wrong no matter who does it or whether there may be valid reasons for doing so. The execution of a convicted murderer is no different from an act of terrorism that results in death. The *talion* is reformulated to read: "A life is a life," rather than "a life for a life." Many are persuaded by the humanistic principle that there is dignity, decency, and goodness in everyone no matter how abominably they may have once behaved. Redemption is always possible; therefore no one deserves to die. Supreme Court Justice William

Brennan, siding with the majority in *Furman v. Georgia*, wrote in a separate concurring opinion that capital punishment is in all cases wrong and unconstitutional, in part because "even the vilest criminal remains a human being possessed of human dignity."[61]

Such expansive generosity in ascribing dignity to everyone regardless of individual merit or evil inclination can test the gag reflex of even the most tolerant and peace loving among us. The constitutional law scholar and political philosopher Walter Berns said it best when he wrote: "What sort of humanism is it that respects equally the life of Thomas Jefferson and Charles Manson, Abraham Lincoln and Adolf Eichmann, Martin Luther King and James Earl Ray? To say that these men, some great and some unspeakably vile, equally possess human dignity is to demonstrate an inability to make a moral judgment derived from or based on the idea of human dignity."[62]

Popular support for the death penalty is being overridden by a hesitant legal system that insists on taking the personal, emotional, and moral out of sentencing decisions. Yet, in many instances, this sanitizing of punishment becomes unbearable for victims and the community. The legal system clumsily magnifies the overall harm by insufficiently punishing the originating source of that harm. Plea bargains distort the truth of how the victim came to be victimized, a whitewashing that makes criminal justice resemble a wheel of fortune or, even worse, a den of shady backroom deal making. In such a transactional environment, every absolute truth, each unrepentant crime becomes negotiable, receiving a downward adjustment to something less felonious and completely unrepresentative of what actually took place. The eye for an eye is now substituted for a lesser organ. The underlying crime and punishment have been reduced to both a lie and a farce. In situations of first-degree murder, the proper punishment is available under the law, but the will to carry it out is sorely lacking.

The South African anthropologist, Lyall Watson, writing in *Dark Nature: A Natural History of Evil*, lamented that the typical jail sentence for manslaughter in the United States is three to five years with the possibility of parole after only eighteen months. Responding to this all too familiar pattern of devaluing crimes in the legal system, he notes, "justice is very often *not* seen to be done and relatives still carry hate and feel an unrequited thirst for revenge. We ignore such passions at our peril, and ought to think twice about dismissing revenge as 'sterile' or somehow unseemly. We lost something of value, a pattern that made evolutionary sense, when we decided to make justice remote and impersonal. Perhaps we should think again and restore once more the old notion of 'just deserts,' of measured retribution that is satisfying and comprehensible to all concerned, because it is totally appropriate to the crime."[63]

Victim Impact Statements

Death penalty executions are grinding to a near halt. But at least sentencing hearings in aggravated felony cases are being used to give voice to the vengeful feelings of victims who are otherwise prohibited from availing themselves of self-help. Victim impact statements—both in their written form and when delivered orally—are yet another side door into the law that invites the emotions of revenge inside the courtroom without the violence and imprecision that society fears in situations of privatized vengeance. Crime victims, and the family members of murdered victims, are given an opportunity during the sentencing phase of the trial once guilt has already been established, to speak directly to the court and articulate the impact that the crime has had on their lives. The state insists on retaining the sole burden and prerogative to punish wrongdoers, but that shouldn't mean that victims must be denied a respectful role in the proceedings or be deprived of having their voices heard in the determination of punishment.

After all, it is the victim who possesses the greatest interest in seeing the wrongdoer paid back for his wrong. The caption *People v. Jones* may be the formalized way that the justice system frames the state's case against a Mr. Jones. But do *all* the "People" really have a score to settle with Mr. Jones? At any given moment district and state's attorneys all across America are prosecuting accused criminals on behalf of the "People," but only one segment of the populace—the victims of the crime—are personally invested in seeing the prosecution and punishment of the wrongdoer carried out to a satisfying conclusion.

As lawyer and social critic Wendy Kaminer observes, "To a victim the notion that crimes are committed against society, making the community the injured party, can seem both bizarre and insulting; it can make them feel invisible, unavenged, and unprotected."[64]

In a legal system that relegates crime victims to the diminished role of witnesses on behalf of the state, victims are entitled to no ownership stake in the process. The stories that brought them to the courtroom have been adopted—co-opted, even—by the state, forever depersonalized, treated more like a banal statistic than an actual lived experience. The victim becomes an afterthought, a buried footnote, and not the center of attention. In a Texas nightclub in 1989, David Lee Herman, a former manager, returned to rob the establishment he once ran. Before leaving the scene of the crime, he forced one of the three women in the office, Jennifer Burns, to strip naked so he could fondle her. "This is where the fun begins," he said before shooting all three women. Herman received the death penalty and was executed. But the dehumanizing experience of being a member of the victim's family never left Paula Foster, the mother of Jennifer Burns. "It was always the state of Texas versus David Lee Herman. You feel like you're not important. [The prosecutor] has no idea of your need to be involved."[65]

At sentencing hearings where victim impact statements are introduced, victims are, essentially, given their own hearing. Quarantined from the guilt phase of the trial, marginalized as overly biased and unreliable, it is only during the sentencing hearings where they finally receive their day in court, such as it is. For a short moment in time, a proper forum is provided for the expression of grief and the dissipation of rage. The wrongdoer might end up escaping a death sentence. He may, ultimately, not be punished commensurate with his crime, equal to what he deserves. The victim might not actually get *even* with the wrongdoer. But with victim impact statements the microphone will be yielded to the victim and he can give full human voice to his loss in a public setting, inside a courtroom, witnessed by a judge, and memorialized as part of a criminal proceeding.

These hearings are held, specifically, in connection with the sentencing of a wrongdoer who has already been found guilty in that same courtroom— part two of his appointment with justice. It is here where the victim seeks to influence the court in imposing the maximum penalty—a reminder that justice done on behalf of the state must also take into consideration the victim's separate need for personalized justice. Victims appear at these hearings at their most damaged and heart-stricken—unreservedly subjective in their bearing. Neutrality is beyond their capacity. After all, their experience with victimhood matters and will continue to matter even as the wrongdoer serves out his or her sentence. The passage of time will be counted on the victim's own clock. With each parole hearing, at every stage at which the status of the wrongdoer's punishment is being reconsidered, the victim will be present once again as a reminder that the criminal act was not directed at some abstract target—the wrongdoer didn't merely just break a law, he or she committed a crime against a specific individual. The consequences of the crime did not disappear with sentencing. The crime had casualties and left an impact on real people.

These hearings are not to be discounted as mere group therapy sessions, the waterworks of family grief at the public's expense. To be sure, their statements are emotional, but that doesn't mean they are not purposeful. Victim impact statements allow for an emotional release that for many people can replicate the experience of revenge—the human encounter, face-to-face, with the full-throated utterance of all that was lost. These statements are made live and in front of a judge, absent the violence of self-help but not without an acoustical cry for help.

Its origins can be traced to the very beginnings of the victims' rights movement. There was a growing disenchantment that many felt about a justice system more focused on the rights of the accused than on the experience of victims, those who encounter the law on a lesser footing than the reception received by the victimizer. The damage done to the victim received no constitutional relief, unlike the due process and equal protection guarantees that are specifically intended for the accused. As an egregious example of this moral imbalance, the accused is permitted to introduce mitigating and character evidence to lesson his punishment, but any evidence of the impact that the crime has had on the victims was once regarded as irrelevant to the crime and far too prejudicial to the accused.

The introduction of victim impact statements humanized the victim and enabled family members to enlighten the court as to the dimensions of their grief and the character of the life that was taken from them. By now such testimony is common in the United States, Australia, and Finland. Victim impact statements in the United States began with the Manson murders in

1969 and the death of Sharon Tate, the pregnant wife of film director Roman Polanski. It was Ms. Tate's mother, Doris Tate, disgusted by the cult status that Manson was achieving and the mere footnote her daughter was becoming, who feared that Manson's cohorts would one day receive parole and her daughter would be forgotten. She organized a public campaign in California against the dismissive, insensitive, and morally inverted manner in which crime victims are treated.[66]

Tate was not alone in her agony. Andrew Serpico's wife, Bonnie, was murdered during an attempted rape in 1979 by James Free. At the trial, the judge insisted that Serpico and his three daughters sit in the back row of the courtroom. Free's mother, however, sat in the front row, beside the jurors, weeping. In an era before victim impact statements, the judge refused to allow Serpico to inform the jury that his wife was the mother of three girls and to somehow express to the jurors the enormity of the loss that each suffered. The judge ruled that it would be too prejudicial to their mother's murderer.[67]

By 1982 the President's Task Force on Victims of Crime recommended that "judges allow for, and give appropriate weight to, input at sentencing from victims of violent crime." The Supreme Court in *Payne v. Tennessee* (1991) ruled that the character of the victim, and the impact of the harm caused to either him or his family, should be taken into consideration by the court, but not during the guilt phase of the criminal trial, where the evidence about the crime and the determination of guilt should be free from emotional, subjective influences.[68] The court recognized that victim impact statements are, by their very nature, emotional and subjective and, therefore, should not be confused with standards of objective proof that govern the determination of guilt in criminal trials. The sentencing phase, however, where punishment flows from proven guilt, is fair game for emotional influences to be on display. There is no mistaking that victim impact statements are written and uttered in the language of grief. At sentencing hearings, subjectivity reigns and emotion echoes all throughout the courthouse. A family member isn't required to supply proof of grief; it is obvious from their statement before the court. Their faces awash in anguish; their pain judged to be true.

During sentencing, where the issues are limited to the degree of punishment, the "human cost" of the wrongdoer's act should factor into his or her penalty. And it should also take account of "each victim's uniqueness as an individual human being." You can't get more subjective, or personal, than that. In his dissenting opinion in *Booth v. Maryland*, the 1987 decision that had initially found victim impact statements to be unconstitutional, Justice Antonin Scalia summed up the reasons behind the public clamor for the victims' rights movement as "an outpouring of popular concern for . . . what its proponents feel is the failure of courts of justice to take into account in its sentencing decisions not only the factors mitigating the defendant's moral guilt, but also the amount of harm he has caused innocent members of society."[69]

And this "taking into account" of the impact on victims the crime has had provides yet another legalized loophole for revenge to make its way into courtrooms. The very thing the law purports to avoid when casting judgment over human beings—the messy, unstable emotions peculiar to revenge—becomes an integral part of the sentencing determination. Rather than remove the personal from the punishment of the guilty, the use of victim impact statements serves to institutionalize revenge by adding a vengeful voice to the punishment process. Not unlike capital punishment, which can resemble revenge, the use of victim impact statements shows legal retribution to be not entirely impersonal. Victims share with the court the impact the crime has had on them and their families, which personalizes the crime and gives victims an ownership stake in the outcome.

In a study conducted in 1987, 54 percent of victims who filed an impact statement and spoke in open court reported that "they felt different after making their statement to the judge," and 59 percent expressed "positive feelings of satisfaction or relief."[70] This form of victim empowerment is particularly acute in cases where judges, in making their sentencing determinations, quote directly from the impact statements, giving true meaning and legal significance to the victim's words. It also demonstrates that the victim's role in the punishment of the wrongdoer is not perfunctory. The experience of speaking to the loss, and having a judge meaningfully listen, humanizes the loss, making it personal to the victim and far less remote to the state.

The Supreme Court in *Payne* reasoned that since the wrongdoer is entitled to put forward mitigating evidence that might persuade the court to reduce the punishment, so, too, should victims be permitted to introduce evidence showing the magnitude of their loss, thereby offsetting whatever sympathies the wrongdoer has managed to evoke in the court. The court ruled that, "just as the murderer should be considered as an individual, so too the victim is an individual whose death represents a unique loss to society and in particular to his family."[71]

Vengeful people are blamed for their lack of maturity and self-control in failing to tame their emotions and suppress their hateful feelings. Yet the presentation of victim impact statements validates those very feelings; in fact, such statements become monuments to those feelings, giving them voice and moral urgency. Perhaps this is why there is still a good deal of push back against the use of victim impact statements. Those opposed to revenge, in principle, and opposed to its camouflage under the guise of victim impact statements, in particular, have argued against their use. Such opposition is yet another assault against emotions playing any role in legal decision making. Punishment should be based on moral blameworthiness alone, it is argued, and not on the character of the victim or on how much his grieving relatives may miss him. Overly articulate and bereft relatives who can fill a courtroom with cascading waves of pity should not be able to tip the scales of justice and increase the punishment of a wrongdoer who haplessly picked a victim whose death will now command the greatest punishment—either because he is more worthy or he is more greatly mourned than another victim. Murder is murder, after all, and equal protection demands equal treatment—even among murderers. It is the wrongful act that determines its punishment, not its consequence.

Observing in an earlier age the unfairness that victims experienced when they came before the law, Supreme Court Justice Benjamin Cardozo wrote in a 1934 opinion, "Justice, though due to the accused, is due to the accuser also. The concept of fairness must not be strained till it is narrowed to a filament. We are to keep the balance true."[72] The imbalance between the rights of the accused and the remoteness of the victim has always been accepted as a staple of constitutional justice. Victims can be prejudiced before the court; the accused, however, must always be judged without prejudice.

When the victims' rights movement finally began to press for more dignified treatment for crime victims, there was the question of how, precisely, to rebalance the scales of justice? Giving victims a voice appeared to be a good idea, but what would such a voice be allowed to sound like? Could it resound with unrestrained wrath, or must it be merciful, as Portia counsels Shylock in Shakespeare's *The Merchant of Venice*? The legal system ordinarily favors the dispassion and disinterest of third-party witnesses, precisely because as nonparties who are not invested in the outcome, they are more likely to be objective and truthful. And they are unlikely to become emotionally unglued. Given the law's preferences for bland neutrality, victim impact statements ought to be the legal system's worst nightmare. These flash points of grief have little purpose other than to throw a spotlight onto the overwrought lives of damaged victims. The hearings can descend into emotionally unmeasured affairs, roller derbies of vengeful feelings that break with the legal system's more customary decorum.

Jeffrie G. Murphy wondered why the outpouring of such feelings should surprise anyone, and, moreover, why anyone would begrudge a family member of the opportunity to speak about the most tragic day of his life—especially if it offers the dual benefit of empowering the victim and informing the court's sentencing decision. He then asks, "Can it be shown to be fundamentally wrong in principle for the suffering that criminals receive from the state to be contingent to any degree on hatreds and desires for revenge felt by their victims? Do criminals have a fundamental right to be shielded from the consequences of such feelings?"[73] Surely the Founding Fathers didn't believe that the Sixth and Eighth Amendments to the Constitution protected wrongdoers not only from the arbitrary and unprincipled abuses of the state but also from the tremors and aftershocks of righteous anger that their victims justifiably feel toward them. The rights owed to the accused cannot possibly extend that far.

All that should matter is that the victim's vengeful wishes not unduly influence the court in punishing the wrongdoer in excess of his moral blameworthiness. The upper limit on the *talion* always applies. The moral universe never wavers in its demand for proportionate punishment; the wrongdoer should not be expected to pay back more than what he owes. But the moral universe also recognizes that victims have a legitimate interest in having their anger satisfied. And the only way for that to happen in a civil society that outlaws private vengeance is to allow victims the right to participate in the punishment.

Of course, that may not be enough for victims. Merely free riding on legal retribution may not fully satisfy the depth of their personal loss. The legal system does all the heavy lifting in enforcing the punishment. In this Hollywood movie, all the glory goes to the state. Victim impact statements exist as a discharger of emotion only. That's all victims get and what the state will allow.

And the value of victim impact statements is limited by other restrictions, as well. In most cases the victim only submits a written statement that may, or may not, be read by the judge during sentencing. The emotional power of the victim's actual voice is generally not required to be heard in open court. Victim impact statements operate only after a guilty verdict is reached and not before, silencing the victim during the pretrial stage of the proceeding and during the entirety of the trial itself, which is precisely when the most important legal decisions are made and facts bearing on guilt are presented—all without the victim's input. Worse still, whether and to what extent victim impact statements must be considered by the court varies widely. In capital cases, some states disallow such statements. The rape victim who survives her attack may not exercise her opportunity to rage against the trauma of the rape, since the trial itself often exacerbates the sense of personal violation and outright fear that she experienced. The victim of an assault knows plenty about the fear that pervades her days and remains imprinted on her life. But her moment to share that suffering with the judge or jury is often too late to alter the sentence.

Moreover, since the vast majority (well over 90 percent) of criminal prosecutions are resolved by way of negotiated pleas, most victims will never get a chance to make a statement in open court that will influence the judge's sentencing decision at all. Far removed from a rampant and unremitting plea-bargaining process, and with no say in decision making, it is the rare victim who will actually receive a day in court—even symbolically. With plea bargains the debt is not only discounted but also immune to the victim's righteous outrage.

And while it is true that other legal remedies, such as civil tort actions, are available to victims, these cases are equally unsatisfying. Just ask the Goldman family of Santa Monica, who, in 1997, obtained a judgment in the amount of $33,500,000 against O. J. Simpson after a jury found him liable for the wrongful death of their son, Ronald. After all these years, the Goldmans have managed to recover only $500,000 of that judgment. Laws shielding pensions and real property from being used to satisfy legal judgments have left the Goldmans still bereft and Simpson, until very recently, remained a wealthy man.[74] Ironically, he now sits in a Nevada jail, but for an altogether different criminal conviction. In 2007, the Goldmans obtained the rights to his book, *If I Did It*, in which Simpson all but confessed to having committed the crime.[75] Other than shedding more light on the truth, it will not contribute much to satisfying the judgment they have against him.

Most victims of violent crime, however, can expect to do even worse than how the Goldmans fared before a civil court. After all, most perpetrators of violent crime are not professional football players and movie stars. They commit violent crimes, in part, because of their dire economic circumstances. Civil lawsuits against violent wrongdoers are likely to receive no better than a token victory. A monetary judgment against an indigent, judgment-proof wrongdoer is valueless, even if the court awards punitive damages as a way of maximizing the wrongdoer's debt. Multiples of zero always produces the same empty sum. A judgment that can never be collected is hardly a fair substitute for what the avenger could have accomplished in settling the score on his own terms.

Besides, a civil judgment is not the same as retributive punishment, and can't possibly accomplish the same aim. A recent study in the Netherlands confirmed that even those who observe a wrong prefer to see the wrongdoer receive his due rather than the victim receive compensation.[76] Victims may have been left with a material loss, but mostly they have been made to suffer, had their self-worth plummet, and had their status as a member of society erode all on account of the actions of another. Compensatory damages, measured in money alone, can never measure up as suitable vindication for damaged pride or bereft loss. What victims wish to see is commensurate suffering, the rebalancing of moral worth, which can only be restored when the wrongdoer is punished in a criminal proceeding. And while punitive damages, which are monetary in nature, appear to embody punitive goals,

CHAPTER 7

plaintiffs who seek punitive damages rarely, if ever, assert their claims in the language of revenge.[77] Perhaps that's because punishment that is focused entirely on the payment of money never feels sufficiently punitive.

Perhaps civil lawsuits, by definition, owing to a certain civility, can never truly function as an alternative to revenge. The theory of tort law known as "civil recourse," pioneered by a colleague of mine, taps into the "primitive 'instinct' of retributive justice."[78] But civil recourse theory makes clear that "it is about *not getting even*"—indeed, it's "what the state gives us in place of getting even."[79] Revenge, however, is unapologetically about getting even. Despite sharing some of the vindicating elements of vengeance, civil lawsuits, which cast judgment only by ordering the payment of compensatory damages from wrongdoers who may have no ability to pay, are actually poor substitutes for the raw emotional power of revenge. Vengeance is often framed in the language of redeeming debts, but this sort of debt is not connected to a dollar sign. Vengeance, generally, has very little to do with money and everything to do with denouncing and punishing wrongdoers. If courtrooms are where such punishments should take place rather than in more personalized arenas, then it is best left to a criminal court, not a civil one.

Another limitation of victim impact statements is that it's not at all clear whether judges actually value the emotion that these statements deposit inside their courtrooms. The victim's experience might end up being more performative than purposeful, the statements having no impact on judges, exerting little influence on them—a misnomer from the outset. Judges who preside over criminal trials may become inured to all that raw emotion or, worse, dismissive of it. They are empowered to punish wrongdoers based on many factors, including the persuasiveness of the victim's anguish and grief. But what if the purported safety zone for vengefulness is nothing but an echo chamber—there only for the victims to vent, without any true effect on the actual legal process? Judges might become deaf to the victim's pleas. All that anger and grief becomes the legal equivalent of shouting into the wind.

The problem, as discussed throughout this book, is that the law has a systemic, near pathological aversion to the emotional life of human beings. Just because emotion might be permitted limited access inside courtrooms doesn't mean that judges will know what to do with it. Revenge, after all, and its connection to justice, is always an internal, emotional, and moral phenomenon. If victim impact statements are to serve as vicarious substitutes for revenge, their full moral force will be wasted unless the emotion is not simply listened to but also acted on.

Unfortunately, so very often that is not the case. The people whose job it is to evaluate the emotional force of these statements are themselves constitutionally ill equipped to deal with tears. Judges take pride in their ability to exist solely in the world of reason; they show little patience or appreciation for the emotional sphere. Only a sissy judge would keep a box of Kleenex beside him on the bench—no reason to coax the waterworks out of witnesses, or himself, for that matter. And anger, the rocket fuel of revenge, is the most unacceptable emotion of all.

Mary Lay Schuster and Amy Propen collaborated on a recent report for the Association for the Study of Law, Culture, and Humanities, in which they examined judicial responses to victim impact statements. The researchers came away with some very disturbing findings. Feelings of anger, especially if it comes across as vengeful, are very much unwelcome in courtrooms and many judges find such emotions to be unproductive. Angry victims are regarded as dishonest, out of control, or simply unable to gain any perspective on the crime. Worse still, judges perceive the victim's expression of anger as an unwillingness to move on with his or her life. For instance, they detest listening to the very words that one would naturally expect to hear in these minitrials of grief: "lock him up forever and throw away the key." In one case where the wrongdoer killed a man and then sexually assaulted, kidnapped, and attempted to murder the victim's girlfriend, the judge was apparently turned off when the woman, who was, after all, a victim herself, ended her statement by saying, "The time has come to lock up Satan."

Here is how one judge described just how unmoved he is by the emotions of anger and rage: "People get up, and I can tell that they are overstating something, or they have a vengeful purpose behind it, or they want the world and in particular the defendant to be responsible for all their life's problems." Another judge plagued by similar deficits in emotional intelligence, added, excessive anger "can certainly backfire in the sense that of the judge's reaction because sometimes victims don't understand that their hatred of the defendant will convey itself to the judge, which undermines the credibility of what they are saying in their sense of objectivity."[80]

Okay, some judges are not only emotional morons, they also have trouble with the English language.

Why *should* crime victims be objective? Surely we can't expect them not to vocalize their feelings of anger in the very forum in which they have been invited to express their rage. Victims can't very well check off the many ways in which they have been damaged with the same bland affect as if reciting a grocery list. These are sentencing hearings, after all, and victims naturally wish to be heard. Judges fear that anger expressed so openly threatens the precious decorum they maintain over their courtrooms. But such self-importance about courtroom etiquette has not served the judiciary well, and has, in fact, contributed to an erosion of respect from the general public. It would be far better for everyone if judges allowed the heartbreaking words of victims to penetrate the thick skin of their own emotional detachment.

What a bizarre paradox: Victim impact statements can actually prejudice some victims whose emotional response makes them seem out of control in the eyes of the court. After being forced to sit through a trial in silence and now finally given an opportunity to speak, their guileless demeanor ends up disqualifying them as a sympathetic victim. They lose credibility. Victim impact statements were instituted, implicitly, as legal stand-ins for the kind of lawless self-help that society will not accept. A physical retaliation is not permitted, but victims are allowed to have their Inigo Montoya moment: they can announce themselves to the wrongdoer, confront him with what he did, and, short of taking their own revenge, they can request of the court that it deliver the harshest penalty permitted under the law. Meanwhile, in the typically deflating fashion of the legal system, emotionally obtuse judges react negatively to these unguarded moments of grief and end up punishing victims by underpunishing the wrongdoers—all because they found the victims' candor to be disturbing.

Truly listening means accepting the hurt underneath all the words spoken in anger. As Schuster and Propen point out, courts are more sympathetic to compassionate victims, those perceived as more mature and emotionally composed, who can somehow look beyond their own hurt and focus instead on the larger needs of society and the court's own limitations in an imperfect world.[81] But consider this: What kind of people appear at sentencing hearings prepared to withhold their true emotions all for the sake of not giving a judge an unfavorable impression of the victim's true feelings?

Voluntary Manslaughter and Self-Defense

The emotions of revenge appear in various guises in criminal law but are rarely acknowledged for what they are. In the same way that capital punishment and victim impact statements provide a legalized forum in which to articulate vengeful feelings, so, too, can certain crimes offer a backdoor way to behave vengefully without incurring the full cost of revenge.

Take voluntary manslaughter, for instance, which is, essentially, a homicide with an emotional component attached to the crime. Under common law, whether British or American, voluntary manslaughter is a killing committed in the "heat of passion" brought about by some "provocation" without sufficient "cooling time" in which to dissipate the attendant emotions, ultimately giving rise to murder.[82] Those who are found guilty of committing voluntary manslaughter are treated as if they were without choice, emotionally driven to a point of impulsive desperation. Such conduct is distinguished from the wrongdoer who commits premeditated, first-degree murder, or even a criminal act motivated by a reckless disregard for human life. Voluntary manslaughter is essentially the crime of murder mitigated by a passionate response that was provoked by the victim of the crime, who may have been a wrongdoer of another sort.

The term of art "heat of passion," and the way it mitigates premeditated murder to a lesser crime, represents a tacit acknowledgment that emotions that motivate crimes are of a far less detestable nature than crimes that emanate out of wickedness and bad intention.[83] Emotion is the essence of human nature, something that all human beings share. Depravity, by contrast, is special and more rare, possessed by human beings whose wickedness can lead to malice aforethought. As law professors Dan Kahan and Martha Nussbaum pointed out, the man who dispassionately kills his wife's paramour with no greater emotion than his killing of a mosquito, shows that "he invests too little value in fidelity; his act of killing without anger would

235

show us that he invests too little value in others' lives."[84] Killing with emotion is treated more favorably under the law than killing without feeling. This leads to the paradoxical outcome that while emotion is not welcome *inside* courtrooms, a criminal defendant will receive a lesser sentence if his crime was committed while in the grip of emotion *outside* of the courtroom.

Emotion, which serves as the cornerstone of revenge can, in certain cases, supply the critical fact that turns a homicide into the lesser crime of voluntary manslaughter.

Similarly, if too much time passes after the heat of passion first showed itself, the wrongdoer will be denied any defense that his act was not pre-meditated. Once the intensity of emotion subsides, he can no longer claim to have been deprived of his reason. His anger is expected to have cooled and been brought under control.[85] What qualifies as voluntary manslaughter is precisely the kind of righteous rage that is ordinarily associated with revenge—the recognition that no cheek turning is possible, that retaliation, arising from inflamed emotion, is humanly necessary. Anything less demonstrates a lack of honor and personal pride. As one federal appeals court once ruled, "The deliberate killer is guilty of first degree murder; the impulsive killer is not."[86]

Another way to look at it is like this: the wrongdoer who commits a homicide does so in *cold blood*, whereas the person who commits voluntary manslaughter was quite possibly forced to do it as a result of the *hot blood* of passion. The presence of that heated emotion, and its influence over him, reduces his culpability. Under the law, passion can constitute a mitigating circumstance; it receives a discount on the act, reducing it to a lesser crime. Murder in cold blood, by contrast, being committed without emotion, receives no such sympathetic treatment.

Oddly, a legal system that condemns the taking of revenge because of its emotional commitments allows for separate pathways to justice—and more leniency—for crimes motivated by the very same emotions that are active in vengeance. As a further example of how the law takes proper account of human emotion in recharacterizing the nature of a crime, Susan Jacoby has observed that certain crimes that occurred within a family context, among intimates, were treated differently than they would have been had the same crime been committed against a stranger.[87] Wives and girlfriends who kill their violent and abusive husbands and boyfriends, whether they invoke the battered women's syndrome or some other legal defense—or excuse— are punished less severely than a woman who kills a man after an awful first date.

In fact the law used to take even greater account of emotion. There was a time, in most jurisdictions, when men who battered their wives were not regarded as criminals precisely because the connection they had to their victims was personal and emotional. Against a stranger the crime would have been deemed cold-blooded; against an intimate it qualified as a lesser crime—if even a crime at all. And the reason for that mitigation was based entirely on the emotional history that the wrongdoer had with his or her victim. Emotion intervenes to alter the character of the crime. This contradicted the most basic canon of criminal law: punish the act, not its consequence; criminals deserve equal protection under the law, too. A punch is actionable no matter who is on the receiving end of it; a battery is a battery whether committed against a stranger or a spouse. But since the crime against a wife was credited as having been motivated by an emotional connection and carries its own emotional history, it was viewed differently. These very same passions, however, were not unlike the emotions emblematic of revenge, which otherwise received no protection under the law. The legal system persisted in the charade that courtrooms are to be emotion free, and vengeance is wrong precisely because it is too emotional. But this leads to a double standard when emotional complexity among lovers and spouses is accounted for under the law, whereas no such allowance is made for strangers.

Despite all of its protestations to the contrary, the legal system has always made some concessions to the emotional life of human beings. Emotions may have been kept out of courtrooms, but if the exercise of an extreme emotional response was the reason why the defendant ended up in a courtroom, that emotion often served as evidence to lessen the punishment.

Just to see how far this double standard once went, Jacoby pointed out that creepy uncles or psycho fathers who committed acts of sexual molestation against their own children were treated as if the act was less a penal offense than a medical problem—no matter how loathsome the act.[88] In many jurisdictions the matter was referred to a family therapist rather than to a law enforcement officer—that is, treated as a medical problem to be handled within the family. Meanwhile, pedophiles with no family connection to children they molested were rightly viewed as if they had committed an unspeakable, punishable crime. Among intimates, criminal conduct ended up unpunished. The more personal and emotional the relationship, the less legal accountability was expected of the wrongdoer.

In reflecting on this disparate treatment—and separate set of legal protections—that once existed between strangers and family members, Jacoby wondered, "ought people who are bound together, either by formal family ties or by the informal but emotionally binding ties of passion and intimacy, be allowed to take revenge upon each other in ways that would ordinarily be forbidden by law?"[89]

A similar exception that enables revenge to sneak inside courtrooms and influence the legal outcome arises in cases of self-defense. The common law rule is clear: a person can use deadly force that is necessary to protect himself from another's attack, provided that the threat is imminent and unprovoked. But the philosophical basis supporting self-defense is often no different from the justifications for revenge. For instance, the "necessity" requirement is satisfied even if it can be shown that the person could have safely avoided the life-threatening assault merely by stepping aside or, in the most prudent circumstance, simply by running away. Why privilege an attack launched in self-defense if it could have been avoided altogether? The reason has to do with dignity and honor, the very same human values that can create a moral justification for vengeance.

Actually, self-defense offers a legally acceptable way to engage in self-help. Provided that the retaliation is imminent rather than deliberate, there is very little philosophical difference between vengeance and self-defense. Yet vengeance receives no justification under the law, whereas acting in self-defense is a well-established excuse to commit a crime that might have the exact same implications as a revenge killing. The moral justification for vengeance relies on the principle that to do anything less is an insult to one's honor. Self-defense is legally justified, to some degree, for very much the same reason.

In a Supreme Court decision written in the nineteenth century, the justices understood how demeaning and dishonorable it would be for a "*true man* . . . to fly from an assailant, who by violence or surprise maliciously seeks to take his life or do him enormous bodily harm."[90] The rule that permits self-defense is as much about maintaining honor and dignity as it is about self-preservation. Indeed, legal commentators have observed that the No Retreat Doctrine, where a person who is faced with an attack is not required to run away to avoid the harm—even if he could easily do so—is based on "a policy against making one act in a cowardly and humiliating role."[91] Honor and dignity, so vital to the moral legitimacy of vengeance, are equally present in the legal theory of self-defense.

Throughout the United States, variations in how self-defense is treated reflects regional differences on the importance of maintaining one's honor and dignity. The majority of northern states impose a general duty of retreat in response to deadly force. In the south and northwest, the number of states doing so is just a little more than half. Perhaps this explains why the practice of dueling, which served for centuries as the only manly response to an insult, lasted much longer in those regions of the country than elsewhere.

Vigilantism as Preemptive Self-Defense

One understandable outcome of the state's failure to live up to its part of the bargain in the social contract is the occasional presence of vigilantes who insist on doing the bidding of an ineffectual legal system. Paradoxically, the state's obligation to be vigilant on behalf of its citizens is the main reason why we even have vigilantes. After all, the enlightened philosophers of the eighteenth century assigned the job of watchfulness to representative governments who were in possession of newly democratic ideals. Vigilance was owed and vigilance must be delivered on behalf of the citizenry. It soon became obvious, however, that if the government wasn't taking its duty of vigilance seriously, if the state was somehow unable to deliver justice on its watch, then someone else must do so in its stead.

By default, the vigilante becomes the lone member of society sickened by the state's casual, all too familiar breach of the social contract. He or she chooses to act in response to the government's general neglect. The vigilante operates outside of the law and, thereby, becomes a fugitive from the law by having to break the law. It all starts when an ordinary citizen is summoned into duty to avenge, either by way of family honor or moral conviction, or because he, himself, is the owner of the debt that must be collected from the wrongdoer. The vigilante picks up where the government last tried and failed.

Painful as it is for law enforcement officers to acknowledge, a vast majority of Americans do not disapprove of vigilante behavior. In a 1985 Gallup poll, 74 percent believed that vigilantism is "sometimes justified," while 8 percent believed that it was "always justified."[92] Of course, this poll was taken shortly after the 1984 Bernard Goetz subway shooting in New York City. Goetz, a middle-aged man, defended himself in an attempted subway robbery by firing an unlicensed firearm at four young men, nearly killing them all. He had been victimized once before and was determined to not let it happen again. Indeed, it was the law's failure that had ennobled Goetz as a justified vigilante; the legal system's broken promise turned lawlessness into righteousness for the price of a subway token.

Goetz was charged with attempted murder, assault, reckless endangerment, and the criminal possession of a deadly weapon. He was convicted of only the latter charge. The jury acquitted him of the more serious offenses under New York's self-defense statute. The would-be robbers were all African-American and had criminal records that they improved on after recovering from their injuries. Each ended up in jail for other offenses. The jury was nearly all white, half of whom had been victims of street crime.

Of course, this all took place during the peak years of New York City's battle with urban crime. There was a tremendous outpouring of support for Goetz from New Yorkers (and the entire nation) outraged by the lawlessness on the city's streets and the ineptitude of the police in protecting the citizenry from crime.[93] Thousands of dollars were raised for his legal defense. In the age of *Death Wish*, Bernard Goetz was an authentic subway vigilante who had lost faith in the legal system's capacity or willingness to do justice. So he armed himself in case he would one day need to resort to self-help

Goetz was unapologetic in his own defense. The shooting was not premeditated, but it was no accident, either. He had, indeed, prepared himself to fight back in the event of an attempted mugging. He refused to be defenseless in his own city. Finding himself in a situation where his life was

imperiled, he took the law into his own hands and nearly killed the four assailants. He said, "My intention was to murder them, to hurt them, to make
them suffer as much as possible. If I had more bullets, I would have shot 'em
all again and again. My problem was I ran out of bullets." He then added, "I
was gonna, I was gonna gouge one of the guy's eyes out with my keys after-
wards," but said he stopped when he saw the fear in the mugger's eyes. Goetz
allegedly told one of his assailants who he had already shot, "You look al-
right. Here's another."[94] Defense attorneys argued that such statements were
examples of the "extreme emotion" under which the crime took place.

And it was doubtless the emotion of the jury that resulted in Goetz's acquittal of the more serious charges. Law professor George P. Fletcher wrote
that the verdict captured the public mood of a morally outraged society
tired of feeling helpless, which led a jury to find for "the right of decent
citizens to hold their ground against the terrorizing effects of the mugging
subculture."[95] Goetz benefited under the law from his emotional response
to an imminent, unprovoked assault, manifested in a mindset to defend
himself as much against violence as dishonor.

Most people regarded this disturbing case of frontier justice in the inner-
city subway as an example of the deteriorating conditions of urban life, a
tragic consequence of the failure of law enforcement to uphold its duty to
protect the people. The Guardian Angels, a citizens patrol group that rode
the subways of New York City, was a direct outgrowth of this fear. And they,
too, were accused of engaging in vigilante behavior—watching over strap-
hangers, ordinarily the job of transit cops.

The verdict stood as a bold statement by the jury—a shrieking pronouncement of communal anxiety—in rejecting the prosecution's attempt
to punish Goetz. Everything was upside down: the government made no
apologies for the high crime rate and the menacing dangers that accompanied any luckless trip on the subway. Yet the government was insistent that
Goetz possessed no right to defend himself. He, alone, had deputized himself to perform police work, which was best left in the hands of experienced
officers of the law. The police, the men in blue, were deemed "New York's
Finest" even though there was massive failure throughout the ranks of the
NYPD. "Finest" was a gigantic exaggeration, certainly in those grittier days
of urban crime. Nonetheless, the prosecution regarded Goetz as an outlaw

who must be taken off the streets. Most certainly he should no longer be permitted to venture underground with a gun. The public, however, saw Goetz as an urban folk hero, a man who stood up for himself and held his ground against four muggers.

No wonder the *Death Wish* films were so popular throughout the 1970s and early 1980s, when the Wild West had taken up permanent residency in many inner cities across the United States. The logic of the legal system seemed delusional. And the jury in the Goetz case spoke directly to that delusion by spray painting a plea to the legal system in the manner of subway graffiti artists: "Do your job, and if you can't, or won't, then don't complain if ordinary citizens are forced into the position of having to do it for you, and for themselves."

The Goetz jury was not alone in delivering messages of disgust with the legal system and support for a vigilante who, in the absence of the law, must, by necessity, become the law. Jurors, either through jury nullification or with the full blessing of the court, have, on occasion, treated those who ultimately took the law into their own hands sympathetically. In 1992, Lance Thomas of Los Angeles killed five men and wounded another who attempted to rob his store. A jury found that all the killings were justified. A grand jury in New York dismissed all charges against Kenny Mendoza in connection with his shooting of an intruder who threatened his pregnant girlfriend.[96] Were these cases of self-defense, voluntary manslaughter, or revenge rewarded—or preemptive strikes against the legal system itself?

Even jurisdictions that impose a general duty to retreat when confronted with violence provide for an exception in cases where someone is holding his ground against an attacker in his own home. The principle here, once again, is to spare a homeowner from the indignity of not being permitted to defend himself in the one absolute place where he has a right to be and where no retreat is possible or expected—in his own home. In many jurisdictions, the same act of self-defense while one is a guest in someone else's home would not lead to the same legal defense. The rule generally does not apply to shield nonowners precisely because they are understood to have no emotional attachment to someone else's home, and no humiliation should arise when retreating from the home of another. The law would not, however, impose such an emotional hardship on the actual homeowner.

But if criminal law is primarily focused on the act rather than its consequence, why should it matter whether a person is forced to defend himself at home rather than elsewhere? The reason for any difference at all reinforces the moral principle that dignity matters to human beings. To be compelled to act in a cowardly manner in one's own home is a true deprivation of dignity. Conceptually, a self-defender is like an avenger who is attacked in his own home—and is given legal protection to do so. The avenger, in all cases, however, remains a lawbreaker and is given no benefit of the doubt or room for excuse.

Self-defense, and its connection to revenge, has a similar role to play in the crime of rape. Typically, the best way to rebut a defense by the alleged rapist that the sexual intercourse was consensual is to show that the rape victim fought back against her attacker. Rape victims have a far better chance of seeing the rapist punished under the law if they resisted the attack. It is not an element of the crime that they show resistance. Indeed, the law once made such a requirement an element of the crime, but that is no longer the case. Nonetheless, a rape victim who fights back supplies the most important aspect of proof. For this reason, a prosecutor with a rape victim who was left unbruised after the attack has a difficult burden to overcome in actually proving nonconsent. The rape victim isn't required to resist, but if she does, she becomes a more credible witness, and her bruised body serves as compelling evidence of the crime.

In the years before the law changed, courts wanted to see that the victim exerted "utmost resistance." Without such proof, courts believed that they were left with nothing more than murky "he said, she said" scenarios. And prosecutors were more disinclined to take on such cases. But even today, rape victims are in a far better position of seeing justice done if they fought back against their attacker because resistance supplies proof that the alleged sex crime was nonconsensual. Nonconsent is the one key element of the crime of rape. But proving the absence of consent is too high a burden without establishing resistance, even though such retaliatory action might expose the victim to further harm.

Why then does the rape victim's resistance become factually, if not altogether legally, necessary?

Rape is not only a physical violation, it is also an insult to the victim, an implication of promiscuity, a stigma that she was taken advantage of sexually and must now be thought of as a damaged, unworthy woman. And in the most vulgar of male fantasies, the rape victim actually enjoyed having sex even if it wasn't her idea at the outset. Self-defense in such instances plays better in court in rebutting consent and establishing that the victim was defending her honor and standing up for herself.[97] Putting up a struggle is what juries want to hear presented as evidence. The honorable rape victim is permitted, if not required, to perform an act of self-defense that appears to be indistinguishable from self-help.[98] The honorable victim, however, male or female, who resorts to self-help in cases that do not involve rape, is an avenger whose act is legally indefensible. The only difference in such cases of self-defense is the immediacy of the retaliation. In all other respects, the victim's actions and motives are the same.

As law professor Kenworthey Bilz frames it, "a true man would not pusillanimously wait for someone else to protect him; a pure woman would not run the risk that others would believe intercourse under the circumstances was consensual."[99] The rape victim is most certainly not required to make such a showing of self-defense. But without such evidence, she may be forced to endure a great deal more indignity under cross-examination. She will be characterized as the woman who didn't properly and forcefully say "no" at the time, and only now wants to punish an innocent man for her own earlier indiscretion.

The same defense of honor that is expected of rape victims morally applies to avengers. Legally, however, avengers cannot defend their honor unless they find themselves under imminent attack. However, if honor is the value that the law is ultimately protecting in cases of self-defense, why then can't vengeance also receive a similar legal excuse or affirmative defense? After all, vengeance is justified only when it amounts to a proportionate retaliation against another's wrong. Aside from the timing of the retaliation, the very same emotional elements are deemed exculpatory in both self-defense and revenge.

In looking at these various examples it is clear that self-defense provides a legal basis for granting a right of retaliation that otherwise does not exist. It demonstrates, once more, that the legal system has a sweet spot for honor crimes, for situations in which the attack is as much an assault on human dignity as it is an injury to the body. And the result is the privileging of self-defense in ways that legally makes it resemble revenge. Self-defense operates like yet another surreptitious way for the legal system to allow vengeance access inside courtrooms—although, as usual, it is referred to by another name. Given this apparent contradiction, it is difficult to see why vengeance is deemed so anathema to justice when retaliations delivered in self-defense are celebrated as the very embodiment of justice. The same moral principle is always at work—the defense of honor, which is not unlike the way the heat of passion can mitigate a murder while similar emotions present during an act of revenge are condemned as barbaric. Self-defense ends up as a legal excuse, while vengeance is always lawless and without justification.

All the while legal distinctions are being made despite the very slight differences between them. And these invariably turn out to be unprincipled distinctions because they lead to unequal treatment. The avenger is reclaiming his honor; the protective homeowner is defending hers. The avenger is no less bound by moral duty and guided by honor than the homeowner. Avengers refuse to be defined by the wrongdoer's act; the man who repels a deadly attack performs a similar safeguarding of personal dignity. The avenger will not be taken advantage of or treated like a mere plaything; the rape victim will not allow the rapist to believe—or a future juror to conclude—that she consented to what was a sexual predatory attack. Each is responding to another's wrong, and each might end up with a violent outcome. The only difference is that the avenger is taking the law into his or her own hands, while those who resort to self-defense are given a legal defense to the very same act that would be actionable if performed by a lawless avenger. Should the immediacy of the retaliation make that much of a difference when the emotional element, and the imperative of honor, are present in both situations?

Juries have been shown to be more sympathetic to husbands who end up killing their wives' paramours than say, a trash-talking lout at a bar. In many cases the husbands are only found guilty of voluntary manslaughter for which the court finds a reasonable excuse or explanation on account of an extreme emotional disturbance. But historically the legal principle that was often invoked to justify such a killing was yet another versatile application of self-defense. Catching your wife in bed with her lover and then immediately taking retaliatory action against him has a lot more to do with honor and dignity than self-defense. The same was true of the father who killed the man who ravaged his unmarried daughter. But a *true man* knows that a betrayed husband has an obligation to defend his own lost honor, and a father must avenge the rape of his defiled daughter. Yet in neither of these cases was the husband or father repelling a physical attack. The paramour and the rapist presented very little of a physical threat to the avenging husband or father. Juries of an earlier era essentially ignored the elements of self-defense and misapplied the defense to enable husbands and fathers to commit murder, not in retaliation for an imminent attack, but solely for the sake of reclaimed honor.

But even the modern rule, which gives betrayed husbands a license to commit voluntary manslaughter against their wives' paramours if the husband is found to have been suffering from an extreme emotional disturbance, is yet another fiction and double standard. What we see time and again is that emotion matters in certain preselected cases—such as with betrayed husbands. But the law, generally, won't take account of such raw feelings of anger or displays of heated emotion. The real principle at work seems to be that the very same emotions that ignite the taking of unlawful revenge can also, under certain circumstances, inflame retaliations that the law will look on more favorably. What appears to be an obvious case of premeditated murder is mitigated to manslaughter in the first degree. A man so dishonored and emasculated is given some license to take his liberties, immediately, against someone who caused him such shame. On a more global scale, no doubt America's war in Afghanistan involved similar emotional justifications.

Juries are more sympathetic to cuckolds than garden-variety avengers because of the emotional violation and decimated dignity they endured. These legal outcomes end up legitimizing a first strike that in other contexts would constitute murder in the first degree. No such similar legal loophole exists outside of the bedroom—especially in barrooms when two macho strangers get in a fight because one of them made an unwanted pass at the other man's wife. In cases of infidelity experienced by surprise, the emotions of vengeance are recharacterized as an "extreme emotional disturbance." And what looks like revenge is magically renamed voluntary manslaughter.

WHEN SELF-HELP IS PERMISSIBLE

Legally, a husband gets away without having to pay the price for committing a more violent crime. What results is a more acceptable moral outcome. But it's just vengeance dressed up to look respectable. Why not just call it what it is?

Temporary Insanity

Finally, there is yet one more special passageway offered under the law that gives cover to revenge: the range of defenses known as temporary insanity, irresistible impulse, and diminished capacity. Revenge attacks that can be characterized as emanating from a temporarily deranged mind will be excused. A legal defense by way of insanity, however, might look to another as a revenge strike that should otherwise be inexcusable under the law. Of course, the insanity defense has had a long ignominious history. Many believe that the entire defense, in whatever variety it presents itself, is all concocted and contrived, a cynical tactic defense attorneys reflexively use to avoid having their clients held legally accountable for their actions. Some states have abolished the defense altogether. After John Hinckley was found to be legally insane and acquitted on the charge of attempting to assassinate President Ronald Reagan in 1981 (all somehow tied to an imaginary love affair he had with the actress Jodi Foster), the general mood for the defense soured even further.

The insanity defense can be traced to the *M'Naughten* case in London in 1843, which gave rise to a test bearing its name. To establish a defense on the ground of temporary insanity, "it must be clearly proved that, at the time of the committing of the act, the party accused was laboring under such a defect of reason, from disease of the mind, as to not know the nature and quality of the act he was doing, or, if he did know, that he did not know what he was doing was wrong." Since then there have been various modifications to the standard, and even to the definition of the defense itself. The "irresistible impulse" insanity defense, for instance, added volitional impairment to the test. By invoking "the science of psychiatry," the 1954 Supreme Court decision in *Durham v. United States* dispensed with both the M'Naughten test and the one based on "irresistible impulse" and created a new rule that the "accused is not criminally responsible if his unlawful act was the product of mental disease or mental defect."[100]

Appreciating all the cynicism surrounding these theories and their impact on justice, Steven Pinker refers to the insanity defense as "dueling rent-a-shrinks and ingenious abuse excuses." He writes, "The *Durham* decision and similar insanity rules, by distinguishing behavior that is a product of brain condition from behavior that is something else, threatens to turn every advance in our understanding of the mind into an erosion of responsibility."[101] As Pinker sees it, the moral outrage that many feel is based on the fallacy that because someone can't be deterred from committing a crime—either because he or she is acting under an uncontrollable impulse or is overcome with a mental disease—he or she should not be held personally responsible for his or her actions. He argues that even for those criminal defendants who have brain damage or suffer from other forms of psychopathology, "we do not have to allow lawyers to loose them on the rest of us."[102]

The insanity defense works on the presumption, as a matter of law, that a wrongdoer who commits an act while under the influence of a diseased mind can't be held personally accountable. But why must one necessarily cancel out the other? Insanity, temporary or otherwise, should not be tantamount to blanket innocence. Law professor and criminologist Norval Morris wondered why, for instance, should mental illness, even if taken to be genuine rather than feigned, be entitled to a special defense whereas extreme social adversity is not?[103] "Social adversity is grossly more potent in the pressure toward criminality, certainly toward all forms of street crime as distinct from white collar crime, than is any psychotic condition."[104] And yet extreme conditions of poverty, for instance, do not furnish a legal excuse or affirmative defense for criminal behavior, whereas the insanity defense automatically does. The conditions of the wrongdoer's diseased mind could be completely fabricated, whereas poverty is not so easily staged. The same is true for blindness and deafness: neither would reasonably furnish an absolute excuse from a criminal act. And yet we are all sympathetic to human beings who manage under such impairments.

The insanity defense, meanwhile, is both used and abused in instances of murder where a wrongdoer is deemed not responsible for his crime. Insanity is rarely invoked as a defense in cases of burglary, theft, or rape even though an insane person is as capable of committing an act of lesser severity where his judgment is impaired through some form of mental sickness. The insanity defense surfaces most frequently to avoid murder convictions and death sentences. This only deepens the public's cynicism toward the legal system—the general feeling that the system is itself rigged, that it can be gamed by lawyers in conspiracy with mental health professionals. Many factors and social circumstances influence criminal behavior, but only mental impairment results in an absolute excuse. The psychological is favored over the social despite each having some bearing on human life. It is for this reason that some have argued that rather than supplying an absolute special defense, mental disorder, to the extent to which it even exists, should serve only as a mitigating factor, making it no different from the more general defenses of self-defense or duress. Mental defect would then apply only to the degree of culpability and should not constitute an automatic exonerating defense.

But a more serious moral problem with the insanity defense is not that it can be feigned but that it is sometimes applied to those wrongdoers who were perfectly rational and righteous in their actions, and the insanity plea is encouraged by the legal system as the only way to avoid a death sentence. This twisted outcome is responsible for yet another type of cynicism, another way for the insanity defense to be manipulated to an immoral end. On the one hand the insanity defense is asserted to protect wrongdoers who don't deserve it; and on the other it distorts the truth and dishonors the actions of avengers who were completely of their right minds when they committed the crime and are proud of their actions. With justified vengeance not available as a legal defense, avengers are encouraged to pretend to have been temporarily insane. An act arising out of honor is debased by lies or mitigated circumstances. The avenger would prefer to own up to, if not extol, what she did and why she did it. Instead, as a concession to a legal system that will not allow vengeance to serve as a legal excuse, the avenger is advised to lie and dishonor the virtue of her deed.

Susan Jacoby tells the story of Francine Hughes, who, in 1977, took revenge against her abusive husband by pouring gasoline around the bed while he was asleep, burning him alive. Years of victimization and violence resulted in one redemptive act of escape for herself and her four small children. On the final day of his life, James Hughes beat Francine, forced her to have sex with him, and then burned all of her schoolbooks in their backyard. She was taking business classes at a local community college. She wanted a new life; James was quite satisfied with the one she was living. The only way to protect herself and save her children was to gain her freedom by killing him. The story of Francine Hughes was made into an Emmy- and Golden Globe–nominated television movie, *The Burning Bed* (1985), starring Farrah Fawcett.

Francine Hughes was charged with premeditated murder, but a jury in Lansing, Michigan, acquitted her by reason of temporary insanity. A short while later she was released from custody altogether when a psychiatrist pronounced her to be sane. So much for all that scientific evidence that was produced at trial showing that she had not been of sound mind when she committed the act. Of course, the jury only ruled that she was "temporarily insane," so there was no reason to treat her as if she had a permanent condition.

Jacoby points out that the use of the insanity defense in such instances is merely a way for the legal system to avoid having to exact a harsh penalty when the facts call out for more compassionate and merciful treatment.[105] In essence, the legal system finds yet another way to sanction revenge. But surely this outcome is not consistent with equal protection under the law. Francine Hughes committed a capital crime but was nevertheless ultimately excused from all personal responsibility and avoided any legal consequence from her actions. James Hughes may have been a vile and loathsome husband, but did he deserve to die, and to be killed in such a gruesome manner? He was burned alive while asleep. Emotionally, jurors refused to punish Francine commensurate with her crime—or perhaps they didn't regard her actions as criminal. Should she have been made to burn in her bed, as well? The jurors allowed her to exploit a legal defense that gave her a pass on a revenge killing—one that was no doubt deserved. Other avengers, however, either because they were less sympathetic or because a jury was unwilling to apply the insanity defense in their favor, would have been convicted of murder and perhaps even received a death sentence.

The insanity defense offered these Michigan jurors an emotional escape hatch through which they avoided having to hold Francine Hughes legally accountable for murdering her husband. The moral outrage of Francine Hughes's domestic dilemma, and the natural emotions that a jury inevitably applied to this case, allowed this crime to be treated as if it was not a crime at all. She was very quickly released from a mental facility, miraculously pronounced cured. This sequence of events gives the appearance of a legal system that apparently looked the other way so that Francine Hughes could avenge her miserable marriage.

At the time of this murder trial, battered woman's syndrome was not widely known. Feminists disapproved of the Hughes verdict not because they didn't believe Francine to be innocent. They knew that her vindication was not an act of insanity. For years she had been subjected to repeated torment by her menacing, imprisoning husband. When she finally had the courage to pour gasoline around his bed, she had never been more rational, right-minded, and thoroughly sane in her entire life. Why should she cheapen the dignity of her act by claiming that she suffered from some temporary mental impairment? This was an act of liberation; it was the product of a righteous mind, not a diseased one.

The very emotions that Francine Hughes called on to kill her husband are indispensable to revenge. Her actions were rational and deliberate, in the same way that vengeance is not incompatible with sound thinking. Yes, of course there are psycho avengers who can't control themselves and who give vengeance a bad name. They start blood feuds; they treat the *talion* like a slot machine; they act without either justification or any sense of proportion. And they won't listen to reason. They become the poster children for revenge run amuck, and they scare society back into the arms of the state's monopoly over revenge. But no matter how one regards their actions, reckless though they may have been, these actions aren't necessarily indicative of insanity and won't be treated as justified revenge. Michael S. Moore refers to such false avengers as "unhinged by powerful emotional storms."[106] Susan Jacoby writes that this is precisely what Heinrich von Kleist had in mind when he wrote the novel *Michael Kohlhaas*.[107] One thing is for certain: this example of irrational, implacable vengeance is not what animated Francine Hughes.

Some believed that a more traditional theory of self-defense was a more appropriate defense strategy for Francine Hughes's lawyer to pursue. The fact that James Hughes was not imminently violent was offset by the deplorable backstory of their marriage: his violence was pervasive and perpetual, capable of surfacing at unpredictable moments—without the slightest provocation. Francine's deed was more akin to a preventative, preemptive strike: the legal justification available to nations under international law. In 2011, in New York, a Queen's County jury acquitted Barbara Sheehan of murdering her husband even though she used two guns and fired eleven bullets while her allegedly abusive husband was shaving. The evidence showed that she had been the victim of a sustained pattern of violent abuse over many years. The jury believed that she reasonably feared for her life and killed her husband in self-defense, even though it didn't appear as if his first strike was in any way imminent. Her husband's brother, dissatisfied with the verdict, said this about the jury: "People make decisions based on emotion."[108]

Yes, they do. And sometimes the law supports those emotional leanings.

Preemptive self-defense, or, as in the legal theory that apparently acquitted Barbara Sheehan, battered woman's syndrome, essentially recognizes the right of a wife to kill a husband before the next battery arises—even though the retaliation is clearly premeditated and the abuse is not technically imminent. But that is an artfully reimagined reading of the law of self-defense. Barbara Sheehan's act far better resembles old-fashioned vengeance: the just deserts owing to a most deserving husband.

Could a similar argument be made in support of a rape victim who manages to kill her rapist *after* the assault? In such cases she would undoubtedly be charged with homicide and not retroactive self-defense. Why the disparate treatment? Why shouldn't both classes of women receive the same legal defense? After all, each was assaulted sexually by overpowering males who could not be stopped the first time. Is it because, once again, crimes committed in the context of intimate family relationships are treated differently under the law? In this case, the rapist is a stranger who receives more rights than a violent husband who rapes his wife every day. (Is there any wonder why there are so few women willing to come forward with rape allegations, and even fewer convictions of such crimes?) Wives can murder the husbands who repeatedly rape them at any point after the last assault; rape victims of a single assault, however, cannot retroactively avenge themselves against their less familiar attackers. Deep emotion is once again taken into account, the very same emotions that are most active in vengeance. However, outside the context of those family relationships, the legal system would judge the conduct to be a lawless act of revenge, and it would be granted no excuse and shown no sympathy.

Western nations that make no allowance for capital punishment are equally confused on what to do in cases where the avenger is perfectly sane, but where the legal system's response to the crime is itself crazy making. In July 2004, Vitaly Kaloev killed the Swiss air traffic controller who, two years earlier, was negligently responsible for a cargo plane's midair collision with a passenger jet. Kaloev's wife and children were passengers on that plane.

Kaloev received an eight-year sentence from a Swiss court for stabbing the man to his death. For the first two years after the collision, the air traffic control company, Skyguide, refused to take responsibility or apologize. Kaloev finally snapped. His lawyer argued that Kaloev acted under diminished capacity. The sentence was reduced, and he was finally released a few months after four employees of Skyguide were found guilty of negligence and manslaughter. Three of the four were sentenced to only one year in prison; the fourth merely had to pay a fine. Given the premeditated act and absent provocation or a situation of self-defense, Kaloev ended up spending very little time in jail—all due to his attorney having mounted a successful temporary insanity defense. The four men responsible for killing his family, however, spent virtually no time in jail.[109] The problem is that Kaloev was *not* temporarily insane; he was simply a man whose family was taken away from him without even an acknowledgment of his loss, much less an apology. As for the Swiss legal system and its handling of this matter, no one is prepared to vouch for its sanity.

The application of the insanity defense in the case of Francine Hughes (and even, to some degree, in the Swiss case) once more establishes that crimes committed in a familial context or against family members—driven by emotional bonds and passionate feelings—can, at times, be judged very differently from other crimes. When the legal system allows itself the privilege, vengeful impulses can find a home within the law, inside the very same courtrooms that otherwise banish emotion from its marbled walls and condemn vengeance as unworthy of any favor.

But, to those who live outside of courtrooms, it all appears to be a charade, a complete lack of honesty within the law. Each of these loopholes is ultimately a sham, a way to disguise vengeance as mitigation rather than redemption. Heat of passion or mental impairment is invoked as an excuse. But the entire time the avenger was wholly rational while engaged in a premeditated, intentional act of righteous sanity.

Hamlet might have acted insane, but he wasn't doing so in order to convince a Danish court to legally excuse him pursuant to a plea of temporary insanity. There is honor in payback; there is absolutely no honor in proclaiming "the devil made me do it" or "I was hearing strange voices in my head" or in creating the pretense that some alchemy of "animal spirits" were at work, conspiring to rob the wrongdoer of his sound mind. For the righteous avenger, the revenge impulse was irresistible not because of some mental defect but because of moral necessity. The avenger's mental capacity was not diminished but, rather, enhanced—all in the service of honor.

In the film *A Time to Kill*, an African-American man in the Deep South whose ten-year-old daughter was raped, urinated on, and battered by beer bottles thrown at her body, ends up killing the two men who scarred his daughter's life forever. His attorney seeks to assert a defense of not guilty by reason of insanity. The crime occurred in a state where the death penalty was available. Surely a Southern jury will gladly convict a black man who kills a white man—regardless of the reason. And the father is likely to be executed for this crime should he be found guilty.

The defendant does not wish to undergo the psychological testing necessary to establish that he had gone temporarily insane on seeing his daughter so visibly violated and left for dead. He also knows he was most decidedly *not* insane on that day; he was mad, for sure, but not suffering from madness. His act in avenging his daughter was necessary, not delusional. In fact, his mental clarity had never been more acute, his moral compass never more accurate. What kind of a father would hide behind a temporary insanity defense when his daughter had suffered that much pain and had undergone such a nightmarish experience? He could not properly reclaim the honor of his family and redeem the debt owed to his daughter if his actions in avenging the crime were attributed to a mental defect rather than an absolute moral duty.[110]

Noting the dilemma that righteous avengers face given the appeal of the temporary insanity defense, Susan Jacoby observes, "By obfuscating the motives and questioning the rationality of one who commits an act of revenge, they deny the avenger his or her dignity in exchange for freedom."[111]

And such a bargain, where dignity is exchanged for freedom, was not one this father was prepared to make. He acted out of honor and would not deny the moral force of his deed simply to avoid going to jail—or even the electric chair. If there were an act of insanity, it would be in asserting the insanity defense, not in forsaking it.

Of course, these decisions are much easier to make in art than in life. The daughter in *True Grit*; the father in *A Time to Kill*; Hamlet, the avenging son whose very name is synonymous with conflicted vengeful duty: they are all fictional. They can afford making bold statements by undertaking righteous acts. Would an actual father risk a death sentence as a testament of fatherly love? Well, let's return to a real example: Would it have been saner for Francine Hughes to remain in the same house with her violent husband, exposing her children, and herself, to daily trauma and the possibility of a violent death? If the answer is no, why then couldn't her vengeance have simply been recorded as justice, rather than insanity, in a court of law?

EIGHT RELEASE REVENGE

In the summer of 2008, Cambodians readied themselves for a unique public trial, the first of its kind, perhaps anywhere. It involved the prosecution of five former leaders of the Khmer Rouge. These men, now all aged, decrepit, and far from threatening, were once part of a gang of genocidal thugs— not quite as talented as the Nazis in such gruesome affairs, but surely no amateurs in matters of mass murder. From 1975 to 1979, the Khmer Rouge killed over 1.7 million Cambodians, fully one-quarter of the population— murdered by way of execution, torture, starvation, and overwork from forced-labor brigades. (The Nazis, by comparison, killed two out of every three Jews of Europe, and a high percentage of homosexuals and Gypsies, as well.)

What made this trial different, however, different from Nuremberg, different from Israel's prosecution of Adolf Eichmann, was that it was established as a hybrid tribunal—as both a criminal proceeding and a civil trial. Therefore, the complaining party, the plaintiff, was not just Cambodia, as a nation, but hundreds of its citizens who had been victims of the Khmer Rouge. No other country devastated by genocide had ever undertaken such a trial before where the victims themselves were parties to the action.[1] Cambodians responded to this trial with great anticipation and promise. The trial offered the people their own Nuremberg moment, their own South African Truth and Reconciliation Commission—even though the class of defendants was small, comprising only five elderly Khmer Rouge leaders.

Of all the differences between those earlier efforts at achieving post-atrocity justice and this Cambodian spectacle, the most significant was that actual victims were being given an opportunity to have a voice and play a role in the proceedings. Upward of thirteen hundred Cambodians applied to take part in the trial as designated official victims. And as victims in this special proceeding, they would be permitted to bring their own separate civil actions against the five men. Roughly half of the victims sought their own civil remedies. Unlike typical victims in international tribunals, or even the victims that crowd into American courthouses, these Cambodians were not relegated to the backbenches of the courtroom, called on merely to offer testimony about the crime on behalf of the state. No, they were to about receive a far more dignified official role as actual plaintiffs, true parties to the action.

And there was more. As plaintiffs to a civil action attached to the criminal case, they were permitted to participate in the investigation, to be represented by their own lawyers, to call their own witnesses, and even to question the accused. Indeed, even more astoundingly, given the treatment customarily afforded to victims, these parties—actual partners in the prosecution with the state—were allowed to address the court personally without so much as having their voices filtered through their counsel. By their very presence, in such an elevated position of importance in a legal proceeding conducted in front of the entire nation, they stood face-to-face and confronted the aged men whose hands, now wrinkled and arthritic, would never be able to wash clean all that Cambodian blood. Fortunately, this human confrontation was buffered by the apparatus of law. The confines of the proceeding made sure that this encounter would never become violent.

Ly Monysar, one of the victims who applied for official victim status said, "Only killing them will make me feel calm. I want them to suffer the way I suffered. I say this from my heart." Sok Chear admitted that if she had a choice, she would prefer to slice the five elderly men of the former Khmer Rouge and pour salt in their wounds. And if permitted even further liberties, she would beat and torture them, then top it all off with electric shock in order to get them to speak the truth of what they had done to her family.[2] Fortunately, for the defendants, who no doubt deserved all of this and more, Sok Chear, as one of the official victims, would have to satisfy herself with a far less violent, although still meaningful, role.

What was most unusual about this innovative tribunal was that it fully empowered victims—but only within the context of a trial. It offered victims and avengers the very thing implicitly promised under the social contract of enlightened societies: a true and respectful day in court, in exchange for the forfeiting of their right to seek private vengeance. They would be heard, in open court, in a criminal proceeding that had the power to punish. There would be a direct encounter between the offenders and the victims—without filters and procedural barriers, and without grandstanding lawyers sucking up all the oxygen. These complaining parties may not have gotten all they had wanted, but a full hearing they would receive.

And this hearing would comport with all the furnishings of legal justice, which meant that the plaintiffs would not be granted a license to resort to violence. And yet they would nonetheless still feel avenged. The sensation of moral relief comes with having their private cause of action adjudicated, and with the knowledge that the wrongdoers would be punished on their behalf. Indeed, these victims were about to be afforded the same center stage position in the trial as would be provided to the accused.

And from that position of empowerment and focal attention, victims were able to tell their stories of what had happened to them and their families and to speak to their outrage—openly and without interruption or prejudice. While many had filed companion civil actions against the five men, their claims were forever hitched to a monumental criminal proceeding. The endgame was still punishment, not solely compensation. But even with civil recourse sitting shotgun, the symbolic restitution they received was not meaningless. They did not reap large restitution checks, but memorials were erected and museums renamed to acknowledge their individual losses. Cultural memory, and the honoring of the dead, turned out to be the most valuable civil remedy of all. And they were satisfied—without receiving much in the way of traditional monetary relief and without inflicting the kind of torture and commensurate suffering they believed the wrongdoers otherwise deserved.

Commenting on the novelty of this proceeding and the inclusion of those who would in the ordinary course have been silenced and unavenged, Diane Orentlicher, special counsel to the Justice Initiative, said, "There has been a growing recognition, after 15 years of international and hybrid courts like this one, not to exclude victims from the justice that is being dispensed on their behalf."[3]

In spite of a bloodied past that could very well have turned into a bloodbath, a Cambodian courtroom somehow managed to hold all of that consolidated emotion and rage without incident. All violence was averted, held in check by a system of justice that set limits but not without appreciating its obligation to help victims discharge their vengeful feelings and emotionally recoup their losses.

We don't know whether the Cambodian architects of this proceeding ever read Aeschylus or whether they were familiar with *Eumenides*, the third portion of the *Oresteia* trilogy, but they seemed to have captured the very essence of Athena's role for the Furies in public trials. The Cambodian trial featured not just a dry presentation of facts assembled by state prosecutors and defense counsel. What was most active in these proceedings were the emotions of the victims, the full sweep and variety of their anger and indignation, welcomed into the courtroom—not dismissed, interrupted, deemed irrelevant, silenced, admonished, browbeaten, but fully represented, as if the trial would have no meaning unless these raw feelings were on full display. The Cambodian legal system was being asked to host all of those feelings in its grandest courtroom—to endure the anger and to listen to the sadness. Why? Courts are morally bound and it should be legally incumbent upon them to do so; to do anything less only invites vigilante justice. The message was sent throughout the country: the court is open for business, and, when it came to Cambodia's darkest tragedy, it means business.

It was particularly interesting that the trial took place in Cambodia, given the nation's long-standing twist on the *talion*, where an eye for an eye had always been reinterpreted as a head for an eye.[4] Culturally, they always believed that victims were entitled to more. The Cambodians have taken the *talionic* formula, modified it with modern principles of legal as well as restorative justice, and found a better way to achieve measured justice in the most transcendent of all trials—precisely because it took into account the full measure of what victims needed to feel satisfied.

In the United States, and in many countries around the world, there is no statute of limitations on murder—legally and morally (although, regrettably, there is for rape and robbery). And the burden to punish the guilty—to ensure that they do not get away with murder—is always greater with mass murder. To undertake and give voice to such trials invariably invites a perfect storm of amassed emotion—on display with the entire nation watching. There can be no limitation on how long these victims are permitted to hold onto their grief; no demand should be made to put it behind them so they can move on with their lives.

Human beings can't simply forget, and they should not be made to do so. And it is folly to assume that victims will not possess feelings of righteous anger and rage toward those who had committed unspeakable crimes against them. This is especially true in societies where criminals do not receive their due and victims never receive vindication. Citizens will invariably internalize all the failures of justice—the empty promise, the lost opportunity. As Susan Jacoby astutely observes, "To permit vindictive rage to dominate one's entire existence is assuredly destructive, but vengeful anger is at its most powerful and pervasive when there are no mechanisms for releasing it through legitimate channels."[5]

And that's what courtrooms are for: legitimate channels to release vengeful anger and where private pain can receive a public hearing. But that's not how we understand it in the United States. We have courtrooms, for sure, and they are grand, and spacious, but they have a very different purpose. In America, courtrooms are the home court for lawyers to prance and preen, object and cross-examine, approach the bench or sit at their tables and stew with mock resentment. It is in such gladiatorial arenas where the hired guns and the sharks meet scowl-to-scowl to scorch the earth. Courtrooms are where cases are quickly dispensed and not where victims feel welcome. Courtrooms are conveyer belts of judicial efficiency and not deliberative places of moral inquiry dedicated to the search for the truth.

This recent Cambodian model, however, demonstrates the very essence of what a courtroom can be and what a legal system can do, and must do, in fulfilling its obligation to its people. The fault lies not with the untamed emotions of victims and their always active, vengeful imaginations. The problem is the law's failure to do what is just and what citizens reasonably expect: the delivery of justice that avenges wrongs.

In Supreme Court Justice Potter Stewart's concurring opinion in *Furman v. Georgia*, he wrote, "The instinct for *retribution is part of the nature of man*, and channeling that instinct in the administration of justice serves an important purpose in promoting the stability of a society governed by law. When people begin to believe that organized society is unwilling or unable to impose upon criminal offenders the punishment they 'deserve,' then there are sown the seeds of anarchy, of self-help, vigilante justice, and lynch law" (emphasis added).[6]

We all know that the Supreme Court justice was addressing an elemental truth: the natural history of humankind—our most natural inclinations—depends on revenge as an instinctual necessity, the very first principle of moral order. And in forfeiting the right to avenge—a right so precious and unique to humankind—men and women had every reason to believe that the state would punish wrongdoers in accordance with their moral blameworthiness. But that expectation has gone unfulfilled, and a great deal of broken trust now exists between citizens and the legal systems that have failed to protect them. And even worse, vindication has virtually no meaning in modern American courtrooms.

Actually, the pervasive malfunction of legal systems throughout the world has led to a circular revenge paradox. And it goes something like this: Revenge is moral, but it can leave behind a big mess. In the eyes of civilization, it is perceived as always lethal, never satisfied—vengeance as virus that knows no cure. The state fears all manner of self-help that is retaliatory and violent in nature, as well as the different varieties of vigilante and frontier justice. It is believed that individuals who are personally invested in payback are unable to set limits, to take the proper measure of their losses, to stay within the bounds of proportionality, and to move on with their lives. What is feared is not so much revenge but its repercussions—the social costs of spillover and excess. Moral revenge presents great risks, which is why legal retribution, imperfect though it may be, is the default position for the delivery of justice.

Ironically, however, the state, in taking on the duty of retribution through the rule of law, not only divests the emotional experience that epitomizes revenge, but adds insult to injury by subtracting from the finely tuned equilibrium of the *talion*. The state does not pay enough attention to numbers and ends up collecting too little on the debt. The score is unsettled; the disarmed avenger never gets close to even. Victims are shortchanged, cheated out of what they deserve.

Citizens begin to see that courts are actually poor proxies for revenge. Plea bargains feel like pennies on the dollar to victims with massive unpaid claims; they are bargains only from the perspective of wrongdoers. And in taking too little, in sloughing off on its retributive duties, the state inadvertently welcomes the return of the righteous avenger. It brings about the very thing it abhors the most, the very thing it never wanted to see again—all due to its own neglect, the all too casual treatment of victim suffering. The legal system might not lose any sleep over the *talionic* deficits it runs, but the moral universe has a keener eye for measurement, and avengers are notoriously unable to sleep.

And that sense of being cheated—this time by the institution that was entrusted with the task of making things right—ironically provides victims and vigilantes with the moral authority to move the revenge meter from "not enough" to something more commensurate with what is actually "deserved." The fear of excess revenge drives judicial philosophy and economy, but the reality of trivialized punishments reignites the victim's dormant, but always present, revenge instinct. Without the law's failure, the avenger would remain in a permanent state of retirement.

The moral imperative of getting even bears no relationship at all to what accounts for civil and criminal justice in America. We never ask victims at the conclusion of a trial or legal process whether they feel vindicated and, if they are not altogether satisfied, what would make them feel better—what more could be accomplished under the law. Legal systems smugly proclaim that justice has been done when, in fact, no such justice has occurred at all. What is meant by "justice" is simply administrative, efficiency-enhancing justice—a legal matter that received a docket number and a final disposition but with little regard for the moral legitimacy of the outcome or the relative satisfaction of the true parties to the action.

But it doesn't have to be this way. The answer is not to do away with legal systems and return to the purported Dark Ages of vengeance, but to redeploy legal systems correctly, more humanely, and with a greater appreciation of the moral universe. Courtrooms have to become true houses of justice, where the therapeutic, restorative, emotionally complex feelings of vengeance are integrated into the legal relief granted. The signatures on the social contract signify mutual obligation. Therefore, these obligations must be taken seriously. Citizens surrender private vengeance; the government provides justice that takes accounts of the human need for moral closure. That mandate has never quite registered with the state. It is time to finally hold law enforcement and the judiciary accountable for doing their jobs. And an essential part of those jobs is to avenge the crimes committed against its citizens, to give victims a truer sense that justice is being done on their behalf—that *they*, and not some abstract legal principle or proclaimed state interest, are the reasons why we have public courtrooms in the first place. Like it or not, law enforcement officers and the caretakers of the judicial process serve as surrogates for victims who are looking to the law to do what an old-school avenger would never tolerate leaving undone.

Recognizing the morally corrosive effects of depersonalizing the prosecution of crimes, Jeffrie G. Murphy has written that "revenge ought to be institutionalized by the state; that is, that the state, taking on the personae of crime victims, should elevate (at least some of) the private grievances of individuals to the stature of public grievances."[7]

There are many possible ways to accomplish this aim of doing a better job in prosecuting and punishing the guilty with the victim in mind. And the rewards are many. In addition to earning renewed trust, the legal system would show itself as an entity capable of feeling and less hostile to human emotion. Victims would experience the difference in treatment instantly. Instead of the legal system's usual display of clinical coldness and emotional dispassion, the law would appear to be acting in solidarity with the victim's suffering. Even the imperfections of constitutional justice, with its focal point on the rights of the accused and the burdens placed on the state, which often result in the acquittal of wrongdoers, would be less profoundly felt if victims became true partners in the pursuit of justice.

What we have now is morally intolerable. The legal system is broken; it has been broken for a long time. Regrettably no one has the heart, or the common decency, to say it out loud. Far too many victims walk away from legal proceedings embittered. Few leave ennobled or vindicated. A new paradigm in which victims become genuine stakeholders in the cases brought on their behalf would have immeasurable value in reestablishing a connection between justice and what actually awaited citizens as they ascended the steps of courtrooms all across America.

The legal system's monopoly on revenge is missing the passion of the avenger. It isn't worthy of the public's trust without it, and it can't regain its broader mandate if it doesn't reclaim it. Because of the wide range of emotions that aren't permitted to lubricate the legal machinery of the state, justice always seems to be grinding in gridlock and lacking moral purpose.

A number of legal scholars and moral philosophers have speculated on what would happen if justice and vengeance shared a greater institutional symmetry—if revenge was introduced, formally, into the conversation about justice, and where victims became part of that conversation.[8] Legal systems would dispense with all pretense of emotionally detached, solely reason-based decision making. The old fears about private vengeance would be cast aside. As Walter Berns suggests, if vengeance produces a mess, it will be tidied up by the state. And victims will be pleased to see the state finally act with moral indignation rather than with the cold calculus of robotic legalism.[9] Such reform, Berns notes, might even result in ancillary deterrence benefits. After all, once potential wrongdoers are introduced to a new sheriff in town in the form of an avenging legal system, they will come to understand that the state is not out solely for legal retribution. The law will take on the passions, and show the human face, of moral revenge. Wrongdoers will have an extra incentive not to break the law lest they be forced to come up against a legal system that aligns the interests of justice with the restorative benefits of vengeance.

If the legal system can adopt a new look, it will no longer be familiar just to trained lawyers but also to regular people. Revenge is justice with a human face, and the legal system must be called on to provide justice that is recognizably human. When the law serves the emotional needs of victims, it carries with it the moral authority of revenge.

One way to accomplish this is for courtrooms to be opened up to victims so that they can appear not as witnesses and spectators but as equal partners. Victims must have their day(s) in court because that's what courtrooms are for. Courthouses are the true forums for the beaten and betrayed. This is where the wounded naturally come, where they seek both legal and emotional relief. And it is for this reason that they must be made to feel welcome. Perhaps most important of all, courthouses must become places where the role of the victim and the rights of the victim are taken seriously.

Law professors Stephanos Bibas and George P. Fletcher have each, separately, lamented the absence of human involvement in the law and have taken aim at what might be its worst culprit: plea bargains.[10] Most criminal cases never make it to trial. They are tragically resolved through plea bargains that offer wrongdoers unjustified discounts on punishments that ought to have been paid in full. It is during this pretrial stage that marginalized victims wait helplessly as lawyers and prosecutors engage in the cynical sport of trading down on the punishment that is otherwise deserved. The negotiations all take place in secret, beyond the reach of victims and galaxies away from the general public. There is hardly any accountability—to the victim or the public. And prosecutors are not required to explain publically how the rule of law can be so subverted. The bargain-basement punishments that hardcore criminals receive every day simply cannot be reconciled with the strict laws that remain so fixedly on the books.

We have come a long way from the morality plays of colonial times when courtrooms were routinely used for the ventilation of private grievances made public.[11] Citizens served as their own lawyers, spoke in plain English, and made themselves heard about the harms and indignities they wished to see resolved in a court of law. Nearly everyone agreed that such an outlet was preferable to becoming an outlaw. The courtroom served as an appropriate substitute for private vengeance because, like revenge, the endgame of the proceeding was vindication for the victim. That was the whole point. The ultimate ruling couldn't merely just comport with the law. It had to make common sense and feel emotionally right to the complaining party as well. And in such a civilized setting, even if the outcome was less then satisfactory, at least victims were treated with dignity and respect, knowing that their participation was both welcome and necessary. Victims didn't rush out of courtrooms feeling that their only alternatives now were either frontier or poetic justice.

But this is no longer the case. Victims are always cast aside on the periphery of decision making. And from the vantage point of exclusion, vengeance always looks more appealing than placing one's faith in the law. Indeed, the widely perceived futility of the legal system leads to the worst kind of law-lessness: self-help where the law is never even given a chance to make things right—the avenger preemptively denies the legal system the opportunity to fail, knowing that relying on the law is a waste of time. In the murky under-belly of the pedophilic priests and the Penn State sexual abuse scandals, the world was reminded of how helpless parents of sexually abused children can end up feeling, and how poor their legal remedies are. Jerry Sandusky, who was sentenced to 30 to 60 years in prison for his sexual molestation of at least ten boys over a fifteen-year period, seemed by many to have been underpunished for his crimes. He was by no means the first coach to have exploited his access to young boys. But he may have been among the most fortunate in having avoided the righteous revenge of his victims.

In 1984, Jeff Doucet, a karate coach in Louisiana, kidnapped one of his students, Jody Plauche, then eleven years old, took him to Disneyland, and sodomized him for ten days. After being arrested, Doucet was flown back to Baton Rouge but, unlike Sandusky, he never made it for his appointment with legal justice. Gary Plauche, the sexually abused boy's father, waited at the airport by a bank of telephones near the gate, removed a .38 snub-nosed revolver from his right boot, and fired a bullet into Doucet's brain from three feet away.[12] A father's justice trumped any chance of Doucet receiving the more conventional treatment of legal retribution, which all too often is unreliable and insufficient from the standpoint of victims.

So here was a display of moral revenge at its most improvisational, with the legal system given scant opportunity to run its usual course. Gary Plauche treated himself to the most selfish form of self-help. But might his intervening actions have been avoided altogether had he believed that he could experience the same vindication in a court of law as he managed to achieve by lurking in an airport with a gun?

In his important book *The Machinery of Justice*, Bibas writes, "Partici-pants see the law as more fair and legitimate when they have some control over the process and feel they have been heard, whether or not they control ultimate outcomes. A participatory role and fair and respectful treatment would go a long way toward addressing victim's grievances, regardless of outcomes."[13]

Even with a bureaucracy as impenetrable as the legal system, there are various crevices through which victims' voices can be heard. Under the current criminal justice model, victims are shielded from the legal process until the very end, after guilt has already been established. Only then, and not in every case, will they be heard, during sentencing, where they can finally, and openly, express their grief. But there is a long, interminably grueling, and uneven road that runs from the arrest of a suspect to the punishment of a wrongdoer. Empowering victims and giving them a genuine sense of involvement in the legal process requires that they be permitted to participate in the pretrial stages of the case. It is at pretrial where prosecutors make the pivotal decisions that culminate in whether the case will even to proceed to trial. In the vast majority of cases, the heavy lifting is done outside the presence of the judge, involving only the prosecution and defense counsel as they haggle and horse trade, trying to arrive at some plea agreement—an agreement to which the victim is most certainly not a party or participant. His views are not solicited; her wishes are not honored.

Victim impact statements already validate the victim's need to address the court and speak to his or her loss. (But, generally, only in capital murder cases.) Instead of merely having these statements read by the judge, they should be read aloud—by the parties making them. And instead of having the crime's impact elicited only during the sentencing phase of the trial, there is no reason why victims can't speak with, ask questions of, respond to the lawyers, and even the defendant, during the plea-bargaining stage, the guilt phase of the trial, and, finally, during the sentencing hearing. Consigning victims to make their appearance only at the end of the proceeding when guilt has already been decided reduces them to an afterthought. The legal system doesn't want to hear from victims until sentencing, in part, because it abhors emotional histrionics, which would be unfair to the accused, and also because it doesn't wish to expose victims to cross-examination, which would be required under the confrontation clause of the Sixth Amendment. But the finger of accusation is most profoundly pointed when the wrongdoer must defend himself of the charges brought against him, and not when he or she has already been judged guilty. That's what it means to stand in judgment of another, and that's the posture victims wish to take.

The role of the public prosecutor could stand for some reform, too, if not a complete overhaul of attitude. Prosecutors should be required to consult with victims before they drop charges against a wrongdoer, enter into a plea bargain, or decide whether to appeal a sentence. The pretrial stage should not be such a black hole to victims. Of course, many prosecutors would claim that they are already under an obligation to inform victims about the progress of the case. Yet many victims complain that such encounters are perfunctory, occurring so far after the fact that they have no real meaning. The Jodie Foster film *The Accused* (1988) is a ruefully accurate depiction of the wide gap between plea bargaining and victim involvement. The victim can end up being among the last to know that the wrongdoers who caused her harm have cut a deal that will result in an unconscionable underpunishment.[14] But even when prosecutors remember to call the victim to alert her of the status of the case, this is not the same thing as meaningfully consulting with her and accepting that no decision can be made without her approval.

Acknowledging the back deal nature of the plea-bargaining process, Bibas writes, "Currently, plea bargains work through brute force. Defendants promise to give prosecutors their pleas, and prosecutors in turn trade bargaining chips as a matter of unreviewable executive grace. They need not explain their actions nor have any particular reason for doing so. Plea bargains need to become less an exercise in power and more a discourse of reason."[15]

And during criminal trials, prosecutors should be reminded that they are standing before the law not only in their representative capacities as the state's lawyer, but also on behalf of the victim. The victim is the only party in a criminal proceeding not represented by a lawyer. Everyone believes, implicitly, that the state's attorney is also looking out for the victim—but that is simply not the case. Private attorneys who are retained to represent the victim are not permitted to participate in criminal trials. They can make speeches outside, on the courtroom steps, playing to the press, but they may not actually address the court. Indeed, there is generally little cooperation between the district attorney's office and the victim's private attorney. He or she often receives even less information than the victim himself. If private lawyers can't play a more constructive role, then prosecutors should announce themselves formally as the attorney for the people, *and* the victim as well.

If victims were to become equal partners with the state, if they were convinced to buy into the benefits of legal retribution over moral revenge, if they were offered a true ownership interest in the case, then at least decisions binding on them will have happened with their participation and under their watch. The more of a participatory role the victim is given, the less likely he or she will walk away from a legal proceeding believing that private vengeance is the only solution to his or her problem—even if the legal outcome turns out to be less than satisfactory. A courtroom environment that treats victims with dignity, offers them a seat at the table, listens to what they have to say, involves them in decision making, gives them an opportunity to address the court, and allows them to express their emotions, is a legal system that recognizes a higher calling for its courtrooms.

Forfeiting the right to avenge privately doesn't mean that vengeance cannot take place in another form, and in a different forum. In a civilized society, courtrooms are the places where victims can localize their grief and settle their scores. But that only works if the legal system accepts its duty as designated avenger, if it embraces its role as even-tempered surrogate. Courtrooms can't serve a score-settling function when plea bargains overwhelmingly outnumber public trials, victims' voices are marginalized, and the punishment of wrongdoers is more of a crapshoot than a moral imperative.

Victims must have legal standing in criminal cases to question judicial rulings. And they should have an independent right to appeal lower-court decisions even if the government is satisfied with the outcome. In cases of violent felonies, the victim should be granted a right to appeal a sentence, or the right to an interlocutory appeal of an especially revolting plea bargain that has the potential of transforming a calmly composed victim into an irate vigilante.

As law professor Lee Eisenstat points out, prosecutors and judges continually make decisions that are binding on victims, and yet victims are without legal standing to challenge those rulings.[16] Prosecutors determine how to try the case, and even whether to try the case. Those tactical decisions might result in an acquittal—without ever having received the victim's input. And the victim is forever stuck with and bound by those decisions. Judges make rulings on evidentiary matters, Fourth Amendment challenges on the gathering of evidence, and the admissibility of that evidence. Those rulings end up being dispositive of what ultimately happens at trial. Victims are expected to sit stone-faced throughout. As Eisenstat has written, "Victims deserve the right to be actively involved in decisions regarding punishment, even if they are motivated by revenge."[17]

And it's possible to go even further. Victims can be given the right of a veto that he or she can exercise at the pretrial stage.[18] If the victim is satisfied with the negotiated plea as it is presented, if he or she believes it to be fair and, perhaps most important, if he or she participated in arriving at the plea, then the victim can sign off with a release, as a party to the criminal trial, indicating that he or she consents to the terms of the plea arrangement. Should the victim reasonably find the plea bargain to be too lenient, he or she should then be free to withhold consent, refuse to sign the release, and exercise his or her veto power. Subject to the rules governing speedy trials, if the prosecutor and wrongdoer cannot agree on an offer that the victim can accept, the case must go to trial. This model of justice adopts the retributive elements of just deserts and combines it with a victim's preference, a right of refusal, reasonably exercised—just like any party to a civil action, acting in good faith, can do.

This retained veto power doesn't only have to operate at the pretrial stage. Victims could actually exercise this veto over all prosecutorial and sentencing decisions in cases of violent crime. The state might be satisfied with the verdict, but it is the victim, after all, who is required to live with it. And if he or she can't, then an avenue of appeal should be made available, otherwise the simmering flame of the avenger might beckon with the promise of vindication.

There is no evidence that, if such reforms are adopted, victims will insist on harsher penalties by taking full advantage of their veto rights. As discussed earlier, human beings have a long cultural and genetic history of applying the law of the *talion* faithfully and honorably. When it comes to punishment, citizens have a far better understanding of proper measurement than do legal systems. The victim is the quintessential keeper of the books. Legal systems, with their administrative efficiency rationales, have a tendency to fudge the books, or even worse, cook them. No one can possibly know what the victim is owed better than the victim himself. As William

Ian Miller points out, "People like to dismiss these victims' rights groups as a bunch of crazed, vengeful, red state lunatics. I think they could be on to some deep moral sense that the wronged party has been undervalued in our fastidious concern not to undervalue the dignity of the wrongdoer. I think we may be in a zero-sum game here. Any anxious dignity you might confer on the wrongdoer is subtracted from the victim. Unless you find a way of making that up, victims and their kin will feel forgotten or undervalued. They're not getting the price right."[19]

Besides, if there is any concern about the victim's possible vindictiveness, that's what legislatures are for—to establish sentencing guidelines, the modern-day versions of tribal societies, meticulously setting forth *talionic* equivalences for every known loss or injury. As they do now, legislatures set the appropriate level of punishment in criminal cases, subject to some judicial discretion, which includes taking account of aggravating or mitigating circumstances.

Gary Plauche, who most deliberatively executed the man who sexually abused and kidnapped his son, was given a seven-year suspended sentence, five years of probation, and 300 hours of community service.[20] The judge ruled that under the exceptional circumstances of this case, and with no prior criminal history, Plauche was surely no threat to the community. The only serious threat he posed was to anyone who dared violate his child. Presumably it didn't occur to the court to treat this father's lawless act as if it was a separate, more serious crime than Jeff Doucet's act of molestation against Plauche's son. The court exercised its discretion in ruling that a father's vengeance might in some situations deserve the most mitigated of punishments.

And in civil cases, damages in tort, along with worker's compensation laws, are subject to a range of liability, which can also include the assessment of punitive damages. Judges are not without guidelines in knowing when a victim has gone too far in his or her request for justice. Indeed, judges can play a role as referees in determining that the victim's proposed remedy is unjust. The victim can be empowered, but she must not hold all the power. Mandatory sentences, judicial oversight, and sound judgment can still supervise and regulate the ultimate penalty.

Victims should become true parties to criminal proceedings, serving in the role of coprosecutors, or plaintiffs in criminal actions, always reserving the right to bring an independent civil suit at the conclusion of the criminal trial. Hearing from the victim earlier than the sentencing phase, and in a way that transcends the cookie-cutter dimensions of the victim impact statement, means, for one thing, that he or she should be permitted to make an opening statement—orally and directly to the jury. The jury needs to hear from the victim, not just the prosecutor. The victim has a slightly different story to tell, and it is not irrelevant for the occasion—a story of loss and hardship that establishes the emotional link between the victim and the crime being prosecuted before the court. And victims should be permitted to direct questions to the witnesses and conduct their own cross-examination—if they are willing and up to the task. Because victims lack the necessary trial skills, this is where the hiring of separate counsel would be most useful and appropriate. But even if represented by counsel, their open court statements should be made in their own voices.

Yes, surely there are Sixth Amendment challenges to allowing victims to address the jury. If not subject to cross-examination, these statements might violate the accused's right to confront those witnesses who are testifying against him. But if the victim is truly serving in the capacity as coprosecutor, then, arguably, his or her unsworn statement is not in the nature of testimony but, rather, is purely prosecutorial.

The Sixth Amendment notwithstanding, the question of how to integrate the victim into an actual criminal trial is a uniquely American problem. As George P. Fletcher points out in his book *Justice for Some*, many countries in Europe permit injured parties to join in criminal proceedings where they assist the government in its prosecution and simultaneously pursue their own civil remedies. The role embodied by victims in American courtrooms is a different story entirely, however, largely owing to a different choreography between the judge and the attorneys. The axis of influence in American courtrooms tilts in a divergent direction. In Europe, the judge is the center of the legal universe. He or she calls the witnesses to testify and determines the relevant facts—most often without the aid of a jury. He or she directs questions to the witnesses and the parties to the dispute. The attorneys and the parties are recruited into the service of assisting the court in discovering the truth so that the court can make a ruling.[21]

In the United States, by contrast, truth is more fungible and relative, largely because the lawyers for each side set the tempo of the trials. The American adversarial system regards the discovery of the truth as a jousting match between lawyers. The actual truth is of lesser value than the process that is set in motion in search of relevant facts. The facts are found by the jury, but only after the lawyers have presented their cases, called their witnesses, and made their arguments. A trial is a performance piece where the lawyers put on a show for the judge and jury. And the stakes are high because trials are zero-sum, winner-take-all affairs. Both sides can't win. Little cooperation is shown among attorneys. Truth seeking takes a backseat to gladiatorial conquest. With the stage set, there is no room at the front tables for laypersons with an insufficient command of legalese. A victim without a law degree is clearly the odd man out, and judges are reduced to ringmasters in what sometimes can resemble a legal three-ring circus.

But in such a circus, featuring lawyers, judges, and victims, it is the victim who should always be given the center ring and the brightest spotlight. The victim's encounter with the legal system must recapture the dignity and self-worth that was lost on account of the wrongdoer's conduct. Law and vengeance are equal opportunity vindicators. By choosing a legal path to justice, the victim is nonetheless expecting the same outcome—vindication. And in order for victims to experience the vindication that comes from revenge, they must be able to simulate the experience of vengeance by participating fully in the prosecution of the accused. They need to be able to confront the wrongdoer and give voice to their private suffering, in the most public of all settings—a criminal trial.

Indeed, as George P. Fletcher has suggested, the whole point of a trial is to stand by the victim, to demonstrate, publically, that his pain was not forgotten. Fletcher writes: "A just legal system must stand by its victims. We may neither deter future offenders, nor rehabilitate present inmates, nor achieve justice in the eyes of God. But by seeking to punish the guilty, we do not abandon the innocent who suffer. We do not become complicitous in the crimes committed against them. We seek justice not only for offenders but for all of us."[22]

What it means to do justice is not just moving the machinery of the legal system, pushing buttons, pulling levers, and punching the clock at the end of the day. Doing justice means doing right by the victim. What we offer instead is justice that is patronizingly tangential to what victims need—and far too removed from what vengeance once offered.

I am under no illusions that such a broad mind-shift in legal reform is easily attainable. Prosecutors and defense attorneys like the ground rules as they are presently played. Actually, they all but invented them. Raw meat-eating zealous advocacy is the bread and butter of the bar. The more complicated, convoluted, and inaccessible the system is, the better, as far as the bar is concerned. Victims should be unseen and unheard. "Let the lawyers work it all out," is what we are told. They know from such things, those unknowable procedures and opaque rules that shed no light on the meaning of the law.

And as for judges, they already feel overburdened; adding an obligation to have victims leave their courtrooms satisfied and avenged would be, truly, well beyond their pay grade. Isn't that kind of service better left for mental health professionals anyway? And law schools spend no time teaching young lawyers about the emotional life and moral claims of their future clients. Moral outcomes are most certainly not what lawyers and judges strive to achieve. If revenge is ultimately moral, if vindication is a moral remedy that victims prize above all else, then avengers will find only a dead end if they are looking for justice in the law. But such moral roadblocks have not served society well over the years. Citizens who return from courtrooms with vengeance beating even more palpably in their hearts are a danger to themselves and to us all.

Finally, reducing the centrality of plea bargains in the criminal justice system—giving victims a meaningful day in court rather than a marginalized existence outside of court—would require building more courthouses and adding more judges. And they would need to be far better, more humanized judges. Who's going to pay for all that? I don't know. What I do know is that when this nation is determined to go to war, no cost is too great to prevent our resolve or lessen our purpose. And when banks must be bailed out because they have been allowed to grow into behemoths of corporate irresponsibility, no one can now doubt that their capital will be magically restored as a reward for their failure. The physical and moral health of millions of victims and their search for justice are equally deserving of such a blank-check commitment from their government.

Seeing an opportunity for courtrooms to play a more meaningful role in the lives of victims, Charles K. B. Barton has written that "taking victim rights and victim justice seriously requires, among other things, the validation of the legitimacy of victim resentment and anger. It also requires acknowledgment of the moral legitimacy of victims' need for retributive justice . . . [and] victim empowerment . . . where victims can express their legitimate feelings of resentment and anger, forums where they can demand satisfaction in terms of adequate restoration, apologies, or retributive justice in a controlled and civilized manner."[23]

Barton refers to this process as the "moral *permissibility* of institutionalized revenge," where revenge becomes part of the institutional framework of a legal proceeding. Indeed, revenge can look a lot like restorative justice, where victims and their families participate in the punishment of wrongdoers. Revenge that is more sanitized than dangerous. Through the restraining filter of the legal system, old-school blood vengeance can live on, harmlessly, as a court proceeding. Citizens wear suits rather than body armor. They express their resentment with words rather than with fists. Disarming the public is more than simply taking away their weapons; it also means discharging their rage, providing a forum where people can safely unload their grief. Outlawing vengeance only works if the law offers a genuine and meaningful alternative. The only way to put private avengers out of business is to create an essential, procedural equivalence—all encapsulated under the rule of law and with the legal system as sanctioning body—between justice and vengeance. Only then will victims come to accept that self-help can still be served but not by ignoring the greater good.

Offering victims an active role that replicates the emotional experience of revenge is critical to the reform of the legal system. It would restore a feature of justice that once existed, one where moral revenge and legal retribution were not so far apart. In the United States, before the late nineteenth century, the state was happy to supply the courtrooms, but the responsibility of tracking down and capturing suspected wrongdoers fell on the victim. Many prosecutions were privately initiated. As Mattie Ross discovered in

True Grit, there were courtrooms and traveling judges, but law enforcement and criminal trials were spotty in the Wild West. There was simply too much wide-open space for US marshals to cover, very few lawyers, and judges who were stuck somewhere along the circuit, traveling from courthouse to courthouse on a slow horse. And there wasn't enough courage and grit to go around. If she was going to obtain justice for her father by getting even with his murderer, she was going to have to arrange to track him down and kill him or return him to face trial—herself. Nearly all cowboy Westerns romanticize the *posse comitatus*, that obligatory moment where a roundup of horse-riding, gun-toting fellow neighbors take to the prairies or mountains, giving chase to wrongdoers in the absence of a more reliable, and professional, method of law enforcement. The lynch mob, yet another motif of the Wild West, was never accorded the same respect and always emerged at the movie's most ominous moment.

Victims were once equal partners with legal systems. And they were trusted to act with measure and restraint. They weren't banished and reduced to the outsider status of bitterly unavenged victims. Restoring rights to victims in a new paradigm of legal justice, one in which they are given equal billing in criminal trials, is simply a modern way of reviving the practice of earlier eras when the state, and its citizens, were in the same business of tracking down and punishing wrongdoers. In such instances, the avenger was not reviled but, rather, respected for having the courage to stand up for himself, get up on a horse, and trot off in search of the wrongdoer who had made dust of his self-worth.

And the avenger's neighbors, hardwired with the same brain circuitry and familiar with the rough terrain, were compelled to help out, to altruistically race off to punish on behalf of another; to do anything less was morally wrong and downright uncivilized. Everyone was fully engaged and determined to bring about justice. But this kind of justice sure resembled revenge, and that's because it was that, too. The state hadn't merely outsourced the task of punishment to its righteously vindictive citizens. The lynch law gave way to the court of law. The state maintained those courthouses, roving judges, and, in many cases, public prosecutors who took over once the posse had returned with a wrongdoer who was very much alive and ready for his court date. When the twentieth century settled into postindustrial, modern life, the American legal system came to mistrust its citizen avengers, and victims lost faith in criminal justice precisely because it left them feeling alienated and sorely unavenged.

And it's so easy to see why. Steven Eisenstat laments that "how our law has (d)evolved from the laudable purpose of seeking to eliminate the ravages of revenge, to where today, the law denies victims standing to even petition courts to enforce punishments which have been lawfully imposed upon convicted wrongdoers."[24]

The flashpoints of the law's failure are abundantly clear: the lack of standing, the casting aside and marginalizing of victims who, in a moral universe, would be the center of attention, the trivialized punishments through plea bargaining, the acquittals of the guilty due to procedural error. In revenge movies, victims are instantly transformed into avengers once the legal system fails in its obligation to punish the guilty—and where there is no alibi for its failure. Outside of Hollywood films, however, where real life can get in the way of a moral solution, the answer to the law's failure is a patronizing instruction to victims to simply go home, forget about it, and get it out of their heads. No further legal recourse is available under criminal law. There is no appeal to another, higher authority. And certainly no vindication is to be found through self-help, which will be treated as a separate and, in many cases, a more serious punishable offense.

Victims must be given a right in criminal proceedings to seek redress. And the only way to do that is to make them parties to the action, with a seat at the prosecutorial table and their names plastered right alongside "the People" or "the State."

Revenge was never quite the problem that justified its wholesale banishment from civilized society. The problem had always been the inadequacy of lawful outlets in which victims could replicate the essential feelings of revenge. The legal presumptions about vengeance always had it wrong: it's not possible, emotionally, to ignore injustice, unfairness, indignity, dishonor, and disrespect. If human beings had no emotional reaction to moral injury, if no anger arose from the infliction of pain, loss of property, and breaches of trust, there would be no need for legal systems at all.

Walter Berns has considered wisely what would happen if, in response to criminal activity, there was no community outrage, no concern about crime, if everyone was guided by the principle of self-interest, of going it alone—every man for himself when it came to crime.[25] In such a case, Berns speculates that there would be an easy solution to the government's breach of the social contract: treat it as a real contract where the government would have to pay actual damages for its breach. In exchange for the state's inability to keep the peace and protect the people, it would be required to pay for its nonperformance—each time it failed. Tens of thousands would file individual claims showing damages directly resulting from the state's failure. The government would have to protect itself from such widespread and perpetual liability, but at least the social contract would then have material, and not just symbolic, value.

Subject to so many legal claims, the state might have to purchase general liability insurance. The government would essentially take out insurance on behalf of its entire citizenry. In fact, insurance would replace the need for police, prosecutors, and judges. The cost of the yearly premiums might actually be cheaper than the cost of maintaining law enforcement agencies, along with justice and penal systems, on both the state and federal levels. Instead of apprehending, prosecuting, and punishing wrongdoers, the government, with the help of its insurers, and subject to a deductible, would simply compensate victims of crime and the families of murdered citizens for their losses and traumatic experiences.

Thankfully, we don't live in such a world where there is no moral outrage, anger, and indignation about crime. Citizens wish not to be insured against the monetary losses that arise from violent crime, but to be protected from the actual criminals. No amount of compensation is valued over the knowledge that the state is duty-bound to apprehend and punish the guilty. Citizens *are* angry about crime, and there *is* moral outrage when wrongdoers go unpunished. No one who has given up the right to avenge wants to let the government off the hook so easily. Injustice is itself a moral crime and not an insurable event. The state has an obligation to keep the peace, and avenging the innocent is part of that peacekeeping commitment. The problem is that the legal system has never been comfortable stepping into the shoes of the avenger and acting on behalf of the victim.

The law has to get it right: it has to do its job of making the right arrest and delivering the right punishment. But the legal system must also understand what may happen if it gets it wrong—gets it terribly wrong. If the law fails and a wrongdoer is released back into society unpunished, or insufficiently punished, then a righteous avenger is likely to surface. Morally, the avenger is expected to make things right. He has a duty to discharge. And he won't be easily deterred.

Yes, of course, the avenger then, too, will have committed a crime. But it is not a crime without justification. Moral outrage sets vengeance in motion. The avenger's retaliation is neither an ordinary crime nor an unexpected one. Therefore, it should not be treated as if the backstory of vengeance is irrelevant to motive. Indeed, the backstory supplies the entire motivation for the avenger's act—a motive not to commit a crime, but to avenge one. The avenger would not have acted, would not have been compelled to right a wrong, had the wrongdoer not acted first and had justice been adequately fulfilled. The legal system, thus, becomes a secondary accomplice. The avenger's march toward justice was brought about by its own failure, which must always be kept in mind in deciding how to now judge the avenger when he or she is brought before the law.

If states can find meaningful ways for victims to participate in criminal proceedings, it is less likely that avengers will require another chance at vindication. But some will. And if the legal system can't be reformed in ways that include a participatory role for victims, then botched prosecutions will doubtlessly always become invitations for the return of the avenger. Given that human beings cannot live with injustice and that legal systems are prone to make mistakes, state legislatures should pass revenge statutes, very much in the same way that they presently enact hate crime laws. The latter allows for enhanced penalties for crimes committed against a protected class of discriminated citizens where animus becomes part of the crime. The former would protect the righteous avenger who was compelled to perform his duty after the legal system left him with no other choice.

Such institutional failure should never be lost on courts when standing in judgment of avengers who otherwise would not have broken the law. The appropriate remedy is not to mischaracterize an act of justified vengeance as either a moment of temporary insanity or a bout of extreme emotional disturbance. The intent is clear; the motive is obvious—taking the life of the wrongdoer was deliberate even if impulsive. A reduced charge of manslaughter is a legal fiction. And any legal excuse cheapens the moral force of the act.

Instead, revenge statutes should function not unlike the affirmative defense of self-defense. The act was justified. Under these special circumstances, an act of revenge could be treated no differently from the way provocation and self-defense presently operates under the law. Revenge is a form of self-defense held in abeyance, without the imminence requirement. The wrongdoer received his due, in due time. A justified revenge killing is not the same as ordinary, premeditated murder. And judges and juries, as fellow human beings, can make that determination as a finding of fact: Was the defendant justifiably motivated by revenge? Did the legal system's own failure to punish the guilty unleash the moral necessity of this act of retaliation? Such a determination is not too difficult for juries to make. In deciding whether to convict a defendant of a hate crime, juries are required to find bias, a search that benefits from emotional intelligence. The same is true with revenge. Was the defendant responding to an unavenged moral injury? Moral outrage as a response to injustice is fundamental to our moral development; it is lodged in the very genetic fabric of our DNA. Juries, and audiences to revenge films, possess this basic insight in common.

We know there are vast differences between the imagined slight and true moral injury. And we know when revenge is a sham, when its purported justification has been widely exaggerated and exceeded. Even if judges and juries choose not to acquit by reason of a revenge defense, but to hold the avenger responsible, mitigation of the punishment may still be appropriate—the avenger is entitled to a downgraded penalty—from murder to manslaughter.

Most important, however, a revenge affirmative defense should never be conflated with—or intellectually mangled by—an act committed under the exonerating spell of extreme emotional disturbance, temporary insanity, or diminished capacity. The avenger's duty is an honorable and obligatory one. He or she doesn't undertake the role lightly. When vengeance must be done because justice has otherwise failed and honor cannot be restored any other way, the act is infused with moral purpose and performed with a clear head. It is the product of a sound mind and a righteous heart. The outcome might still be punishable under the law, if not subject to a legal excuse or justification, but it should not be trivialized and misunderstood, made false by a fiction that the avenger was without his mental faculties, that he didn't know what he was doing, that he had no intention to stand up for himself. The criminal justice system is at least required, in its legal pronouncements, to provide a much more intellectually honest assessment of what happened and why.

Because, in the end, isn't that what we all most want from the law: a respect for the truth and the capacity to make things right?

ACKNOWLEDGMENTS

In a book that is essentially about acknowledging and repaying debts, I must extend a debt of gratitude to the many friends and family who assisted in easing the burden of having a book hanging over my head: Hugo Barreca, Paul and Judy Berkman, Sandee Brawarsky, Asha Curran, Marjory Dobbin, Eva Fogelman, Robert Goldblum, Sol Haber, Tom Hameline, Angela Himsel, Robert Hollweg, Tracey Hughes, Annette Insdorf, Carolyn Jackson, Myrna Kirkpatrick, Andrea and Bill Kirsh, Gary Klein, Andy Kovler, Jim Leitner, Karen Mauskop, Ellen Pall, Pearl Pantone, Brett Paul, Paula and Maya Rackoff, Danny Retter, Solenne Rose, Joel Seidemann, Bret Stephens, David Stern, Ivan Strausz, Esther Tendy, and Susan Wolfson.

Also due thanks are my longtime agent and friend, Ellen Levine, who continues to watch over this literary career, and my editors for this book, David Pervin, whose vision and support hovers over this book still, and Christie Henry, a most redoubtable and inspiring publisher and friend. I would also like to thank Yvonne Zipter and Carrie Adams for their dedicated editorial and promotional efforts on my behalf.

I had a crack team of research assistants from Fordham Law School who assisted in preparing this book to be written, loyal former students who are now friends: Claire Evans, Ilana Ofgang, Megan Rockwell, Jared Stanisci, and especially, Kate Moore and Aaron Retter. And I was assisted by one of Fordham's law librarians, Theodore Pitts.

I also had a Dream Team of teenage daughters who pitched in at critical times and without the inducement of a reward: Zofii and Elska, who I thank for their flawless inputting, and Basia Tess, for her meticulous endnoting. And, finally, a full-throated thank you to Roslyn, who simply lovingly makes it all easier.

NOTES

Chapter One

1. Joseph Berger, "Jewish Prayers Are Modernized in New Book," *New York Times*, September 16, 2010, http://www.nytimes.com/2010/09/17/us/17prayer.html.

2. George W. Bush, "Remarks to the Federal Bureau of Investigation Employees," The American Presidency Project, September 25, 2001, http://www.presidency.ucsb.edu/ws/index.php?pid=65083#axzz1zfbNBDKM.

3. Jeffrie G. Murphy, *Getting Even: Forgiveness and Its Limits* (Oxford: Oxford University Press, 2003), 4.

4. "Rewards for Justice Program," US Department of State, http://www.state.gov/m/ds/terrorism/c8651.htm.

5. Peter Baker, Helene Cooper, and Mark Mazzetti, "Bin Laden Is Dead, Obama Says," *New York Times*, May 1, 2011, http://www.nytimes.com/2011/05/02/world/asia/osama-bin-laden-is-killed.html?_r=1&pagewanted=all.

6. Austin Knoblauch, "Favre Says He Isn't Out for Revenge against Packers," *Los Angeles Times*, October 1, 2009, http://latimesblogs.latimes.com/sports_blog/2009/10/brett-favre-revenge-packers-vikings.html.

7. Sean Leahy, "Not about the Revenge for Brett Favre vs. Packers? Analysts Don't Buy It," *USA Today*, October 5, 2009, http://content.usatoday.com/communities/thehuddle/post/2009/10/not-about-the-revenge-for-brett-favre-vs-packers-analysts-dont-buy-it/1.

8. Mike Vandermause, "Minnesota Vikings QB Brett Favre's Motivation vs. Green Bay Packers? Revenge, ESPN's Old Pros Say," *Green Bay Press-Gazette*, October 4, 2009.

9. Leahy, "Not about the Revenge."

10. Charlotte Bercaw, "Mother Feels Pity as Case Is Closed," *Beacon-News* (Aurora, IL), November 20, 1985.

11. Martha Bellisle, "DUI Victim: 'My Son's Life Is Worth More Than Three Months,'" RGJ.com, February 3, 2010, http://www.rgj.com/article/20100214/NEWS/2140351/DUI-victim-My-son-s-life-worth-more-than-three-months-.

12. L. L. Brasier, "Gunman Convicted in Landscaper's Death," *Detroit Free Press*, April 23, 2010, A6.

13. Not to be confused with the "self-help" aisle in a local bookstore, although while one deals with private justice and the other refers to human betterment, they both ultimately mean that a person is capable of taking it on himself to improve on something that simply doesn't feel right—whether it is low self-esteem or an unvindicated wrong.

14. William Glaberson, "Reliving Horror in a Test for the Death Penalty," *New York Times*, January 18, 2010, http://www.nytimes.com/2010/01/19/nyregion/19cheshire.html ?pagewanted=all.

15. "CBS News Transcripts," *CBS Evening News*, November 8, 2010; and Laura Italiano, Reuven Fenton, Erin Calabrese and Perry Chiaramonte, "Juror Speaks Out as Conn. Family's Killer Gets Death Penalty," *New York Post*, November 9, 2010, 4.

16. Tony Rizzo, "Reflection and Remorse as Execution Looms for Convicted Killer," *Kansas City Star*, October 18, 2010, reprinted at http://www.mcclatchydc.com/2010/10/17 /102168/reflection-and-remorse-as-execution.html.

17. Amazon.com, "An Interview with Tom Clancy regarding His Book 'Rainbow Six,'" Seeli.com, reprinted at Internet Archive Wayback Machine, July 11, 2004, http://web .archive.org/web/20070711033207/http://www.seeli.com/Daniel/leisure/tcinterview.php.

18. Jeanne Brooks, "Jenny Sanford Says She's Moving on and Her Book Isn't Revenge," *GreenvilleOnline.com*, February 14, 2010.

19. Karl Vick, "9/11 Jury Duty Poses Wrenching Questions for New Yorkers," *Washington Post*, November 30, 2009, http://www.washingtonpost.com/wp-dyn/content /article/2009/11/29/AR2009112902668.html.

20. Dena Potter, "DC Sniper Execution: Victims, Witnesses Will Watch," *Huffington Post*, November 5, 2009, accessed July 3, 2012, http://www.huffingtonpost.com/2009/11/05 /dc-sniper-execution-victi_n_346906.html.

21. Jena McGregor, Steve Hamm, David Kiley, "Sweet Revenge: The Power of Retribution, Spite, and Loathing in the World of Business," *BusinessWeek*, January 22, 2007, reprinted at http://www.msnbc.msn.com/id/16638145/ns/business-us_business/t/sweet -revenge/.

22. Derek Scally, "I Can't Escape My Dreams, Holocaust Survivor Tells Trial," *Irish Times*, January 20, 2010, http://www.irishtimes.com/newspaper/world/2010/0120/1224262713029 .html.

23. Catrina Stewart, "Twisted History of John Demjanjuk," *National* (United Arab Emirates), November 29, 2009, http://www.thenational.ae/news/world/europe/twisted -history-of-john-demjanjuk.

24. Susan Jacoby, *Wild Justice: The Evolution of Revenge* (New York: Harper & Row, 1983), 2.

25. Diana B. Henriques, "Madoff Is Sentenced to 150 Years for Ponzi Scheme," *New York Times*, June 29, 2009, http://www.nytimes.com/2009/06/30/business/30madoff .html?pagewanted=all; Thane Rosenbaum, "In the Courtroom: Torment and Dante's Hell," *Jewish Daily Forward*, July 1, 2009, http://forward.com/articles/108797/in-the-courtroom -torment-and-dante-s-hell/.

26. Benjamin Weiser, "Judge Explains 150-Year Sentence for Madoff," *New York Times*, June 28, 2011, http://www.nytimes.com/2011/06/29/nyregion/judge-denny-chin-recounts -his-thoughts-in-bernard-madoff-sentencing.html?pagewanted=all.

27. Thane Rosenbaum, "Penn State's Tragedy Enabled by Coaches and Others Who Looked Away," *Daily Beast*, November 12, 2011, http://www.thedailybeast.com

/articles/2011/11/12/penn-state-s-tragedy-enabled-by-coaches-and-others-who-looked-away.html.

28. Tim Rohan, "Sandusky Gets 30 to 60 Years for Sexual Abuse," *New York Times*, October 9, 2012, A1.

29. Lester Munson, "A Just, but Lacking, Sentence," *ESPN.com*, October 9, 2012, http://espn.go.com/espn/otl/story/_/id/8482696/jerry-sandusky-sentence-just-harsher -represent-crimes.

30. Ibid.

31. Steven Erlanger, "14 Convicted in Jew's Killing Will Be Retried in France," *New York Times*, July 13, 2009, A4.

32. Eleanor Harding, "Paralysed DJ Sami Sharif's Dad: 'This Is a Miscarriage of Justice,'" *Guardian* (London), September 10, 2010, http://www.yourlocalguardian.co.uk /news/8376917.DJ_s_dad___This_is_a_miscarriage_of_justice_/.

33. Irwan Firdaus, "Indonesia Anti-Graft Official Convicted in Killing," *Boston Globe*, February 11, 2010, http://www.boston.com/news/world/asia/articles/2010/02/11 /indonesia_anti_graft_official_convicted_in_killing/.

34. "PCGG: Justice, Not Vengeance, Should Govern Marcos Settlement," abs-cbnNews .com, May 12, 2010, http://www.abs-cbnnews.com/nation/05/12/10/pcgg-justice-not -vengeance-should-govern-marcos-settlement.

35. On exile, see Martin H. Pritikin, "Punishment, Prisons, and the Bible: 'Does Old Testament Justice' Justify Our Retributive Culture?" *Cardozo Law Review* 28 (2006): 754; Steven Eisenstat, "Justice and Law: Recognizing the Victim's Desire for Vengeance as a Justification for Punishment," *Wayne Law Review* 50 (2005): 1134–35.

36. Robert C. Solomon, "Justice and the Passion for Vengeance," in *What Is Justice? Classic and Contemporary Readings*, ed. Robert C. Solomon and Mark C. Murphy (New York: Oxford University Press, 2000), 252.

37. Cesare Beccaria, *On Crimes and Punishment*, trans. Henry Paolucci (1764; repr., New York: Bobbs-Merrill, 1963), 58.

38. Ibid.

39. Solomon, "Justice and the Passion for Vengeance," 255.

40. Thane Rosenbaum, "Evening the Score in Afghanistan," *Wall Street Journal*, October 20, 2009, http://online.wsj.com/article/SB10001424052748704500604574481822068068860.html.

41. Bruno Heller and Ashley Gable, "Flame Red," *The Mentalist*, season 1, episode 9, directed by Charles Beeson, aired December 2, 2008 (Burbank, CA: Warner Brothers).

Chapter Two

1. Steven Pinker, *How the Mind Works* (New York: W.W. Norton, 1997), 497.

2. *The Godfather*, directed by Francis Ford Coppola (Los Angeles: Paramount Pictures, 1972).

3. Eisenstat, "Revenge, Justice and Law," 1116–18 (see chap. 1, n. 31).

4. *Coker v. Georgia*, 433 U.S. 584 (1977), 592.

5. Peter A. French, *The Virtues of Vengeance* (Lawrence, KS: University Press of Kansas, 2001), 226.

6. Jacoby, *Wild Justice*, 189, 199–203, 214 (see chap. 1, n. 24).

7. Aaron Sorkin, "A Proportional Response," *The West Wing*, season 1, episode 3, directed by Marc Buckland, aired October 6, 1999 (Burbank, CA: Warner Brothers).

8. *Munich*, directed by Steven Spielberg (Universal City, CA: Universal Pictures, 2005).

9. Michael Walzer, *Just and Unjust Wars: A Moral Argument with Historical Illustrations* (New York: Basic Books, 2006); Steven Pinker, *The Blank Slate: The Modern Denial of Human Nature* (New York: Viking, 2002), 325.

10. Thane Rosenbaum, "For Israel, Every Day Is Groundhog Day," *Jerusalem Post*, January 14, 2009, http://www.jpost.com/Opinion/Op-EdContributors/Article.aspx?id=129331.

11. Thane Rosenbaum, "Is Israel Immoral to Retaliate against Gaza?" *Daily Beast*, November 24, 2012, http://www.thedailybeast.com/articles/2012/11/24/is-israel-immoral-to-retaliate-against-gaza.html.

12. Pete Townsend, "Behind Blue Eyes," recorded by The Who, *Who's Next*, Decca MCA, 1971.

13. French, *The Virtues of Vengeance*, 227.

14. William Ian Miller, *Eye for an Eye* (New York: Cambridge University Press, 2006), 21.

15. *The Secret in Their Eyes*, directed by Juan Jose Campanella (2009; Buenos Aires, Argentina: Tornasol Films).

16. Laura Miller, "The Fine Art of Revenge: A legal scholar says that 'eye for an eye' justice is a lot more humane than you think," *Salon*, February 20, 2006, accessed July 6, 2012, http://www.salon.com/2006/02/20/miller_45/.

17. Pinker, *How the Mind Works*, 496.

18. Miller, "Fine Art of Revenge."

19. Miller, *Eye for an Eye*, 141–42.

20. William Ian Miller, *Bloodtaking and Peacemaking: Feud, Law and Society in Saga Iceland* (Chicago: University of Chicago Press 1990), 5, and "Choosing the Avenger: Some Aspects of the Bloodfeud in Medieval Iceland and England," *Law and History Review* 1 (1983): 159–204; Emily Sherwin, "Compensation and Revenge," *San Diego Law Review* 40 (2003): 1398.

21. Jack Ewing and Alan Cowell, "Demjanjuk Convicted for Role in Nazi Death Camp," *New York Times*, May 12, 2011, http://www.nytimes.com/2011/05/13/world/europe/13nazi.html?_r=1.

22. Berel Lang, "Holocaust Memory and Revenge: The Presence of the Past," *Jewish Social Studies*, n.s., 2 (1996): 17.

23. Miller, *Eye for an Eye*, 93–99, 101.

24. Solomon, "Justice and the Passion for Vengeance," 255 (see chap. 1, n. 32).

25. French, *Virtues of Vengeance*, 110–11.

26. Solomon, "Justice and the Passion for Vengeance," 254.

27. Charles K. B. Barton, *Getting Even: Revenge as a Form of Justice* (Chicago: Open Court, 1999), 61.

28. Carey Goldberg, "Families Hope Freeway Killer's Execution Ends Their Years of Pain," *New York Times*, February 22, 1996, http://www.nytimes.com/1996/02/22/us/families-hope-freeway-killer-s-execution-ends-their-years-of-pain.html?pagewanted=all&src=pm; Susan Bandes, "When Victims Seek Closure: Forgiveness, Vengeance and the Role of Government," *Fordham Urban Law Journal* 27 (2000): 1600.

Chapter Three

1. Juliet Macur, "Etiquette Debate Follows Lead Change," *The New York Times*, July 20, 2010, B11–12.
2. Solomon, "Justice and the Passion for Vengeance," 253 (see chap. 1, n. 32).
3. French, *Virtues of Vengeance*, 94–95 (see chap. 2, n. 5).
4. "The Presidential Debate: Transcript of the Second Debate between Bush and Dukakis," *New York Times*, October 14, 1988, http://www.nytimes.com/1988/10/14/us /the-presidential-debate-transcript-of-the-second-debate-between-bush-and-dukakis .html?pagewanted=all&src=pm.
5. Julie Carpenter, "Hell Hath No Fury Like a Woman Scorned," *Express* (London), June 5, 2009, http://www.express.co.uk/posts/view/105505/Hell-hath-no-fury-like-a -woman-scorned/.
6. Ibid.
7. French, *Virtues of Vengeance*, 95.
8. Murphy, "Forgiveness and Resentment," 18 (see chap. 2, n. 8).
9. Richard A. Posner, *Law and Literature: A Misunderstood Relation* (Cambridge, MA: Harvard University Press, 1988), 33.
10. Thane Rosenbaum, "The Writer's Story, and the Lawyer's," *New York Times*, August 20, 2000, http://www.nytimes.com/books/00/08/20/bookend/bookend.html.
11. Thane Rosenbaum, "The Case of the Loopy Lawyers: Frat-Party Antics and Self-Doubt Are the Stuff of Today's Legal Dramas; Where's Atticus Finch?" *Wall Street Journal*, June 18, 2011, C3, and "Where Lawyers with a Conscience Get to Win Cases," *New York Times*, May 12, 2002, C23.
12. Thane Rosenbaum, *The Myth of Moral Justice: Why the Legal System Fails to Do What's Right* (New York: Harper Collins, 2004), 48.
13. Thane Rosenbaum, ed., *Law Lit, from Atticus Finch to* The Practice: *A Collection of Great Writing About the Law* (New York: New Press, 2008).
14. Patricia Cohen, "Next Big Thing in English: Knowing They Know That You Know," *New York Times*, April 1, 2000, C1.
15. Jacoby, *Wild Justice*, 178 (see chap. 1, n. 24).
16. Manohla Dargis, "Wearing Braids, Seeking Revenge," *New York Times*, December 22, 2010, C1.
17. *Braveheart*, directed by Mel Gibson (Los Angeles: Paramount Pictures, 1995).
18. *The Patriot*, directed by Roland Emmerich (Culver City, CA: Columbia Pictures, 2000).
19. *Mad Max*, directed by George Miller (Melbourne: Village Roadshow Pictures, 1975).
20. Paul Gerwitz, "Aeschylus' Law," *Harvard Law Review* 101 (1988): 1047.
21. Ibid.
22. Murphy, *Getting Even*, 20 (see chap. 1, n. 3).
23. Gerwitz, "Aeschylus' Law," 1048.
24. Jeffrie G. Murphy, "Getting Even: The Role of the Victim," *Social Philosophy and Policy* 7, no. 2 (1990): 215n11.
25. Solomon, "Justice and the Passion for Vengeance," 260.

26. *Legally Blonde*, directed by Robert Luketic (Beverly Hills, CA: MGM Pictures, 2001).

27. Eisenstat, "Revenge, Justice and Law," 1139–40 (see chap. 1, n. 31).

Chapter Four

1. Benedict Carey, "Payback Time: Why Revenge Tastes So Sweet," *New York Times*, July 27, 2004, http://www.nytimes.com/2004/07/27/science/payback-time-why-revenge -tastes-so-sweet.html?pagewanted=all&src=pm.

2. Benedict Carey, "Wired for Justice," *New York Times*, October 7, 2008, D1.

3. Lawrence Van Gelder, "Margaret Truman Daniel, President's Daughter and Popular Author, Dies at 83," *New York Times*, January 30, 2008, B6.

4. Patricia Cohen, "Calculating Economics of an Eye For an Eye," *New York Times*, July 29, 2008, E3.

5. Natalie Angier, "Thirst for Fairness May Have Helped Us Survive," *New York Times*, July 5, 2011, D2.

6. Anne McIlroy, "Payback Pays Off: Why Revenge Is So Sweet," *Globe and Mail* (Toronto), February 4, 2006, F1.

7. Tania Singer et al., "Empathic Neural Responses Are Modulated by the Perceived Fairness of Others," *Nature* 439, no. 26 (2006): 466–69.

8. Cohen, "Calculating Economics."

9. John Cassidy, "Mind Games: What Neuroeconomics Tells Us about Money and the Brain," *New Yorker*, September 18, 2006, 30, http://www.newyorker.com/archive/2006/09 /18/060918fa_fact?currentPage=1.

10. John Roach, "Brain Study Shows Why Revenge Is Sweet," *National Geographic News*, August 27, 2004, http://news.nationalgeographic.com/news/2004/08/0827_040827_ punishment.html; Dominique J.-F. de Quervain et al., "The Neural Basis of Altruistic Punishment," *Science*, August 27, 2004, 1254.

11. Cassidy, "Mind Games."

12. Cohen, "Calculating Economics."

13. de Quervain et al., "Neural Basis," 1254.

14. McIlroy, "Payback Pays Off."

15. Steven Pinker, *The Better Angels of Our Nature: Why Violence Has Declined* (New York: Viking, 2011), 537.

16. Cassidy, "Mind Games."

17. Carey, "Payback Time."

18. Cassidy, "Mind Games."

19. Ibid.

20. de Quervain et al., "Neural Basis," 1254–55.

21. Alexander Strobel et al., "Beyond Revenge: Natural and Genetic Bases of Altruistic Punishment," *NeuroImage* (2010), doi:10.1016/j.neuroimage.2010.07.051.

22. Ibid.

23. John Cassidy, Patricia Cohen, and Christopher Shea, "Drunken Ultimatums," *New York Times Magazine*, December 13, 2009, 34.

24. McIlroy, "Payback Pays Off."

25. Angier, "Thirst for Fairness."

26. Carey, "Wired for Justice."

27. Cassidy, "Mind Games."

28. Brian Knutson, "Sweet Revenge?" *Science*, August 27, 2004, 1246.

29. Roach, "Brain Study."

30. Michael S. Moore, "The Moral Worth of Retribution," in *Responsibility, Character, and the Emotions: New Essays in Moral Psychology*, ed. Ferdinand Schoeman (Cambridge: Cambridge University Press, 1987), 190.

31. Cassidy, "Mind Games."

32. Pinker, *How the Mind Works*, 496 (see chap. 2, n. 1).

33. Lyall Watson, *Dark Nature: A Natural History of Evil* (New York: Harper Collins, 1995), 201.

34. Rose McDermott et al., "Monoamine Oxidase A Gene (MAOA) Predicts Behavioral Aggression Following Provocation," *PNAS* 106, no. 7 (2009): 2118.

35. On the warrior gene's response to resentment and spite, see ibid., 2122.

36. Jon Elster, "Norms of Revenge," *Ethics* 100 (1990): 862.

37. Posner, *Law and Literature*, 29 (see chap. 3, n. 9).

38. Kenworthey Bilz, "The Puzzle of Delegated Revenge," *Boston University Law Review* 87 (2007): 1083–85.

39. Ibid., 1078–82.

40. On tit for tat, see Watson, *Dark Nature*, 77–83.

41. Solomon, "Justice and the Passion for Vengeance," 256 (see chap. 1, n. 32); Azar Gat, "The Human Motivational Complex: Evolutionary Theory and the Causes of the Hunter-Gatherer Fighting," *Anthropological Quarterly* 73, no. 2 (2000): 77–78.

42. Solomon, "Justice and the Passion for Vengeance," 256.

43. Kevin M. Carlsmith, Timothy D. Wilson, and Daniel T. Gilbert, "The Paradoxical Consequences of Revenge," *Journal of Personality and Social Psychology* 95 no. 6 (2008): 1316–17, 1323.

44. Ibid., 1323.

45. *Munich*, directed by Steven Spielberg.

46. Robert Nozick, *Philosophical Explanations* (Cambridge, MA: Belknap Press, 1981), 367–68.

47. Miller, *Eye for an Eye*, 150 (see chap. 2, n. 13).

48. Mario Gollwitzer and Markus Denzler, "What Makes Revenge Sweet: Seeing the Offender Suffer or Delivering a Message?" *Journal of Experimental Social Psychology* 45 (2009): 840, 843–44.

49. *The Princess Bride*, directed by Rob Reiner (Century City, CA: Twentieth Century Fox Pictures, 1987).

50. *Law Abiding Citizen*, directed by F. Gary Gray (Beverly Hills, CA: Overture Films, 2009).

51. Miller, *Eye for an Eye*, 143–44.

52. Ibid.

53. Bilz, "Puzzle of Delegated Revenge," 1076–78.

54. French, *Virtues of Vengeance*, 69 (see chap. 2, n. 5).

55. Ibid., 161, Jeffrie G. Murphy, "A Paradox in Locke's Theory of Natural Rights," *Dialogue* 8 (September 1967): 256–71.

Chapter Five

1. Sonia Kruks, "Why Do We Humans Seek Revenge, and Should We?" *Durham University Insights*, 2, no. 9 (2009).

2. Simone de Beauvoir, "An Eye for an Eye," in *Simone de Beauvoir: Philosophical Writings*, ed. Margaret A. Simmons (Urbana: University of Illinois Press, 2004), 245.

3. John Locke, *Second Treatise of Government*, chap. 2, sec. 7 (1690); French, *Virtues of Vengeance*, 164 (see chap. 2, n. 5).

4. Paul H. Robinson and John M. Darley, "The Utility of Desert," *Northwestern University Law Review* 91 (1997): 454–55.

5. Jeremy Bentham, *An Introduction to the Principles of Morals and Legislation*, ed. J. Burns and H. L. A. Hart (London: Athlone P., 1970), 11–12; Ronald J. Rychlak, "Society's Moral Right to Punish: A Further Exploration of the Denunciation Theory of Punishment," *Tulane Law Review* 65 (1990): 322–24; Mary Sigler, "Just Deserts, Prison Rape, and the Pleasing Fiction of Guideline Sentencing," *Arizona State Law Journal* 38 (2006): 563–64.

6. Jeremy Bentham, "Principles of Penal Law," in vol. 1 of *The Works of Jeremy Bentham*, ed. John Bowring (New York: Russell & Russell, 1962), Robinson and Darley, "The Utility of Desert," 454.

7. Beccaria, *Essay on Crimes and Punishments* (see chap. 1, n. 33).

8. Sigler, "Just Deserts," 563.

9. Immanuel Kant, *The Metaphysics of Morals*, trans. Mary Gregor (Cambridge: Cambridge University Press, 1996), 105.

10. French, *Virtues of Vengeance*, 208.

11. Moore, "Moral Worth" (see chap. 4, n. 31).

12. Walter Berns, *For Capital Punishment: Crime and the Morality of the Death Penalty* (New York: Basic Books, 1979), 154.

13. Pinker, *Blank Slate*, 181 (see chap. 2, n. 9).

14. Jeffrey M. Jones, "Understanding American's Support for the Death Penalty," June 3, 2003, http://www.gallup.com/poll/8557/understand-Support-Death-Penalty-Remains-High-74.aspx.

15. Solomon, "Justice and the Passion for Vengeance," 257 (see chap. 1, n. 32).

16. Nozick, *Philosophical Explanations*, 366–68 (see chap. 4, n. 47).

17. Francis Bacon, "Of Revenge," *Essays or Counsels, Civil and Moral* (London, 1625).

18. Nozick, *Philosophical Explanations*, 374–80.

19. Jean Hampton, "The Retributive Idea," in *Forgiveness and Mercy*, by Murphy and Hampton, 122–47 (see chap. 3, n. 8).

20. Ibid., 125.

21. Murphy, "Forgiveness and Resentment," 18, 25 (see chap. 3, n. 8).

22. Moore, "Moral Worth," 181–82.

23. Immanuel Kant, *The Metaphysical Elements of Justice*, trans. John Ladd (Indianapolis: Bobbs-Merrill, 1965), 102.

24. Matthew H. Kramer, *The Ethics of Capital Punishment* (Oxford: Oxford University Press, 2011), 184–85.

25. *Unforgiven*, directed by Clint Eastwood (Burbank, CA: Warner Bros. Pictures, 1992); Miller, *Eye for an Eye*, 147–49, 158 (see chap. 2, n. 13).

26. Alexander Volokh, "n Guilty Men," *University of Pennsylvania Law Review* 146 (1997): 173.

27. French, *Virtues of Vengeance*, 163.

28. *Snyder v. Phelps*, 562 U.S. __ (2011).

29. The examples of cases on Neo-Nazis, racists burning crosses, and protestors burning the American flag are, respectively, *Collin v. Smith*, 578 F.2d 1197 (7th Cir. 1978); *RAV v. City of St. Paul*, 505 U.S. 377 (1992); and *Texas v. Johnson*, 491 U.S. 397 (1989).

30. Adam Liptak, "Supreme Court Term Offers Hot Issues and Future Hints," *New York Times*, October 2, 2010, http://www.nytimes.com/2010/10/03/us/03scotus.html?page wanted=all.

31. "Mother Gets 10 Years for Slaying Molester Suspect," *New York Times*, January 8, 1994, http://www.nytimes.com/1994/01/08/us/mother-gets-10-years-for-slaying-molester -suspect.html.

32. Ibid.

33. Associated Press, "Accused Molester Is Killed in Court," *New York Times*, April 4, 1993, A30.

34. Eisenstat, "Revenge, Justice and Law," 1144–46 (chap. 1, n. 31).

35. William Glaberson, "Mob Killer and Defector Receives Time Served, and Will Live in Hiding," *New York Times*, October 30, 2010, A17.

36. Miller, "Fine Art of Revenge" (see chap. 2, n. 15).

37. French, *Virtues of Vengeance*, 163.

38. Eisenstat, "Revenge, Justice and Law," 1146–47.

39. Jacoby, *Wild Justice*, 291 (see chap. 1, n. 24).

40. Ibid., 128.

41. Sandy Rovner, "The Ultimate Conflict: Killing the Abuser; a Woman Convicted in Husband's Murder Tells Her Side of the Story," *Washington Post*, August 11, 1987, Z13.

42. Jacoby, *Wild Justice*, 214.

43. *The Brave One*, directed by Neil Jordan (Burbank, CA: Warner Bros. Pictures, 2007).

44. *A Time to Kill*, directed by Joel Schumacher (Burbank, CA: Warner Bros. Pictures, 1996).

45. *In the Bedroom*, directed by Todd Field (New York, NY: Greenestreet Films, 2001).

46. *Sleepers*, directed by Barry Levinson (Burbank, CA: Warner Bros. Pictures, 1996).

47. Barton, *Getting Even*, 69 (see chap. 2, n. 26).

Chapter Six

1. Associated Press, "Hospitals Are Asked to Maim Man as Punishment," *New York Times*, August 20, 2010, A9.

2. Rod Nordland, "Portrait of Pain Ignites a Debate over the Afghan War," *New York Times*, August 5, 2010, A6.

3. Rod Nordland, "In Bold Display, Taliban Order Stoning Deaths," *New York Times*, August 16, 2010, http://www.nytimes.com/2010/08/17/world/asia/17stoning.html.

4. Ibid.

5. Ibid.

6. Associated Press, "60 Lashes Ordered for Saudi Woman," *New York Times*, October 25, 2009, http://www.nytimes.com/2009/10/25/world/middleeast/25saudi.html.

7. "Editorial: Lashing Justice," *New York Times*, December 3, 2007, http://www.nytimes.com/2007/12/03/opinion/03mon2.html.

8. Associated Press, "Saudi Arabia: Lashes for 75-Year-Old Widow," *New York Times*, March 10, 2009, http://www.nytimes.com/2009/03/10/world/middleeast/10briefs-LASHES FORWID_BRF.html.

9. Salman Masood, "Pakistan Moves toward Altering Rape Law," *New York Times*, November 16, 2006, http://www.nytimes.com/2006/11/16/world/asia/16pakistan.html.

10. Salman Masood, "Pakistan Top Court Upholds Acquittals in Notorious Rape Case," *New York Times*, April 21, 2009, http://www.nytimes.com/2011/04/22/world/asia/22pakistan.html?scp=1&sq=salman+masood+mukhtar+upholds+acquittals&st=nyt.

11. Salman Masood, "Vendetta Rapes Continue as Pakistan Resists Change," *New York Times*, October 14, 2006, http://www.nytimes.com/2006/10/14/world/asia/14pakistan.html.

12. Alissa J. Rubin, "For Afghan Woman, Justice Runs into Unforgiving Wall of Custom," *New York Times*, December 1, 2011, http://www.nytimes.com/2011/12/02/world/asia/for-afghan-woman-justice-runs-into-the-static-wall-of-custom.html?pagewanted=all.

13. John Leland and Namo Abdulla, "A Killing Set Honor above Love," *New York Times*, November 21, 2010, A8.

14. Boehm, *Blood Revenge*, 88, 183 (see chap. 6, n. 14).

15. Max Gluckman, "The Peace in the Feud," *Past and Present* 8 (1955): 1–14.

16. Pinker, *Blank Slate*, 327 (see chap. 2, n. 9).

17. Miller, "Fine Art of Revenge" (see chap. 2, n. 15).

18. McIlroy, "Payback Pays Off" (see chap. 4, n. 6).

19. Boehm, *Blood Revenge*, 89.

20. Ibid., 54, Miller, *Eye for an Eye*, 145 (see chap. 2, n. 13).

21. Milovan Djilas, *Land without Justice* (London: Methuen, 1958), 105–7.

22. Elster, "Norms of Revenge," 871 (see chap. 4, n. 37).

23. Ibid.

24. McIlroy, "Payback Pays Off."

25. *True Grit*, directed by Joel and Ethan Coen (Los Angeles, CA: Paramount Pictures, 2010); Thane Rosenbaum, "*True Grit* and the Truth about Revenge," *Huffington Post*, January 27, 2011, http://www.huffingtonpost.com/thane-rosenbaum/true-grit-and-the-truth-a_b_815167.html.

26. Majlinda Mortimer and Anca Toader, "Blood Feuds Blight Albanian Lives," *BBC News*, September 23, 2005, http://news.bbc.co.uk/2/hi/europe/4273020.stm.

27. Epaminontas E. Triantafilou, "In Aid of Transitional Justice: Eroding Norms of Revenge in Countries with Weak State Authority," *UCLA Journal of International Law and Foreign Affairs* 541 (2005): 566.

28. McIlroy, "Payback Pays Off."

29. Laura Blumenfeld, *Revenge: A Story of Hope* (London: Picador, 2003), 66–69.

30. Abby Goodnough and Katie Zezima, "Rhode Island Town Fights the Release of a Child Killer," *New York Times*, March 9, 2011, http://www.nytimes.com/2011/03/10/us/10release.html; Thane Rosenbaum, "Justice? Vengeance? You Need Both," *New York Times*, July 27, 2011, http://www.nytimes.com/2011/07/28/opinion/28rosenbaum.html?_r=1.

31. Miller, "Fine Art of Revenge."

32. Roger V. Gould, "Revenge as Sanction and Solidarity Display: An Analysis of Vendettas in Nineteenth-Century Corsica," *American Sociological Review* 65, no. 5 (2000): 684.

33. Chrisena Coleman, "Yemeni Man Charged in Family Revenge Slay," *New York Daily News*, April 4, 2002, http://www.nydailynews.com/archives/news/yemeni-man-charged -family-revenge-slay-article-1.488462.

34. Lee H. Hamilton, "Outside the Green Zone, the Human Dimension," *New York Times*, September 12, 2008, E34.

35. Ibid.

36. Miller, *Bloodtaking and Peacemaking*, 5 (see chap. 2, n. 19), and "Choosing the Avenger," 159–204 (see chap. 2, n. 19).

37. Blumenfeld, *Revenge*, 75.

38. Ibid., 86–87.

39. "Acid Attacked Woman Rejects Revenge," *News 24*, July 31, 2011, http://www.news24 .com/World/News/Acid-attacked-woman-rejects-revenge-20110731.

40. Shirzad Bozorgmehr, "Victim: Revenge in Iran Acid Attack Is 'Not Worth It,'" *CNN*, July 31, 2011, http://articles.cnn.com/2011-07-31/world/iran.acid.pardon_1_majid -movahedi-ameneh-bahrami-acid-attack?_s=PM:WORLD.

41. McIlroy, "Payback Pays Off"; Blumenfeld, *Revenge*, 62.

42. McIlroy, "Payback Pays Off"; Blumenfeld, *Revenge*, 36.

43. Blumenfeld, *Revenge*, 36; McIlroy, "Payback Pays Off.".

44. Pinker, *Blank Slate*, 325.

45. Trevor Dean, "Marriage and Mutilation: Vendetta in Late Medieval Italy," *Past and Present* 157 (1997): 34.

46. Elster, "Norms of Revenge," 870.

47. James Cowan, *The Hauhau Wars, 1864-72*, vol. 2 of *The New Zealand Wars: A History of the Maori Campaigns and the Pioneering Period* (Wellington: R. E. Owen, Govt. printer, 1955), 180.

48. Dean, "Marriage and Multilation," 33.

49. Alexander Laban Hinton, "A Head for an Eye: Revenge in the Cambodian Genocide," *American Ethnologist* 25, no. 3 (1998): 353, 355, 357.

50. Pinker, *Blank Slate*, 328–29; Eduardo A. Vasquez, Brian Lickel, and Karen Hennigan, "Gangs, Displaced, and Group-Based Aggression," *Aggression and Violent Behavior* (2009), doi:10.1016/j.avb.2009.08.001.

51. Daniel Lord Smail, "Factions and Vengeance in Renaissance Italy," *Comparative Studies in Society and History* 38, no. 4 (1996): 782.

52. Gould, "Revenge as Sanction," 700.

53. Pinker, *The Blank Slate*, 328.

54. Pinker, *How the Mind Works*, 497 (see chap. 2, n. 1); Jacoby, *Wild Justice*, 125 (see chap. 1, n. 24).

55. Gould, "Revenge as Sanction," 684–85.

56. Barton, *Getting Even*, 67 (see chap. 2, n. 26)).

57. Boehm, *Blood Revenge*.

58. Napoleon A. Chagnon, "Life Histories, Blood Revenge, and Warfare in a Tribal Population," *Science*, February 26, 1988, 985.

59. Gould, "Revenge as Sanction," 684.

60. Ibid.

61. Barton, *Getting Even*, 67.

62. Michael Dalby, "Revenge and the Law in Traditional China," *American Journal of Legal History* 25, no. 4 (1981): 268, 286.

63. Ibid., 292, 295, 300.

64. Jared Diamond, "Vengeance Is Ours: What Can Tribal Societies Tell Us about Our Need to Get Even?" *New Yorker*, April 21, 2008, http://www.newyorker.com/reporting /2008/04/21/080421fa_fact_diamond.

65. Ibid.

66. Michael Butler, "'Vengeance' Bites Back at Jared Diamond," *Science*, May 15, 2009, 872–74; Dirk Smillie, "New Guinea Tribesmen Sue the *New Yorker* for $10 Million," *Forbes*, April 21, 2009, http://www.forbes.com/2009/04/21/new-yorker-jared-diamond-business -media-new-yorker.html.

Chapter Seven

1. "Reported Confidence in the Criminal Justice System" and "Respondents' Ratings of the Honesty and Ethical Standards of Lawyers," both in *Sourcebook of Criminal Justice Statistics*, Year 2011, http://www.albany.edu/sourcebook/pdf/t2112011.pdf and http://www .albany.edu/sourcebook/pdf/t2192011.pdf, respectively.

2. Leo J. Shapiro and Associates, *Public Perceptions of Lawyers Consumer Research Findings* ([Chicago]: Litigation Section, American Bar Association, April 2002).

3. Tamar Frankel, "Lessons from the Past: Revenge Yesterday and Today," *Boston University Law Review* 89 (1996): 91–92.

4. Eisenstat, "Revenge, Justice and Law," 1147 (see chap. 1, n. 31).

5. *Eye for an Eye*, directed by John Schlesinger (Los Angeles: Paramount Pictures, 1996).

6. Rosenbaum, *Myth of Moral Justice* (see chap. 3, n. 12).

7. Samuel H. Pillsbury, "Emotional Justice: Moralizing the Passions of Criminal Justice," *Cornell Law Review* 74 (1989): 673.

8. Stephanos Bibas, *The Machinery of Criminal Justice* (Oxford: Oxford University Press, 2012), xviii.

9. Gerwitz, "Aeschylus' Law," 1043–48 (see chap. 3, n. 20); Murphy, *Getting Even*, 20 (see chap. 1, n. 3), and "Getting Even," 215n11 (see chap. 3, n. 24).

10. *Gregg v. Georgia*, 428 U.S. 153 (1976).

11. Lupe S. Salinas, "Is It Time to Kill the Death Penalty? A View from the Bench and the Bar," *American Journal of Criminal Law* 34 (2006): 47.

12. Jeffrey Toobin, "The Mitigator," *New Yorker*, May 9, 2011, 33.

13. Frank Newport, "In U.S., 64% Support Death Penalty in Cases of Murder: Half Say Death Penalty Not Imposed Often Enough," *Gallup Politics*, November 8, 2012, http://www .gallup.com/poll/144284/Support-Death-Penalty-Cases-Murder.aspx.

14. Frank Newport, "In U.S., Two-Thirds Continue to Support Death Penalty: Little Change in Recent Years Despite International Opposition," *Gallup*, October 13, 2009, http://www.gallup.com/poll/123638/In-U.S.-Two-Thirds-Continue-Support-Death -Penalty.aspx; Lydia Saad, "Americans Hold Firm Support for Death Penalty: Only 21% Say

It Is Applied Too Often," *Gallup Crime Survey*, November 17, 2008, http://www.gallup.com /poll/111931/Americans-Hold-Firm-Support-Death-Penalty.aspx.

15. *Furman v. Georgia*, 408 U.S. 238 (1976), 305.

16. Ibid., 343.

17. Salinas, "Is It Time to Kill the Death Penalty?" 57–58.

18. James Q. Wilson, "Hard Times, Fewer Crimes," *Wall Street Journal*, May 28, 2011, C1.

19. Murphy, "Getting Even," 219n19.

20. Hampton, "The Retributive Idea," 125.

21. Goodnough and Zezima, "Rhode Island Town Fights" (see chap. 6, n. 30); Rosenbaum, "Justice? Vengeance?" (see chap. 6, n. 30).

22. "Dad: I'll Kill My Son's Murderer If He's Released," MSNBC.com, March 8, 2011, http://www.msnbc.msn.com/id/41963513/ns/us_news-crime_and_courts/t/dad-ill-kill -my-sons-murderer-if-hes-released/.

23. Goodnough and Zezima, "Rhode Island Town Fights."

24. Ibid.

25. Chris Herring, "Death Penalty in Triple Killing," *Wall Street Journal*, October 9, 2010, A21.

26. William Glaberson, "At Sentencing, Connecticut Killer Says He Is Tormented," *New York Times*, December 3, 2010, A27.

27. Christopher Keating, "Rell Vetoes Bill to Abolish Capital Punishment; Death Penalty," *Hartford Courant*, June 6, 2009, A3.

28. Glaberson, "Reliving Horror," A1 (see chap. 1, n. 14).

29. Donna Fielder, "Family Sought Death Penalty," *Dallas Morning News*, November 20, 2010, http://www.dallasnews.com/incoming/20101120-family-sought-death-penalty.ece.

30. Ibid.

31. Shmuley Boteach, "Suffering Has No Redemptive Value," *Record* (Woodland Park, NJ), November 18, 2010, http://www.northjersey.com/news/opinions/108870359_ Suffering_has_no_redemptive_value.html.

32. Dena Potter, "DC Sniper Execution: Victims, Witnesses Will Watch," *Huffington Post*, November 5, 2009, http://www.huffingtonpost.com/2009/11/05/dc-sniper-execution -victi_n_346906.html.

33. Shannon Brownlee et al., "The Place for Vengeance: Many Grieving Families Seek Comfort and Closure in the Execution of the Murderer. Do They Find It?" *U.S. News and World Report*, June 16, 1997, 24, http://www.usnews.com/usnews/news/articles/970616 /archive_007198.htm.

34. Carey Goldberg, "Families Hope Freeway Killer's Execution Ends Years of Pain," *New York Times*, February 22, 1996, A14; Susan Bandes, "When Victims Seek Closure: Forgiveness, Vengeance and the Role of Government," *Fordham Urban Law Journal* 27 (2000): 1599.

35. Stephen P. Garvey, "Punishment as Atonement," *UCLA Law Review* 46 (1999): 1844.

36. Brownlee et al., "The Place for Vengeance."

37. Ibid.

38. Ibid.

39. Ibid.

40. Walter Rodgers, "America's New Drug of Choice: Revenge," *Christian Science Monitor*, November 29, 2010, http://www.csmonitor.com/Commentary/Walter-Rodgers/2010/1129/America-s-new-drug-of-choice-revenge.

41. Ernest van den Haag, "The Ultimate Punishment: A Defense," *Harvard Law Review* 99, no. 7 (1986): 1668.

42. Brownlee et al., "The Place for Vengeance."

43. John Paul Stevens, "On the Death Sentence," review of Peculiar Institution: America's Death Penalty in an Age of Abolition, by David Garland, *New York Review of Books*, December 23, 2010, http://www.nybooks.com/articles/archives/2010/dec/23/death-sentence/?pagination=false.

44. *Gregg v. Georgia*, 428 U.S. 153 (1976), 183.

45. Berns, *For Capital Punishment*, 174 (see chap. 5, n. 12).

46. *Gregg v. Georgia*, 428 U.S. 153 (1976), 183.

47. Ibid., 184n30.

48. Thane Rosenbaum, "Casey Anthony Verdict: A Jury of Idiots or Hapless Peers?" *Huffington Post*, July 7, 2011, http://www.huffingtonpost.com/thane-rosenbaum/casey-anthony-verdict-a-j_b_892428.html.

49. Ibid.

50. Berns, *For Capital Punishment*, 189.

51. Adam Liptak, "Lifelong Death Sentences," *New York Times*, October 31, 2011, http://www.nytimes.com/2011/11/01/us/death-row-inmates-wait-years-before-execution.html; John Schwartz, "Death Penalty Down in U.S., Figures Show," *New York Times*, December 21, 2010, http://www.nytimes.com/2010/12/21/us/21penalty.html.

52. "Women and the Death Penalty," *Death Penalty Information Center*, April 1, 2012, http://www.deathpenaltyinfo.org/women-and-death-penalty.

53. Stevens, "On the Death Sentence."

54. van den Haag, "The Ultimate Punishment," 1664.

55. For a list of crimes that might constitute the worst of the worst, where the death penalty is perhaps most deserved, *see* Salinas, "Is It Time to Kill the Death Penalty?" 58.

56. Ibid., 102–3.

57. "Revenge Begins to Seem Less Sweet," *Economist*, September 1, 2007, 21.

58. Amy Taxin, "Prosecutor: Revenge Was Motive in Salon Massacre," *Boston Globe*, October 15, 2011, http://www.boston.com/news/nation/articles/2011/10/15/prosecutor_revenge_was_motive_in_salon_massacre/.

59. Salinas, "Is It Time to Kill the Death Penalty?" 47.

60. Murphy, "Getting Even," 212 (see chap. 3, n. 24).

61. *Furman v. Georgia*, 408 U.S. 238 (1976), 273.

62. Berns, *For Capital Punishment*, 163 (see chap. 5, n. 12).

63. Watson, *Dark Nature*, 202 (see chap. 4, n. 34).

64. Wendy Kaminer, *It's All the Rage: Crime and Culture* (New York: Basic Books, 1996), 75.

65. Brownlee et al., "The Place for Vengeance."

66. "Doris Tate," Tate Foundation, http://tatefoundation.com/?q=doris_tate.

67. Brownlee et al., "The Place for Vengeance."

68. *Payne v. Tennessee*, 501 U.S. 808 (1991), 825–27.

69. *Booth v. Maryland*, 482 U.S. 496 (1987), 520.

70. Mary Lay Schuster and Amy Propen, "Degrees of Emotion: Judicial Responses to Victim Impact Statements," *Law, Culture and the Humanities* 6, no. 1 (2010): 77.

71. *Payne v. Tennessee*, 825.

72. *Snyder v. Massachusetts*, 291 U.S. 97 (1934), 122.

73. Murphy, "Getting Even," 213.

74. "Simpson Reported Drawing $25,000 a Month from Trust Pension Fund Is Exempt from Civil Judgment," *Los Angeles Times*, June 13, 1997, http://articles.baltimoresun .com/1997-06-13/news/1997164053_1_simpson-pension-fund-civil-judgment.

75. "O. J. Simpson Book Rights Go to Goldman Family," *New York Times*, August 1, 2007, http://query.nytimes.com/gst/fullpage.html?res=990DEFDA133EF932A3575BC0A 9619C8B63.

76. Jan-Willem Van Prooijen, "Retributive versus Compensatory Justice: Observers' Preference for Punishing in Response to Criminal Offenses," *European Journal of Social Psychology* 40 (2010): 81–82.

77. Anthony J. Sebok, "Punitive Damages: From Myth to Theory," *Iowa Law Review* 92 (2007): 1031.

78. Benjamin C. Zipursky, "Rights, Wrongs, and Recourse in the Law of Torts," *Vanderbilt Law Review* 51, no. 1 (1998): 100.

79. Ibid., 5.

80. Schuster and Propen, "Degrees of Emotion," 92–93.

81. Ibid., 103.

82. Wayne R. LaFave and Austin W. Scott Jr., *Criminal Law*, 2d ed., Hornbook Series (St. Paul, MN: West Publishing, 1986).

83. Dan M. Kahan and Martha C. Nussbaum, "Two Conceptions of Emotion in Criminal Law," *Columbia Law Review* 96 (1996): 315.

84. Ibid., 316.

85. Ibid., 316–17.

86. *Bullock v. United States*, 122 F.2d 213 (DC Circuit 1941), 214.

87. Jacoby, *Wild Justice*, 183–232 (see chap. 1, n. 24).

88. Ibid., 22–23.

89. Ibid., 222.

90. *Beard v. United States*, 158 U.S. 550 (1895), 561.

91. Wayne R. LaFave and Austin W. Scott, Jr., 5.7(f).

92. Elisabeth Ayyildiz, "When Battered Women's Syndrome Does Not Go Far Enough: The Battered Woman as Vigilante," *American University Journal of Gender and Law* 4 (1995): 156–58.

93. Lillian B. Rubin, *Quiet Rage: Bernie Goetz in a Time of Madness* (Berkeley: University of California Press, 1986), 79; Joe Starita, "'Vigilante' Sparks Wave of Hero Worship,'" *Miami Herald*, January 6, 1985, A1.

94. Margot Hornblower, "Intended to Gouge Eye of Teen, Goetz Tape Says; 'My Problem Was I Ran Out of Bullets,'" *Washington Post*, May 14, 1987; Ayyildiz, "Battered Women's Syndrome," 157n130.

95. George P. Fletcher, *A Crime of Self-Defense: Bernhard Goetz and the Law on Trial* (Chicago: University of Chicago Press, 1990).

96. Ayyildiz, "Battered Women's Syndrome," 155–56.

97. Bilz, "Puzzle of Delegated Revenge," 1100–1103 (see chap. 4, n. 39).

98. *Hazel v. State*, 157 A.2d 922 (Md. 1960), 925.

99. Bilz, "Puzzle of Delegated Revenge," 1102.

100. Norval Morris, *Madness and the Criminal Law* (Chicago: The University of Chicago Press, 1982).

101. Pinker, *Blank Slate*, 184 (see chap. 2, n. 9).

102. Ibid., 185.

103. Morris, *Madness*, 61–63.

104. Ibid., 63.

105. Jacoby, *Wild Justice*, 211–16 (see chap. 1, n. 24).

106. Moore, "Moral Worth," 190 (see chap. 4, n. 31).

107. Jacoby, *Wild Justice*, 50–52.

108. Dan Bilefsky, "Wife Who Fired 11 Shots Is Acquitted of Murder," *New York Times*, October 7, 2011, A1.

109. "Russian Vigilante: I Had to Avenge My Family," RT.com, July 2, 2008, http://www .rt.com/news/prime-time/russian-vigilante-i-had-to-avenge-my-family/.

110. *A Time to Kill*, directed by Joel Schumacher.

111. Jacoby, *Wild Justice*, 214–15.

Chapter Eight

1. Seth Mydans, "In Khmer Rouge Trial, Victims Will Not Stand Idly By," *New York Times*, June 17, 2008, A6, http://www.nytimes.com/2008/06/17/world/asia/17cambodia .html?pagewanted=all.

2. Ibid.

3. Ibid.

4. Hinton, "A Head for an Eye," 353, 355, 357 (see chap. 6, n. 49).

5. Jacoby, *Wild Justice*, 181–82 (see chap. 1, n. 24).

6. *Furman v. Georgia*, 408 U.S. 238 (1976).

7. Murphy, "Getting Even," 219 (see chap. 3, n. 24).

8. Barton, *Getting Even*, 85–86 (see chap. 2, n. 26); Bilz, "Puzzle of Delegated Revenge," 1144–45, 1154–55, 1165–70 (see chap. 4, n. 39), Eisenstat, "Revenge, Justice and Law," 1103; George Fletcher, "The Place of Victims in the Theory of Retribution," *Buffalo Criminal Law Review* 3 (1999): 63; Karen Kennard, "The Victim's Veto: A Way to Increase Victim Impact on Criminal Case Dispositions," *California Law Review* 77 (1989): 437–52.

9. Berns, *For Capital Punishment*, 173 (see chap. 5, n. 12).

10. Bibas, *Machinery of Criminal Justice*, 129–65 (see chap. 7, n. 8); George P. Fletcher, *With Justice for Some: Victims' Rights in Criminal Trials* (Reading, MA: Addison-Wesley Publishing, 1995), 241–58.

11. Bibas, *Machinery of Criminal Justice*, xix.

12. Ricky Reilly, "A Father's Justice," ESPN.com, October 10, 2012, http://espn.go.com /espn/story/_/id/8486252/a-father-justice.

13. Ibid., 151.

14. *The Accused*, directed by Jonathan Kaplan (Los Angeles: Paramount Pictures, 1988).

15. Bibas, *Machinery of Criminal Justice*, 160.

16. Eisenstat, "Revenge, Justice and Law," 1143–47.

17. Ibid., 1119.

18. Fletcher, *With Justice for Some*, 193; Kennard, "Victim's Veto," 437–38.

19. Miller, "The Fine Art of Revenge" (see chap. 2, n. 15).

20. Reilly, "A Father's Justice."

21. Fletcher, *With Justice for Some*, 191, 194–96.

22. Ibid., 258.

23. Barton, *Getting Even*, 85–86.

24. Eisenstat, "Revenge, Justice and Law," 1147.

25. Berns, *For Capital Punishment*, 175.

INDEX